Discover Britain's most popular road atlases.

AA essential car accessories

– a comprehensive range of motoring must-haves.

AA

Theory Test
and The
Highway Code

The official questions and answers for car drivers

AA Publishing

Produced by AA Publishing.

© Automobile Association Developments Limited 2008
Reprinted 2002
Second edition with revised questions 2003
Third edition 2004
Reprinted with amendments 2005
Fourth edition with revised questions 2005
Fifth edition with revised questions 2006
Sixth edition with revised questions 2007
Seventh edition with updated Highway Code 2007
Eighth edition with revised questions 2008

ISBN: 978-0-7495-5742-3

Published by AA Publishing (a trading name of Automobile Association Developments
Limited, whose registered office is Fanum House, Basing View, Basingstoke, Hampshire
RG21 4EA; registered number 1878835). A03783

Visit the AA website *www.theAA.com*

Colour separation by Keene Group, Andover
Printed and bound in Italy by Printer Trento

While every effort has been made to include the
widest possible range of questions available at the
time of printing, the Government may from time
to time change, add or remove questions, and the
publisher cannot be held responsible for questions
that may appear on a question paper which were
not available for inclusion in this book.

Your FREE AA driving lesson voucher

With only fully qualified instructors, the new Ford Focus, block booking discounts and a FREE lesson when you buy your first two, you can be sure you're in good hands with the AA driving school.

Call 0800 107 2045

quoting Code 342 AA Theory Test.

Buy 2 lessons, then simply hand the attached voucher to your AA driving instructor at your first lesson to arrange your free lesson.

AA | **driving school**

Grab your FREE AA driving lesson.

Call **0800 107 2045** quoting Code 342 AA Theory Test.

Buy 2 lessons, then simply hand this voucher to your AA driving instructor at your first lesson to arrange your free lesson.

Your Name

Your Pupil Number (Given on calling 0800 107 2045)

(Instructor use only)   AA Driving Instructor Name

(Instructor use only)   AA Driving Instructor Number

Code 342 AA Theory Test

Contents

1
2
3
4
5
6
7
8
9
10
11
12
13
14
15

Introduction

You want to pass the driving test and take advantage of the freedom and mobility that driving a car can give you. Do the following three things and you will achieve your goal – passing the driving test.

Acquire **knowledge** of the rules through your instructor and by carefully studying *The Highway Code*. A key element is to test and reinforce your knowledge.

Take the right **attitude**. Be careful, courteous and considerate to all other road users.

Learn and understand the **skills** of driving by taking lessons from a trained and fully qualified driving instructor.

We're here to help you become a careful and safe driver and we've designed this book to help you take the first steps towards achieving your goal – preparing for your **Theory Test**.

Six essential steps to getting your licence

1. Get your provisional licence

You can apply online for your provisional licence at www.direct.gov.uk/motoring or use form D1 from any Post Office. The driving licence is issued in the form of a two-part document: a photo card and paper counterpart. So that you can legally begin learning to drive, at the appropriate date, you must be in possession of the correct licence documents. Take care when completing all the forms. Many licences cannot be issued for the required date because of errors or omissions on the application forms. You will have to provide proof of identity such as a UK passport; make sure you have all the documents needed.

2. Learn The Highway Code

The Highway Code is essential reading for all drivers not just those learning to drive. It sets out all the rules for good driving, as well as the rules for other road users such as pedestrians and motorcycle riders. When you have learned the rules you will be able to answer most of the questions in the Theory Test and be ready to start learning the driving skills you will need to pass your Practical Test.

3. Apply for and take the test

The driving test is in two parts, the Theory Test and the Practical Test. Once you have a valid provisional licence you may take the Theory Test at any time, but you must pass it before you are allowed to apply for the Practical Test. However, it is important that you should not take your Theory Test too early in your course of practical lessons. This is because you need the experience of meeting real hazards while you are learning to drive, to help you pass the Hazard Perception element of the Theory Test.

You can book your Theory Test by post, by calling or online. Visa, MasterCard, Delta, Visa Electron, Switch/Maestro and Solo cards are all accepted. Application forms are available from test centres, Approved Driving Instructors or by calling the booking number below. Forms need to be sent with a cheque, postal order or credit or debit card details.

By Post DSA (Driving Standards Agency), Booking Department, PO Box 381, Manchester, M50 3UW
By Phone 0870 0101 372
Online www.dsa.gov.uk

4. Start to learn to drive

We recommended that you learn with an Approved Driving Instructor (ADI). Only an ADI may legally charge for providing tuition.

Choose an instructor or driving school by asking friends or relatives who they recommend. Price is important, so find out whether the school offers any discounts for blocks or courses of lessons paid in advance; if you decide to pay in advance, make sure the driving school is reputable. If lesson prices are very low, ask yourself 'why?' Check how long the lesson will last. And don't forget to ask about the car you'll be learning to drive in. Is it modern and reliable? Is it insured? Does it have dual controls?

The most efficient and cost-effective way to learn to drive is to accept that there is no short-cut approach to learning the necessary skills. Agree with your instructor on a planned course of tuition suited to your needs, take regular lessons, and don't skip weeks and expect to pick up where you left off. Ensure the full official syllabus is covered and, as your skills develop, get as much practice as possible with a relative or friend – but make sure they are legally able to supervise your practice. They must be over 21 years of age and have held a full driving licence for at least three years.

5. Apply for and take the Practical Test

Once you have passed the Theory Test, and with your instructor's guidance based on your progress, you can plan ahead for a suitable test date for the Practical Test.

You can book your Practical Test by calling 0870 0101 372 at any time between 8am and 6pm Monday to Friday. You can pay for your test using a credit or debit card and the person who books the test must be the cardholder. If you need to, you can change your practical test appointment by calling the same number or online at www.direct.gov.uk/motoring

Introduction

Make sure you have the following details to hand when booking your Practical Test.

- Theory Test pass certificate number
- driver number shown on your licence
- driving school code number (if known)
- your preferred date
- unacceptable days or periods
- if you can accept a test at short notice
- disability or any special circumstances
- your credit/debit card details

Saturday and weekday evening tests are available at some driving test centres. The fee is higher than for a driving test during normal working hours on weekdays. Evening tests are available during the summer months only.

Telephone bookings and enquiries
0870 0101 372

Facsimile
0870 0102 372

Welsh speakers
0870 0100 372

Minicom
0870 0107 372

6. Apply for your full driver's licence
To obtain a full licence you need to send your Pass Certificate and your provisional licence to the DVLA in Swansea, within two years of passing your Practical Test.

After the Practical Test
The Driving Standards Agency and the insurance industry recognise and seek to reward those drivers who enhance their basic skills and widen their experience by taking further training in the form of the Pass Plus scheme.

This is a six-module syllabus which covers town and rural driving, night driving, driving in adverse weather conditions, and on dual carriageways and motorways. It offers you the opportunity to gain more driving experience with the help of an instructor to hand. An increasing number of insurance companies are prepared to offer discounts to new drivers who have completed the course. There is no test to take at the end of the course.

More information
For more practical information on learning to drive including the Theory Test, Hazard Perception and the Practical Test visit www.theAA.com and www.dsa.gov.uk For information on the Pass Plus scheme visit www.passplus.org.uk

How to use this book

This book is arranged in six sections.

Part 1 explains what to expect and how to prepare for the Theory Test including the Hazard Perception Test.

Part 2 is designed to help you understand each of the 14 topics in the Theory Test. We tell you what type of questions you can expect in each section and give lots of helpful tips.

Each topic is colour coded to its relevant section in Part 3 of this book, which contains all the Theory Test questions.

Experience has taught us that learner drivers find particular questions difficult and are often confused when they see questions which are similar. Reading through the background to each topic, before looking at the questions, will help you to avoid the pitfalls and to group questions together, as you will often find several questions are asking the same thing but in a slightly different way.

Part 3 contains all the official questions for car drivers which appear in the question bank of the DSA. You could be tested on any of these questions when you take your touch-screen Theory Test.

The questions are arranged in topics, such as Safety Margins and Rules of the Road. Each theme has its own colour band to help you

Learn to drive in a modern car with a reputable driving school

How to use this book

find your way around. However, as you start to work through the questions you will soon discover that similar questions on the same topic may appear in different sections. Don't be put off by this, but read each question and the choice of answers very carefully. Similar questions may be asked in a slightly different way to test your knowledge.

Most of the Theory Test questions can be answered if you learn *The Highway Code* (see below). However, you will only find the answers to some questions by talking to your driving instructor and learning about good driving practice on the road.

You'll find all the correct answers to the questions at the back of the book, that way, you can easily test yourself to see what you are getting right and what you will need to work on.

Part 4 contains the complete, official *Highway Code*. *The Highway Code* sets out all the rules and advice on good driving, as well as the rules for other road users such as pedestrians and motorcyclists.

It is essential reading for everybody who uses the road but particularly for learner drivers. The good news is that once you have learned the rules you will be able to answer most of the questions in the Theory Test.

The rules are set out in sections, such as Using the road, or Driving in adverse weather conditions. There are also useful picture-based sections about traffic signs and road markings, and annexes at the end which give advice about topics such as vehicle documentation and first aid. At the back of this section you'll find a complete index to *The Highway Code*, which will help you find all the relevant rules and advice on a particular topic or word.

Part 5 is a short glossary, which explains some of the more difficult words and terms used in the theory questions and *The Highway Code*. It's in alphabetical order and you can use this to check if you're not sure what a chicane is, for example, or what brake fade means.

Part 6 has all the answers to the Theory Test questions.

Part 1
The Theory Test:
What to expect

You have to pass two driving tests before you can apply for a full driving licence – the Theory Test, including Hazard Perception, and the Practical Test. The Theory Test was introduced in 1996 to check that drivers know more than just how to operate a car, and the Hazard Perception element was introduced in 2001 to test learner drivers on their hazard awareness skills.

You are strongly recommended to prepare for the Theory Test and Hazard Perception at the same time as you develop your skills behind the wheel for the Practical Test. Obviously there are many similarities between the two tests and you need the experience of meeting real hazards in order to pass the Hazard Perception element of the Theory Test.

It is all about making you a safer driver on today's busy roads. By preparing for both tests at the same time, you will reinforce your knowledge and understanding of all aspects of driving and you will improve your chances of passing both tests first time.

You have to pass both the Theory Test questions and the Hazard Perception test. At the end of the test they will tell you your scores for both parts. Even if you only failed on one part of the Theory Test, you still have to take both parts again next time.

What to expect in the multiple-choice test

You will have 40 minutes to complete the questions in the test, using a touch-screen to select your answers. The test is a set of 35 questions drawn from a bank of almost 1,000, all of which have multiple-choice answers. In order to pass the test you must answer a minimum of 30 questions correctly within the given time. The Government may change the pass mark from time to time. Your driving school or the DSA will be able to tell you if there has been a change. The questions appear on the screen one at a time and you can return to any of the questions within the 40 minutes to re-check or alter your answers.

Preparing for the Theory Test
Read and get to know *The Highway Code*. It is included in full in this book, and many of the theory questions relate directly to it. Look at the list of Theory Test topics, then read through each topic summary. Now turn to the section containing the questions. Read through the questions and tick your choice of answer(s). Now check your answer(s) against those given in the answer section at the back of the book. If you don't understand the answer, take a note of the question and discuss it with your driving instructor.

Questions marked with an **NI** symbol are those not found in Theory Test papers in Northern Ireland.

Remember
- Don't try too many questions at once.
- Don't try to learn the answers by heart.
- The order of the questions in this book may be different from how they are arranged in the actual test – so don't try to memorise the order.

How to answer the questions

Each question has four, five or six possible answers. You must mark the boxes with the correct answer(s). Each question tells you how many answers to mark.

Study each question carefully, making sure you understand what it is asking you. Look carefully at any diagram, drawing or photograph. Before you look at the answers given, decide what you think the correct answer(s) might be. You can then select the answer(s) that matches the one you had decided on. If you follow this system, you will avoid being confused by answers that appear to be similar.

What to expect in the Hazard Perception Test

After a break of up to three minutes you will begin the Hazard Perception part of the test. The Hazard Perception test lasts for about 20 minutes. Before you start you will be given some instructions explaining how the test works; you'll also get a chance to practise with the computer and mouse before you start the test.

Next you will see 14 film or video clips of real street scenes with traffic such as cars, pedestrians, cyclists, etc. The scenes are shot from the point of view of a driver in a car. You have to notice potential hazards that are developing on the road ahead – that is, problems that could lead to an accident. As soon as you notice a hazard developing, click the mouse. You will have plenty of time to see the hazard – but the sooner you notice it, the more marks you score.

Each clip has at least one hazard in it – some clips may have more than one hazard. You have to score a minimum of 44 out of 75 to

Left: Real road scenes feature in the video clips in the Hazard Perception test
Above: Click the mouse when you spot potential hazards – the pedestrian crossing the side road and the cyclist approaching a parked vehicle (ringed in yellow). Click again as the hazard develops when the cyclist (ringed in red) moves out to overtake the parked vehicle.

pass, but the pass mark may change so check with your instructor or the DSA before sitting your test. (Note that the computer has checks built in to show anyone trying to cheat – for example someone who keeps clicking the mouse all the time.) Be aware that, unlike the Theory Test questions, you will not have an opportunity to go back to an earlier clip and change your response, so you need to concentrate throughout the test.

Preparing for the Hazard Perception test

Who do you think have the most accidents – new or experienced drivers? New drivers have just had lessons, so they should remember how to drive safely, but in fact new drivers have the most accidents.

Learner drivers need training in how to spot hazards because they are often so busy thinking about the car's controls that they forget to watch the road and traffic – and losing concentration for even a second could prove fatal to you or another road user.

Proper training can help you to recognise more of the hazards that you will meet when driving and to spot those hazards earlier. So you are less likely to have an accident. Your driving instructor has been trained to help you learn hazard perception skills and can give you plenty of practice in what to look out for when driving, how to anticipate hazards, and what action to take to deal with hazards of all kinds.

You won't be able to practise with the real video clips used in the official test, of course, but training books and practice videos are widely available.

Part 2
Understanding the theory behind the test

Contents

Section 1
Alertness

The first section in the Theory Test questions is headed ALERTNESS. Alertness is a short section and is a good place to start.

- Alertness means being wide awake and concentrating on what you are doing – driving – not being distracted by mobile phones or loud music.
- Alertness means looking out for hazards.
- Alertness means noticing all road signs and road markings, and acting on the instructions and information they give.

Are you fit to drive?
'Fit' can mean:
- Did you have any alcoholic drinks before you set out?
- Are you under the influence of illegal substances (drugs)?
- Are you feeling groggy or unwell?
- Are you taking prescription medicine that could affect your ability to control the car?
- Are you too tired to drive?

It's unwise to set out on a journey if you're not well, on the basis of 'I'll see how I go – I'll probably be all right':
- Your reactions are likely to be slower.
- You may be unable to judge distances properly.
- Your actions may be less well co-ordinated than usual and it's not legal.

If you are tired, open the window for a few moments to let in some fresh air. If you drive when you are too tired, you risk falling asleep at the wheel – an all too common cause of serious accidents. Driving for long stretches on a motorway at night can be especially dangerous. If you sense that you are losing your concentration, then take a break at a motorway service station. Plan your journey ahead, giving yourself plenty of time for rest stops – at least every couple of hours.

Tackling the questions
Look at the questions in the Alertness section. You'll see that the Alertness questions are all about these
- anticipation
- observation
- signalling
- reversing
- using your mirrors
- concentration
- getting distracted
- feeling sleepy
- using mobile phones

DID YOU KNOW?
The main causes of distraction are:
- Loud music in the car
- Passengers (usually children)
- Events happening outside (such as accidents)
- Using a mobile phone

Now test yourself on the questions about Alertness

Section 2
Attitude

The government road safety organisations believe that the ATTITUDE of learner drivers is extremely important for road safety.

Attitude means
• Your frame of mind when you get in the car
• How you react when you meet hazards on the road
• How you behave towards other drivers

Attitude is a very important part of being a good driver. Your attitude when you are driving plays a big part in ensuring your safety and that of other road users.

Do you aim to be a careful and safe driver or a fast and skilful driver? If you don't want to end up as another road accident statistic, then carefully and safely is the way to go.

Remember that a car is not an offensive weapon, and often people don't realise what a potentially lethal machine they are in control of when they get behind the wheel. You only have to think about this to understand the importance of your attitude when driving.

You'll see that questions in this section are concerned with encouraging you to be a careful and safe driver, and cover:
• Tailgating
• Consideration for other road users, including pedestrians, buses, slow-moving vehicles and horse riders
• Driving at the right speed for the conditions
• When to flash headlights
• The right place, time and way to overtake

And remembering a few dos and don'ts will help you achieve the right attitude for driving and make passing this section of the test much easier.

Good drivers do
• drive at the right speed and for the road and traffic conditions
• observe speed limits
• overtake only when it is safe to do so
• park in correct and safe places
• wait patiently if the driver in front is a learner or elderly or hesitant
• look out for vulnerable road users such as cyclists, pedestrians and children
• concentrate on their driving at all times
• plan their journey so that they have plenty of time to get to their destination

Good drivers don't
• allow themselves to become involved in road rage
• break speed limits
• drive too fast, particularly in wet, foggy or icy weather
• accelerate or brake too harshly
• overtake and 'cut in', forcing others to brake sharply
• put pressure on other drivers by driving too close behind them (this is called 'tailgating'), flashing headlights or gesturing
• allow their attention to be distracted by passengers, mobile phones or loud music, or what is happening on the road, such as staring at an accident

Tailgating

Driving excessively close behind another vehicle is known as tailgating – and it's dangerous! The car in front may stop suddenly (to avoid hitting a child or animal that has dashed out into the road, for example); when this happens the car following runs the risk of crashing into it.

You should always leave enough space between your vehicle and the one in front, so that you can stop safely if the driver in front suddenly slows down or stops.

Rear-end shunts account for a large percentage of all accidents on the road. In these situations, the driver of the car behind is almost always judged to be the guilty party.

So tailgating is potentially expensive as well as dangerous.

Another time when drivers are tempted to tailgate is when attempting to pass a large, slow-moving vehicle. However, keeping well back will improve your view of the road ahead, so that you're better able to judge when it's safe to overtake and the driver of the large vehicle will also be able to see you.

Useful tip

If you are being followed too closely by another driver you should slow down and increase the distance between your vehicle and the one in front. If you slow down or have to stop suddenly, the driver behind may crash into you, but you will have increased your stopping distance and will not be pushed into the vehicle in front of you.

Always remember

- Expect the unexpected, and make provision for the potential errors of other drivers – everyone makes mistakes sometimes.
- Don't create unnecessary stress for other drivers by showing your frustration in an aggressive manner.

If you are driving at the right speed for the road and weather conditions and a driver behind tries to overtake, you should pull back a bit from the vehicle in front so that if the driver behind insists on overtaking, there is less risk of an accident.

Do not try to stop the car behind from overtaking. Do not move into the middle of the road or move up close to the car in front. These actions could be very dangerous.

You should not give confusing signals such as indicating left or waving the other driver on.

Now test yourself on the questions about Attitude

Section 3
Safety and Your Vehicle

When you go through this section you will notice that the questions are a bit of a mixture. They cover a number of topics about SAFETY, including:
- Understanding the controls of your vehicle
- What the car's warning lights tell you
- Tyres – correct inflation, pressures and tread depths
- When to use hazard warning lights
- Passenger safety
- The environment
- Security and crime prevention

Many of the questions in this section are to do with 'legal requirements' and rules regarding parking your car and using lights. Look up all the sections in *The Highway Code* that deal with parking rules. Find out the rules for red routes, white lines and zigzag lines as well as yellow lines.

use your lights, including your hazard warning lights.

A confusing question
One of the most confusing questions in this section asks what kind of driving results in high fuel consumption. The answer, of course, is **bad** driving – especially harsh braking and acceleration. This means you will use more fuel than you should and therefore cause more damage to the environment than is necessary.

BUT many people read the word 'high' as meaning 'good' – as in a level of driving skill – and so pick the wrong answer.

Don't let it be you...

Seat belts
If any of your passengers are young people under 14, you are responsible for making sure that they wear seat belts. You are responsible for them by law, even if you are still a learner driver yourself.

Tips for this section
Learn *The Highway Code* and you will be able to answer most of the questions in this section. In particular make sure you know the rules regarding seat belts, tyres, and when to

Now test yourself on the questions about Safety and Your Vehicle

Safety Margins

Section 4
Safety Margins

Experienced drivers are usually better than new or learner drivers at leaving good SAFETY MARGINS. Learner drivers find it harder to keep their vehicle at a safe distance from the one in front. Therefore the questions in this section cover
- safe stopping distances

and
- safe separation distances (these are the same as safety margins)

What is a safety margin?
A safety margin is the space that you need to leave between your vehicle and the one in front so that you will not crash into it if it slows downs or stops suddenly. They are also called 'separation distances' and are an important part of anticipating road and traffic hazards. When you are learning to drive, you can feel pressured to speed up by drivers behind you.

Don't let other drivers make you cut down on your safety margins. Stay a safe distance ehind the vehicle in front. Then you will have time to anticipate and react to hazards.

The two-second rule
In traffic that's moving at normal speed, allow at least a two-second gap between you and the vehicle in front.

Stopping distances
Many people who are taking their Theory Test get confused about this. You will notice that

some of the questions ask for your overall stopping distance and others ask for your braking distance. These are different.

Overall stopping distance or stopping distance is not the same as braking distance. Stopping distance is made up of thinking distance + braking distance.

In other words, the time it takes to notice that there's a hazard ahead plus the time it takes to brake to deal with it.

Thinking distance
Thinking distance is sometimes called reaction time or reaction distance. If you are driving at 30mph, your thinking distance will be 30 feet (9 metres). That means your vehicle will travel 30 feet (9 metres) before you start braking.

The link between stopping distance and safety margins
You should always leave enough space between your vehicle and the one in front. If the other driver has to slow down suddenly or stop without warning, you need to be able to stop safely. The space is your safety margin.

Safety margins for other vehicles
Long vehicles and motorcycles need more room to stop – in other words, you must leave a bigger safety margin when following a long vehicle or motorbike. When driving behind a long vehicle, pull back to increase your separation distance and your safety margin so that you get a better view of the road ahead – there could be hazards developing and if you are too close he will be unable to see you in his rear view mirror. Strong winds can blow

Thinking Distance   **Braking Distance**

6 metres + 6 metres

= 12 metres (40 feet) or 3 car lengths

9 metres + 14 metres

= 23 metres (75 feet) or 6 car lengths

12 metres + 24 metres

= 36 metres (120 feet) or 9 car lengths

15 metres + 38 metres

= 53 metres (175 feet) or 13 car lengths

18 metres + 55 metres

= 73 metres (240 feet) or 18 car lengths

21 metres + 75 metres

= 96 metres (315 feet) or 24 car lengths

Safety Margins

lorries and motorbikes off course. So leave a bigger safety margin.

Different conditions and safety margins

You may find that one or more questions in your Theory Test might be about driving in 'different conditions'. These questions aim to make sure you know what adjustments you should make to your driving when either road conditions are different from normal, for example, when parts of the road are closed off for roadworks or weather conditions affect your driving.

Road works

You should always take extra care when you see a sign warning you that there are road works ahead. Remember, road works are a hazard and you have to anticipate them.

If you see the driver in front of you slowing down, take this as a sign that you should do the same – even if you can't see a hazard ahead. You still need to keep a safe distance from him. Harassing the driver in front by 'tailgating' is both wrong and dangerous and so is overtaking to fill the gap. It's especially important that you know what to do when you see a sign for road works ahead on a motorway.

- There may be a lower speed limit than normal – keep to it.
- Use your mirrors and indicators, and get into the correct lane in plenty of time.
- Don't overtake the queue and then force your way in at the last minute (this is an example of showing an inconsiderate attitude to other road users).

- Always keep a safe distance from the vehicle in front.

Weather conditions

In bad weather (often called 'adverse' weather), you need to increase your safety margins.

When it's raining you need to leave at least twice as much distance between you and the vehicle in front. When there's ice on the road leave an even bigger gap because your stopping distance increases tenfold.

It's amazing how often drivers go too fast in bad weather. In adverse weather motorways have lower speed limits, but some drivers don't take any notice of them.

When it's icy you should multiply your two-second gap by ten.

Questions that look alike

There are a number of questions about anti-lock brakes in this section. Lots of questions look the same. Some are easy and some are hard. Some of them appear to be the same but they are not.

The questions test two things – your knowledge of the rules of the road and your understanding of words to do with driving.

> **Now test yourself on the questions about Safety Margins**

Section 5
Hazard Awareness

How often does a motorist protest that the accident happened before they had time to realise the person they hit was there? Some accidents will inevitably happen, but part of your instructor's job while teaching you to drive is to help you learn to anticipate problems before they happen.

What is the difference between Hazard Awareness and Hazard Perception?

- Hazard Awareness and Hazard Perception mean the same thing.
- Hazard Perception is the name for the part of the Theory Test that uses video clips. This test is about spotting developing hazards. One of the key skills of good driving, this is called anticipation.
- Anticipating hazards means looking out for them in advance and taking action now.
- Hazard Awareness is about being alert whenever you are driving.

That is why some of the questions in the HAZARD AWARENESS section deal with things that might make you less alert. For example feeling tired, feeling ill, taking medicines prescribed by your doctor or drinking alcohol

Other questions in Hazard Awareness cover noticing road and traffic signs as well as road markings, what to do at traffic lights and when to slow down for hazards ahead.

Why are young male drivers more at risk?

New drivers have a greater than average chance of being involved in accidents. Statistics show that young male drivers have the most accidents.

- Maybe it's because when they first get their licence they want to show off to other drivers.
- Some people think that driving much too fast will earn them 'respect' from their friends.
- Some people think that they are such good drivers that the rules of the road should not apply to them.

Whatever the reason – drivers who don't watch out for hazards are at risk of being involved in an accident. The problem has a lot to do with people's attitude to driving. You'll find more about this aspect of driving in the Attitude part of the Theory Test.

We've already said that young drivers often don't learn to anticipate hazards until they are older and more experienced. The Hazard Perception test aims to 'fill the gap' in hazard perception for young drivers and other new drivers by making sure they have some proper training to make up for their lack of experience.

This should make them safer drivers when they start out on the road alone.

Looking for clues to hazards developing on the road

As you get more driving experience you will start to learn about the times and places where you are most likely to meet hazards. Think about some of these examples.

Rush hour

You know that people take more risks when driving in the rush hour. Maybe they have to drop their children off at school before going to work. Maybe they are late for a business meeting. So you have to be prepared for bad driving, such as other drivers pulling out in front of you.

Dustbin day

Drivers in a hurry may get frustrated if they are held up in traffic because of a hazard such as a dustcart. They may accelerate and pull out to overtake even though they cannot see clearly ahead. You should not blindly follow the lead of another driver. Check for yourself that there are no hazards ahead.

Schoolchildren

Young children are often not very good at judging how far away a car is from them, and may run into the road unexpectedly. Always be on the lookout for hazards near a school entrance.

Parked cars

Imagine you are driving on a quiet one-way street with cars parked down each side of the road. You wouldn't expect to meet any vehicles coming the other way – but what about children playing? They might run out into the road after a football. It would be difficult to see them because of the parked

cars, until they were in the road in front of you.

More examples of hazards

So, what kinds of hazards are we talking about? And what should you do about them?

Road markings and road signs sometimes highlight likely hazards for you.

The list below gives some of the hazards you should look out for when driving along a busy street in town.

After each hazard there are some ideas about what you should be looking out for, and what to do next.

- You see a bus which has stopped in a lay-by ahead.
There may be some pedestrians hidden by the bus who are trying to cross the road, or the bus may signal to pull out. Be ready to slow down and stop.

- You see a white triangle painted on the road surface ahead.
This is a hazard warning sign. It tells you that there is a 'Give Way' junction just ahead. Slow down and be ready to stop.

- You see a sign for a roundabout on the road ahead.
Anticipate that other drivers may need to change lane, and be ready to leave them enough room.

- You come to some road works where the traffic is controlled by temporary traffic lights. *Watch out for drivers speeding to get through before the lights change.*

- You look in your rear view mirror and see an emergency vehicle with flashing lights coming up behind you. *An emergency vehicle wants to pass, so get ready to pull over when it's safe.*

- You see a small child standing with an adult near the edge of the pavement. *Check if the child is safely holding the adult's hand. Be ready to stop safely if the child suddenly steps into the road.*

- You notice dustbins or rubbish bags put out on the pavement. *The dustcart could be around the next corner, or the bin men could be crossing the road with bags of rubbish. Be ready to slow down and stop if necessary.*

- You hear a siren. *Look all around to find out where the emergency vehicle is. You may have to pull over to let it pass.*

You will find out more about the different types of hazards you may encounter, including what to look for when driving on narrow country roads, or in bad (adverse) weather conditions, in the Vehicle Handling section of this book.

> **Always expect the unexpected**
> Don't forget that not all hazards can be anticipated. There are bound to be some you haven't expected.

> **Red flashing warning lights**
> Level crossings, ambulance stations, fire stations and swing bridges all have red lights that flash on and off to warn you when you must stop.

Observation

Another word for taking in information through our eyes is observation. Observation is one of the three key skills needed in hazard perception. The three skills are

- observation
- anticipation
- planning

An easy way to remember this is **O A P** for

Observe
Anticipate
Plan

Talk to yourself!

It's a good idea to 'talk to yourself' when you're learning to drive – and even after you've passed your test. Talk about all the things you see that could be potential hazards. Your driving instructor might suggest this as a way of making you concentrate and notice hazards ahead.

Hazard Awareness

Even if you don't talk out loud, you can do a 'running commentary' in your head on everything you see around you as you drive.

For example, you might say to yourself – 'I am following a cyclist and the traffic lights ahead are red. *When the lights change I will allow him/her plenty of time and room to move off.*'
or
'The dual carriageway ahead is starting to look very busy. There is a sign showing that the right lane is closing in 800 yards. *I must get ready to check my mirrors and, if safe to do so, drop back to allow other vehicles to move into the left-hand lane ahead of me.*'

Note: Don't forget the mirrors! This way, you will notice more hazards, and you will learn to make more sense of the information that your eyes are taking in.

Scanning the road

Learner drivers tend to look straight ahead of their car and may not notice all the hazards that might be building up on both sides. You will spot more hazards when driving if you train yourself to scan the road.

- Practise looking up and ahead as far as possible.
- Use all your mirrors to look out for hazards too.
- Don't forget that you have 'blind spots' when driving – work out where they are and find safe ways of checking all round for hazards.
- Ask your driving instructor to help you with all of this.

Learn your road signs!
Notice the information at the bottom of the first page of traffic signs in *The Highway Code*. It explains that you won't find every road sign shown here.

You can buy a copy of *Know Your Traffic Signs* from a bookshop to see some of the extra signs that are not in *The Highway Code*.

Note: In Wales, some road signs include the Welsh spelling as well as the English, and in Scotland, some signs are written using Gaelic spelling. You'll also see some 'old-style' road signs around, which are slightly different too.

How is learning to scan the road going to help me pass my Theory Test?
- The idea of the Hazard Perception element of the test is to encourage you to get some real experience of driving before you take the Theory Test.
- If you meet real hazards on the road and learn how to anticipate them, you'll learn how to pass the Hazard Perception element of the test.
- In the video test you may not be able to look all around you as you would when driving a car; but the clips will be as realistic as possible in giving you a wide 'view' of the road ahead.

Observation questions

Study some of the pictures in the Hazard Awareness section.

They include photographs of scenes such as

- a cyclist at traffic lights, seen from the viewpoint of a driver in a car behind the cyclist

- what you see as a driver when you are approaching a level crossing

- what you see when coming up to a 'blind bend'

- a view of the road ahead with traffic building up where one lane is closing.

Look out for situations like these when you are out driving with your instructor, and use the practice to improve your hazard awareness.

As well as photographs, there are pictures of road and traffic signs.

What do these signs mean?

What actions should you take when you see these signs?

- If you are not sure, look them up in *The Highway Code*.

- Think about why the square yellow sign with the two children is in the Vehicle Markings section and not with the rest of the road signs.

> Now test yourself on the questions about Hazard Awareness

Section 6
Vulnerable Road Users

Today's new vehicles are becoming safer all the time for the driver inside the car, but sadly this is not always the case for the pedestrian or cyclist outside. Many road users who are not driving cars have nothing to protect them if they are in an accident with a motor vehicle.

The questions in the VULNERABLE ROAD USERS section deal with the following:
- why different types of road users are vulnerable
- what you as a driver must do to keep them safe

Who are vulnerable road users?
The following are all vulnerable road users and you must drive with extra care when you are near vulnerable road users.
- pedestrians
- children
- elderly people
- people with disabilities
- cyclists
- motorcycle riders
- horse riders
- learner drivers and new drivers
- animals being herded along the road

Cyclists
Give cyclists plenty of room. Remember to keep well back from cyclists when you are coming up to a junction or a roundabout because you cannot be sure what they are going to do. On the roundabout they may go in any direction – left, right or straight ahead. They are allowed to stay in the left lane and

signal right if they are going to continue round. Leave them enough room to cross in front of you if they need to. Turn to the section headed Vulnerable Road Users in the Theory Test questions to see some pictures of this. You must also give way to cyclists at toucan crossings and in cycle lanes (see the rules for cyclists set out in *The Highway Code*).

Look out for cyclists!
- It can be hard to see cyclists in busy town traffic.
- It can also be hard to see them coming when you are waiting to turn out at a junction. They can be hidden by other vehicles.

Always be on the lookout for cyclists. Especially, check your mirror to make sure you do not trap a cyclist on your left when you are turning left into a side road. Check your blind spots for cyclists, too.

Controlling your vehicle near cyclists
When you are following a cyclist, you must be able to drive as slowly as they do, and keep your vehicle under control. Only overtake

when you can allow them plenty of room, and it is safe to do so.

Cycle lanes

Cycle lanes are reserved for cyclists and car drivers should not use them. A cycle lane is marked by a white line on the road. A solid white line means you must not drive or park in the cycle lane during the hours it is in use. A broken white line means that you should drive or park in it only if there is no alternative. You should not park there at any time when there are waiting restrictions.

When you overtake a cyclist, a motorcyclist or a horse rider, give them at least as much room as you would give a car.

Cyclists and motorcycle riders

Cyclists and motorcycle riders are more at risk than car drivers because

- they are more affected by strong winds, or by turbulence caused by other vehicles
- they are more affected by an uneven road surface, and they may have to move out suddenly to avoid a pot-hole
- car drivers often cannot see them

Pedestrians

Pedestrians most at risk include elderly people and children. Elderly people and others who cannot move easily may be slower to cross roads – you must give them plenty of time. Children don't have a sense of danger on the road; they can't tell how close a car is, or how fast it is going. They may run out into the road without looking. Or they may step out behind you when you are reversing – you may not see them because they are small.

People who are unable to see and/or hear

A blind person will usually carry a white stick to alert you to their presence. If the stick has a red band, this means that the person is also deaf, so will have no warning of an approaching car either visually or from engine noise.

When to give way to pedestrians

At any pedestrian crossing, if a pedestrian has started to cross, wait until they have reached the other side. Do not harass them by revving your engine or edging forward.

At a crossing with lights (pelican, toucan or puffin crossings), pedestrians have priority once they have started to cross even if, when on a pelican crossing, the amber lights start flashing.

Once a pedestrian has stepped on to a zebra crossing, you must stop and wait for them to cross.

Note: It is courteous to stop at a zebra crossing if a pedestrian is waiting to cross.

Vulnerable Road Users

When you take your Practical Driving Test, you must stop for any pedestrians who are waiting on the pavement at a zebra crossing even if they haven't stepped on to the crossing yet. However, you must not wave to them to cross.

If you want to turn left into a side road and pedestrians have already started to cross the side road on foot, wait for them to finish crossing. People on foot have priority over car drivers.

> **DID YOU KNOW?**
> If a car hits a pedestrian at 40mph, the pedestrian will probably be killed. Even at 30mph, 50% of pedestrians hit by cars will be killed.
> At 20mph, pedestrians have a better chance of surviving. This is why you will find 20mph limits and other things to slow traffic in some residential streets and near school entrances.

Other types of vulnerable road users

Be prepared to slow down for animals, learner drivers, and other more unusual hazards such as people walking along the road in organised groups (for example, on a demonstration, or a sponsored walk). There are rules in *The Highway Code* that walkers must follow. But even if they break the rules, make sure you keep to them.

Animals

Drive slowly past horses or other animals. Allow them plenty of space on the road. Don't frighten them by sounding your horn or revving your engine.

If you see a flock of sheep or a herd of cattle blocking the road, you must
• stop
• switch off your engine
• and wait until they have left the road

People riding horses on the road are often children, so you need to take extra care; when you see two riders abreast, it may well be that the one on the outside is shielding a less experienced rider.

Traffic signs

Look up the Traffic Signs and Vehicle Markings sections in *The Highway Code* and find the following signs
• pedestrians walking in the road ahead (no pavement)
• cycle lane and pedestrian route
• advance warning of school crossing patrol ahead
• school crossing patrol
• elderly or disabled people crossing
• sign on back of school bus or coach

> **Now test yourself on the questions about Vulnerable Road Users**

Section 7
Other Types of Vehicle

We have already come across some of the other types of vehicle that share the road with you and your car including motorbikes and bicycles. The questions in this part of the Theory Test are mostly about long vehicles such as lorries. However, you also need to know what to do about

- buses
- caravans
- trams
- tractors and other farm vehicles
- special vehicles for disabled drivers (powered invalid carriages)
- slow vehicles such as road gritters
- motorway repair vehicles

Important points to remember about these types of vehicle
- Many of them can only move very slowly.
- They cannot easily stop or change direction.

The driver's field of vision may be restricted – this means that car drivers have to allow them plenty of room.

Motorcycles
- Motorcycles are easily blown off course by strong winds. If you see a motorcyclist overtaking a high-sided vehicle such as a lorry, keep well back. The lorry may shield the motorcyclist from the wind as it is overtaking, but then a sudden gust could blow the motorcyclist off course.
- It can be hard to see a motorcyclist when you are waiting at a junction. Always look out for them.

- If you see a motorcyclist looking over their shoulder, it could mean that they will soon give a signal to turn right. This applies to cyclists too. Keep back to give them plenty of room.
- Motorcyclists and cyclists sometimes have to swerve to avoid hazards such as bumps in the road, patches of ice and drain covers. As before – give them plenty of room.

Long vehicles
- Like cyclists, long vehicles coming up to roundabouts may stay in the left lane even if they intend to turn right. This is because they need lots of room to manoeuvre. Keep well back so they have room to turn.
- Take great care when overtaking long or high-sided vehicles. Before you pull out to overtake, make sure you have a clear view of the road ahead.
- A long vehicle that needs to turn left off a major road into a minor road may prepare to do so by moving out towards the centre of the road, or by moving across to the other side.

If you're following them
- Give way, and don't try to overtake – on the right or the left.
- You might need to slow down and stop while the driver of the long vehicle makes the turn.

Buses and trams
- Always give way to buses when they signal to pull out.
- Always give way to trams as they cannot steer to avoid you.
- Don't try to overtake a tram.

Trams are **quiet** vehicles – you cannot rely on approaching engine noise to warn you that a tram is coming.

Take extra care when you see this sign, because trams are sometimes allowed to go when car drivers are not.

Tractors and slow-moving vehicles

• Always be patient if you are following a slow vehicle.

Drivers of slow vehicles will usually try to find a safe place to pull in to let the traffic go past. In the meantime you should keep well back, so that you can see the road ahead. Allow a safe distance in case they slow down or stop.

Slow vehicles are not allowed on motorways because they cannot keep up with the fast-moving traffic. Vehicles not allowed on motorways include

• motorcycles under 50cc
• bicycles
• tractors and other farm vehicles
• powered invalid carriages

> **Now test yourself on the questions about Other Types of Vehicle**

Section 8
Vehicle Handling

The questions in this section test how much you know about controlling your vehicle on different road surfaces and in different weather.

Your control is affected by
• the road surface – is it rough or smooth? Are there any holes or bumps? Are there any 'traffic-calming measures', such as humps or chicanes?
• the weather conditions – you have to drive in different ways when there is fog, snow, ice or heavy rain.

Other questions in this section cover driving on country roads – on narrow and one-way roads, humpback bridges, steep hills, fords. Other questions need practical knowledge, for example, on engine braking, brake fade, and coasting your vehicle – use the Glossary.

This section also has some questions on overtaking and parking.

Road surface

The condition of the road surface can affect the way your vehicle handles. Your vehicle handles better on a smooth surface than on a surface that is damaged, bumpy or full of holes. If you have to drive on an uneven surface, keep your speed down so that you have full control of your vehicle, even if your steering wheel is jolted.

Take care also where there are tramlines on the road. The layout of the road affects the way your vehicle handles.

You may have to adjust your driving for traffic calming measures, such as traffic humps (sometimes called 'sleeping policemen') and chicanes. These are double bends that have been put into the road layout to slow the traffic down. The sign before the chicane tells you who has priority.

Traffic calming measures are often used in residential areas or near school entrances to make it safer for pedestrians.

Weather conditions

Bad weather (adverse weather) such as heavy rain, ice or snow affects the way your vehicle handles. If you drive too fast in adverse weather, your tyres may lose their grip on the road when you try to brake. This means the car may skid or 'aquaplane'. Aquaplaning means sliding out of control on a wet surface.

Driving in snow

In snow, the best advice is do not drive at all unless you really have to make a journey. If you have to drive in snowy conditions, leave extra time for your journey and keep to the main roads. You can fit snow chains to your tyres to increase their grip in deep snow.

Driving in fog

In fog your field of vision can be down to a few metres. Your vehicle is fitted with fog lights to help you see and be seen in fog. But you must know how and when to use them. Look up the three rules about fog lights in *The Highway Code*. You'll see that the key points to remember are:

- Don't dazzle other road users with your fog lights.
- Switch them off as soon as you can see better (as soon as the fog starts to clear).

> **Remember the two-second rule**
> You should double the two-second gap to four seconds when driving in rain, and increase the gap by as much as ten times when there is ice on the road.

Country driving

If you have had most of your driving lessons in a town, you need to know how to drive on narrow country roads. Some are only wide enough for one vehicle ('single-track'), and some are on very steep hills.

Your control of the gears, clutch and brakes will be important if you have to follow a tractor very slowly up a hill. On a steep downward slope you have to make sure your vehicle does not 'run away'.

On country roads you might find humpback bridges and fords. The signs below warn you of these hazards.

- Find out what you must do first after you have driven through a ford.

Vehicle Handling

Technical knowledge

We have already mentioned engine braking. Understanding how engine braking works is part of good vehicle handling.

Note: If you press the footbrake constantly on a long hill, you may get brake fade. If you're not sure, check what that means in the Glossary at the back of this book.

Use the gears to control your vehicle on a downhill slope (or 'gradient'). If you put the vehicle in 'neutral', or drive with the clutch down (called coasting), your vehicle will increase speed beyond what is safe and will not be under proper control.

This sign warns you of a steep hill downwards.

- Travelling in neutral for long distances (known as coasting) is wrong and dangerous – you should not be tempted to do it to save fuel.

Remember that if there is sudden heavy rain after a dry hot spell, the road surface can get very slippery.

> **Now test yourself on the questions about Vehicle Handling**

Section 9
Motorway Rules

Learner drivers aren't allowed on motorways, so you can't get experience of what it's like to drive on them until you've passed your test. However, you do need to know all about MOTORWAY RULES before taking your Practical Test, and your Theory Test will most likely include a question about motorways.

As soon as you pass your driving test you will be legally allowed to drive on motorways. You need to know all the motorway rules in advance, so that you are confident and ready to cope with motorway driving when you pass your test.

There are some major roads and dual carriageways that learners can drive on which are very much like motorways. You may drive on some of these fast roads during your driving test, so that your examiner can see how well you cope with hazards at higher speeds.

When driving on these fast roads you will need some of the very same skills that you will need for motorway driving – for example, using lanes properly, knowing when it is safe to overtake, and controlling your vehicle at speed.

If you are learning to drive with a driving school, you will have the chance to book a motorway lesson with your instructor after you have passed your test. It makes sense to take up this offer before you drive on a motorway alone for the first time.

Motorways and other roads

- On a motorway traffic is moving at high speed all the time.
- All lanes are in use.
- No stopping is allowed on a motorway – traffic only slows or comes to a stop because of accidents or other types of hold-up.
- Some road users are not allowed on motorways. These include
- pedestrians, cyclists and learner drivers
- horses and other animals
- motorcycles under 50cc
- slow-moving vehicles, tractors and farm vehicles and invalid carriages
- You always enter and leave a motorway on the left, via a slip road.
- To the left of the inside lane (left-hand lane) on a motorway is the hard shoulder. You can only drive on this in an emergency.
- Special signs and signals are used on motorways. These include signs above the road on overhead gantries, signs on the central reservation, and amber and red flashing lights.

Checks before your journey

Be extra careful about doing all your regular checks before you set out on a motorway journey. You cannot stop on the motorway to fix small problems, and no one wants to break down in the middle of fast traffic.

Always check
- oil and coolant levels, screen wash container
- tyres and tyre pressures
- fuel gauge
- that all mirrors and windows are free of dirt and grease
- that the horn works

Many of these checks are legally necessary, as well as important for your safety.

How to move on to a motorway

- Join the motorway by building up your speed on the slip road to match the speed of traffic in the left lane of the motorway.
- Use MSM (Mirrors – Signal – Manoeuvre) and move into the flow of traffic when it is safe to do so.

Changing lanes and overtaking

Driving on a motorway needs all the skills you have learned about anticipation and forward planning.

You should
- make good use of all mirrors, and check your blind spots
- signal to move out in plenty of time
- look out for hazards ahead in the lane you want to move to
- not go ahead if it will force another vehicle to brake or swerve
- keep a safe distance from the vehicle in front

Take a break

When you drive on motorways you will sometimes see signs that say 'Tiredness can kill – take a break!' This is very good advice. Motorways are monotonous – boring to drive, with long stretches of road that look the same for miles. A major cause of accidents is drivers falling asleep at the wheel. Plan your journey so that you have time to get out, stretch your legs and have a drink or snack.

The rules you need to know

- Keep to the left-hand lane unless you are overtaking and move back to the left lane as soon as it is safe to do so. Sometimes you need to stay in the centre lane for a time – for example, when a line of lorries is travelling up a hill in the left lane. Stay in the centre lane until you have passed the hazard, then signal left and return to the left lane.
- NEVER
  reverse
  park
  walk
  drive in the wrong direction on the motorway.
- Don't exceed the speed limit. This is normally 70mph, but lower speed limits may be signed when the road is busy, or in bad weather.
- Keep to the correct separation distance (see Safety Margins).
- Don't overtake on the left.
  If traffic is moving slowly in all three lanes you may find that the lane on the left is moving faster than the one to its right for a short time. Or the left lane may be signed for traffic turning off at the next junction only. But these are exceptions to the rule.
- If luggage falls from your vehicle, do not get out to pick it up. Stop at the next emergency phone and tell the police. Posts on the edge of the motorway show the way to the nearest emergency phone. You should use these phones rather than your mobile phone, because the emergency phone connects directly to the police and tells them exactly where you are calling from on the motorway.

- Don't stop on the hard shoulder except in an emergency. The hard shoulder is an extremely dangerous place, as many as one in eight road deaths happen there.

Traffic signs and road markings

Light signals

In *The Highway Code* you'll find the light signals only seen on motorways. Signs above the roadway or on the central reservation are activated as needed to warn of accidents, lane closures or weather conditions. Overhead gantries display arrows or red crosses showing which lanes are open or closed to traffic and which lanes to move to

when motorways merge or diverge. They may also show temporary speed limits.

Direction signs

Direction signs on motorways are blue and those on other major roads are green – other direction signs are white with black print.

Reflective studs

It's useful to know the colours of studs on a motorway; this can help in working out which part of the road you're on if it's dark or foggy. White studs mark lanes or the centre of the road and red studs mark the left edge of the carriageway.

Amber studs are used alongside the central reservation and green studs mark the entry to a slip road.
Note: these markings are also found on some dual carriageways.

Using the hard shoulder
- Stop as far to the left as possible and, if you can, near an emergency phone.
- Emergency phones are situated 1 mile apart and have blue and white marker posts every 100 metres. An arrow on the posts points the direction of the nearest phone.
  - If you are using a mobile phone you can identify your location from the number on the post.
- Switch on your hazard warning lights.
- Use the left-hand door to get out of the vehicle, and make sure your passengers do too.
- Get everyone away from the road – if possible, behind the barrier or up the bank.
- Leave animals in the vehicle unless they aren't safe there.
- Phone the police with full details of where you are, then go back and wait in a safe place near your vehicle.

Section 10
Rules of the Road

'Rules of the Road' is a good way to describe what is in *The Highway Code*.

The questions that come under this heading in the Theory Test include several on road signs and road markings. There are many more road sign questions in the section on Road and Traffic Signs. Several of the topics listed in this section have already come up.

Other questions in this section cover
- speed limits
- overtaking
- parking
- lanes and roundabouts
- clearways
- box junctions
- crossroads
- pedestrian crossings
- towing caravans and trailers

Speed limits
Driving too fast for the road, traffic or weather conditions causes accidents. Make sure that you keep below the speed limit shown on the signs for the road that you are on.

Now test yourself on the questions about Motorway Rules

| 30mph in a built-up area | 50mph on a long, twisty country road | or as low as 20mph in a residential area with speed humps or traffic calming measures |

The right speed for the conditions

If it is raining or there is snow and ice on the road or if you are driving in a high wind you will have to drive more slowly than the maximum speed limit. This will keep you and other road users safe.

- Remember – you have to double the time you allow for stopping and braking in wet weather. Allow even more time in snow and ice.
- You need to be extra careful when driving in fog.

The right speed for your vehicle

Some other vehicles have lower speed limits than cars. You can find out more about speed limits from the table in *The Highway Code*.

The national speed limit for cars on a dual carriageway is 70mph.
This is also the maximum speed for motorway driving.

National speed limit

When you leave a built-up area you will usually see this sign.

- This sign tells you that the national speed limit for this type of road applies here.
- The national speed limit for cars on a normal road (single carriageway outside a built-up area) is 60mph. So on this road you must drive below 60mph even if it is straight and empty.

Street lights usually mean that a 30mph limit applies, unless there are signs showing other limits.

Parking rules

There are some general rules about parking that all drivers should know.

- Whenever you can, you should use off-street car parks, or parking bays. These are marked out with white lines on the road.
- Never park where your vehicle could be a danger to other road users.

Look for special signs that tell you that you cannot park there at certain times of the day or that only certain people may park in that place. Examples include signs showing bus lanes, cycle lanes, residents' parking zones and roads edged with red or yellow lines.

Orange or blue badges are given to people with disabilities. Do not park in a space reserved for a disabled driver, even if that is the only place left to park. A disabled driver may need to park there. You will break the law if you park in that space.

Parking at night

- If you park at night on a road that has a speed limit higher than 30mph, you must switch on your parking lights. You must switch on your parking lights even if you have parked in a lay-by on this type of road.
- When parking at night, always park facing in the same direction as the traffic flow.
- If your vehicle has a trailer, you must switch on parking lights, even if the road has a 30mph speed limit.

Where not to park

You are not permitted to park

- on the pavement
- at a bus stop
- in front of someone's drive
- opposite a traffic island
- near a school entrance
- on a pedestrian crossing (or inside the zigzag lines either side of it)
- near a junction
- on a clearway
- on a motorway

> **Now test yourself on the questions about Rules of the Road**

Section 11
Road and Traffic Signs

When you look up the chapter on ROAD AND TRAFFIC SIGNS in the Theory Test questions you will see that it takes up a lot of pages. This is because most of the questions have a picture of a road sign or marking. You will also see that a lot of questions ask 'What does this sign mean?'

But however differently the questions are worded, it all comes down to how well you know *The Highway Code*. You can try to learn as much of *The Highway Code* as possible, but there are other ways you can get to know the road signs.

As you walk or drive around, look at the road signs you see in the street, and the different markings painted on the road surface.

On foot

Look at the signs and signals that all road users must obey, whether they are in a car or walking. For example, when you use a pedestrian crossing, check what kind of crossing it is (such as a pelican, toucan or zebra crossing).

Check whether you know the following

- What are the rules for pedestrians and drivers coming up to the crossing?
- What kinds of crossings are controlled by traffic lights?
- What is different about a zebra crossing?

Road and Traffic Signs

During your driving lessons

If you are having a driving lesson look well ahead so that you see all the signs that tell you what to do next. Obey them in good time.

During your test

When you take your test the examiner will tell you when to move off, when to make a turn and when to carry out one of the set manoeuvres. The examiner will expect you to watch out for lane markings on the road, and signs giving directions, and to decide how to react to these yourself.

Signs

If you see several signs all on the same post, it can be confusing. The general rule is to start at the top and read down the post. The sign at the top tells you about the first hazard you have to look out for.

If you are a passenger in a car on a motorway, look at the motorway signs, because you need to know them, even though you can't drive on a motorway yet yourself.

Check that you can answer the following:
What colour are the signs at the side of the motorway?
What do the light signals above the road tell you?
What signs tell you that you are coming to an exit?

Shapes of signs

Road and traffic signs come in three main shapes. Get to know them. You must learn what the signs mean.

Circles

Signs in circles tell you to do (blue) or not do (red) something – they give orders.

Triangles

Signs in triangles tell you of a hazard ahead – they give warnings.

Rectangles

Signs in rectangles tell you about where you are or where you are going – they give information.

There is only one sign which is octagonal – that is, it has eight sides. This is the sign for STOP. The eight-sided shape makes the sign stand out.

> Now test yourself on the questions about Road and Traffic Signs

Section 12
Documents

This is quite a short section in the Theory Test questions. It is also different from the other sections, because it does not deal with either your driving skills or knowledge of *The Highway Code*.

It covers all the paperwork and the laws that you need to know about when you start learning to drive.

In this section there are questions about
- driving licences
- insurance
- MOT certificate
- Vehicle Excise Duty (tax disc)
- Vehicle Registration Document (log book)

This section also covers who can supervise a learner driverand changes you must tell the licensing authority about

Driving licence
If you are learning to drive, you need a provisional licence.
- You must have a valid licence to drive legally.
- All licences now have two parts – a photo card and a paper document.
- Your signature appears on both parts of the licence.
- Take good care of your provisional licence. If you lose it by mistake, you can get another one but you will have to pay a fee, and wait for the new licence to come.
- When you pass your test you can apply for a full licence.

Insurance
You must have a valid insurance certificate that covers you at least for third party liability. If you are learning with a driving school, you are covered by their insurance while you are in the driving school car. When you are in your own or anybody else's car, you must have insurance. Third party insurance cover usually comes as 'Third Party, Fire and Theft'. It is a basic insurance policy that will pay for repairs to another person's car and allows you to claim on the other driver's insurance if you are in an accident that was not your fault. If you have comprehensive insurance, the policy will pay for repairs to your vehicle even when the accident was your fault.

MOT certificate
Cars and motorcycles must have their first MOT test three years after they are new and first registered. After that, they must have an MOT test every year.

The MOT test checks that your vehicle
- is roadworthy – that is, all the parts work properly and the vehicle is safe to drive
- keeps to the legal limits for exhaust emissions – that is, the level of poisons in the gas that comes from the exhaust

If your vehicle is more than three years old you must not drive it without a valid MOT certificate – unless you are on your way to get an MOT and you have booked it in advance.

Vehicle Excise Duty (tax disc)

Your vehicle must have an up-to-date tax disc on the windscreen. The disc shows that you have paid Vehicle Excise Duty up to the date on the disc (you can pay for 6 or 12 months at a time). If you don't renew your tax disc within a month of the old one expiring you will be automatically fined. If you are not going to renew your tax disc (if you don't use your vehicle or keep it on a public road) you must inform the DVLA by completing a Statutory Off Road Vehicle Notification (SORN).

Vehicle Excise Duty is the tax that the government charges you to drive your vehicle on the roads. It is also sometimes called road tax. When you get your tax disc, you must show proof that your vehicle is insured, and that it has a valid MOT if required.

Vehicle Registration Document/Certificate

The Vehicle Registration Document/Certificate has all the important details about you and your vehicle, such as the make and model of the vehicle. It also has your name and address as the registered keeper of the vehicle. It is a record of the vehicle's history and is sometimes called 'the log book'.

DVLA

The Driver and Vehicle Licensing Agency is known as the DVLA. You must tell the DVLA if you are going to keep your car off road and are not renewing your tax disc, when you buy or sell a car and if you change your name or your address.

This is because your details go on to the Vehicle Registration Document/Certificate and you are legally responsible for the vehicle (car tax, parking fines, etc) until you have notified the DVLA that it is off road or you have sold it.

Supervising a learner driver

As a learner driver you cannot drive on your own. If you are not with your driving instructor, you must be supervised by a person who is at least 21 years old, has a full licence for the kind of car you drive and has had that licence for at least three years. Note that if a person has a licence to drive an automatic car only, they cannot supervise a learner in a manual car.

Now test yourself on the questions about Documents

Section 13
Accidents

The questions in this section are about helping anyone who is hurt in a road accident. Some people think they might do more harm than good if they try to help. But if you have a basic knowledge of first aid you won't panic and if you are first on the scene at an accident, you could even save a life. Look up Accidents and First Aid in *The Highway Code*.

The Theory Test questions in this section cover
- what to do when warning lights come on in your vehicle
- what to do if you break down
- safety equipment to carry with you
- when to use hazard warning lights
- what to do – and what not to do – at the scene of an accident
- what to do in tunnels

Basic first aid
What to do at an accident scene
- Check that you are not putting yourself in danger before you go to help somebody else. You may need to warn other drivers of the accident.
- Check all vehicle engines are switched off.
- Make sure no one is smoking.
- Move people who are not injured to a safe place. If the accident has happened on a motorway, if possible get uninjured people away from the hard shoulder, behind the barrier or on to the bank.

- Call the emergency services. You will need to tell them exactly where you are, and how many vehicles are involved in the accident. On motorways, use the emergency phone which connects directly to the police and tells them exactly where you are.
- Do not move injured people – unless there is a risk of fire or of an explosion.
- Give essential first aid to injured people (see below).
- Stay there until the emergency services arrive.

The ABC of first aid
This tells you what three things to check for when you go to help an injured person
A is for Airway
B is for Breathing
C is for Circulation

Airway
If an injured person is breathing, but unconscious, if possible place them in the recovery position. If they are not breathing, first make sure there is nothing in their mouth that might be blocking the airway.

Breathing
If you have checked the airway and they are still not breathing, then give first aid as follows
- lift their chin
- carefully tilt their head back to open their airway

- pinch their nose and blow into their mouth until their chest rises

Repeat this every 4 seconds until the person can breathe alone, or until help arrives.

Circulation

'Circulation' here means 'bleeding'. If a person is bleeding, press firmly on the wound for up to 10 minutes, until the bleeding slows or stops. You can raise an injured arm or leg to reduce the bleeding – as long as the limb is not broken. If you carry a first aid kit use a sterile dressing over the wound.

Other ways to help

- Do speak in a calm way to the injured person.
- Do try to keep them warm and as comfortable as possible.
- Do not give them anything to drink.
- Do not give them a cigarette.
- Don't let injured people wander into the road.

The AA's advice on safety if you break down
If you are on a non-motorway road

- Try to get your vehicle off the main road. At least, get it right to the side of the road or on to the verge.
- If the vehicle is in a place where it might be hit by another vehicle, get any passengers out and to a safer place.
- Switch on the hazard warning lights to warn other drivers.
- If you have a red warning triangle, place it at least 45 metres behind your car to warn other traffic (but don't use it on a motorway).

- If you are a member of a motoring organisation such as the AA, call them and tell them where you are and what has happened. Wait with your vehicle until the patrol arrives.

If you are on a motorway

- If possible, leave the motorway at the next exit. If you can't get that far, drive on to the hard shoulder. Stop far over to the left, and switch on your hazard warning lights.
- Get everyone out of the vehicle, using the nearside doors (but leave pets in the vehicle). Get them to sit on the bank, well away from the traffic.
- Use the nearest orange emergency phone to call the emergency services and tell them where you are and what has happened (for your safety, face the oncoming traffic while you are on the phone).
- Go back to your vehicle and wait on the bank near by until help arrives.
- Do not cross the motorway on foot or try to do repairs yourself – even changing a wheel. This is too dangerous on a motorway.

> **DID YOU KNOW?**
> Before driving into a tunnel you should tune into a local radio station and listen to the traffic reports in case there are any accidents or problems in the tunnel.

Now test yourself on the questions about Accidents

Section 14
Vehicle Loading

This last section, called VEHICLE LOADING, is the shortest of all. It covers a mixture of the following
- how to load your vehicle safely
- using a roof rack
- towing caravans and trailers
- child restraints and safety locks

When you have passed your test you can tow a trailer, if the combined weight of the vehicle and trailer is less than 3,500kg. So you need to know the rules about towing.

Towing
When you get your first full driving licence, check it to see how much you are allowed to tow. Do not tow any trailer that comes to more than that weight. The weight of a trailer should be no more than 85% of the weight of the car that is to pull it. But it is best to stay well below that top weight, because towing a trailer will affect the way your vehicle handles. When you are towing, you need to allow more room when overtaking and more time to brake and stop.

When you are turning at a roundabout or junction you will need to think about where you are on the road.

When towing a heavy load, you might need to blow your tyres up to more than the normal pressures. Check your vehicle's handbook for advice. Remember to change back to the normal tyre pressures when you finish your journey.

Roof racks
If you attach a roof rack to your car, it will make a difference to the way in which your vehicle handles. Any load that is carried on a roof rack must be tied down securely.

- The roof rack makes your vehicle taller, so more vulnerable to strong winds.
- You will increase your fuel consumption.
- You need to change the way you drive to allow for the extra weight.

To find out more, look up the parts of *The Highway Code* that deal with Loads and Towing.

Loading a trailer
If the weight of the load is arranged properly, this should cut down the risk of losing control, swerving and snaking.
- Try to spread the weight evenly when you load your trailer. Do not put more weight towards the front, or the back, or to one side.
- It is against the law to have a load that is sticking out in a dangerous way.
- Don't forget that if you park a vehicle with a trailer overnight, it must have lights.

A vehicle towing a trailer
- must not go over a maximum speed limit of 60mph
- must not use the right (outside) lane on a motorway

If you are going to buy a trailer, make sure it fits your car's tow bar. Tow bars must keep to EU regulations, and must have electric sockets to connect to the lights on the trailer.

Snaking

'Snaking' means moving from side to side. A caravan will snake if it is not properly attached or loaded, or if the car pulling it is going too fast.

If you are towing a caravan or trailer and it starts to snake
- slow down – stop pressing the accelerator (do not brake suddenly)
- get back in control of the steering
- then brake gently

You are responsible for passengers in your vehicle

There are also questions in the Vehicle Loading section about the safety of passengers. As the driver, you are responsible for making sure your vehicle is not overloaded – and this applies to people and animals as well as to luggage. Remember that all passengers must wear a seat belt (unless they have a medical certificate saying they should not wear one) and that all children under the age of 14 must wear a seat belt or be strapped into a child seat or other 'restraint' suitable for their age. (See the section on Child Restraints in *The Highway Code*).

Children

Children must not sit in the space behind the back seat of a hatchback car, and no passengers should sit in a caravan while it is being towed.

Pets

Pets should be kept under careful control. You might keep them and you safe with a special harness, or if they are kept behind a screen in a hatchback which would stop them being thrown forward in the event of an accident.

> Now test yourself on the questions about Vehicle Loading

Part 3 Theory Test Questions

Contents   **Page**

1 Before you make a U-turn in the road, you should

Mark one answer

- [ ] **A.** give an arm signal as well as using your indicators
- [ ] **B.** signal so that other drivers can slow down for you
- [ ] **C.** look over your shoulder for a final check
- [ ] **D.** select a higher gear than normal

2 As you approach this bridge you should

Mark three answers

- [ ] **A.** move into the middle of the road to get a better view
- [ ] **B.** slow down
- [ ] **C.** get over the bridge as quickly as possible
- [ ] **D.** consider using your horn
- [ ] **E.** find another route
- [ ] **F.** beware of pedestrians

3 When following a large vehicle you should keep well back because this

Mark one answer

- [ ] **A.** allows you to corner more quickly
- [ ] **B.** helps the large vehicle to stop more easily
- [ ] **C.** allows the driver to see you in the mirrors
- [ ] **D.** helps you to keep out of the wind

4 In which of these situations should you avoid overtaking?

Mark one answer

- [ ] **A.** Just after a bend
- [ ] **B.** In a one-way street
- [ ] **C.** On a 30mph road
- [ ] **D.** Approaching a dip in the road

5 This road marking warns

Mark one answer

- [ ] **A.** drivers to use the hard shoulder
- [ ] **B.** overtaking drivers there is a bend to the left
- [ ] **C.** overtaking drivers to move back to the left
- [ ] **D.** drivers that it is safe to overtake

6 Your mobile phone rings while you are travelling. You should

Mark one answer

- [ ] **A.** stop immediately
- [ ] **B.** answer it immediately
- [ ] **C.** pull up in a suitable place
- [ ] **D.** pull up at the nearest kerb

7 Why are these yellow lines painted across the road?

Mark one answer

- **A.** To help you choose the correct lane
- **B.** To help you keep the correct separation distance
- **C.** To make you aware of your speed
- **D.** To tell you the distance to the roundabout

8 You are approaching traffic lights that have been on green for some time. You should

Mark one answer

- **A.** accelerate hard
- **B.** maintain your speed
- **C.** be ready to stop
- **D.** brake hard

9 Which of the following should you do before stopping?

Mark one answer

- **A.** Sound the horn
- **B.** Use the mirrors
- **C.** Select a higher gear
- **D.** Flash your headlights

10 What does the term 'blind spot' mean for a driver?

Mark one answer

- **A.** An area covered by your right-hand mirror
- **B.** An area not covered by your headlights
- **C.** An area covered by your left-hand mirror
- **D.** An area not covered by your mirrors

11 Objects hanging from your interior mirror may

Mark two answers

- **A.** restrict your view
- **B.** improve your driving
- **C.** distract your attention
- **D.** help your concentration

12 Which of the following may cause loss of concentration on a long journey?

Mark four answers

- **A.** Loud music
- **B.** Arguing with a passenger
- **C.** Using a mobile phone
- **D.** Putting in a cassette tape
- **E.** Stopping regularly to rest
- **F.** Pulling up to tune the radio

13 On a long motorway journey boredom can cause you to feel sleepy. You should

Mark two answers

- **A.** leave the motorway and find a safe place to stop
- **B.** keep looking around at the surrounding landscape
- **C.** drive faster to complete your journey sooner
- **D.** ensure a supply of fresh air into your vehicle
- **E.** stop on the hard shoulder for a rest

14 You are driving at dusk. You should switch your lights on

Mark two answers

- [ ] **A.** even when street lights are not lit
- [ ] **B.** so others can see you
- [ ] **C.** only when others have done so
- [ ] **D.** only when street lights are lit

15 You are most likely to lose concentration when driving if you

Mark two answers

- [ ] **A.** use a mobile phone
- [ ] **B.** listen to very loud music
- [ ] **C.** switch on the heated rear window
- [ ] **D.** look at the door mirrors

16 Which FOUR are most likely to cause you to lose concentration while you are driving?

Mark four answers

- [ ] **A.** Using a mobile phone
- [ ] **B.** Talking into a microphone
- [ ] **C.** Tuning your car radio
- [ ] **D.** Looking at a map
- [ ] **E.** Checking the mirrors
- [ ] **F.** Using the demisters

17 Your vehicle is fitted with a hands-free phone system. Using this equipment whilst driving

Mark one answer

- [ ] **A.** is quite safe as long as you slow down
- [ ] **B.** could distract your attention from the road
- [ ] **C.** is recommended by *The Highway Code*
- [ ] **D.** could be very good for road safety

18 Using a hands-free phone is likely to

Mark one answer

- [ ] **A.** improve your safety
- [ ] **B.** increase your concentration
- [ ] **C.** reduce your view
- [ ] **D.** divert your attention

19 You should ONLY use a mobile phone when

Mark one answer

- [ ] **A.** receiving a call
- [ ] **B.** suitably parked
- [ ] **C.** driving at less than 30mph
- [ ] **D.** driving an automatic vehicle

20 You must not use a hand-held phone while you are driving. Using a hands-free system

Mark one answer

- [ ] **A.** is acceptable in a vehicle with power steering
- [ ] **B.** will significantly reduce your field of vision
- [ ] **C.** will affect your vehicle's electronic systems
- [ ] **D** could distract your attention from the road

21 What is the safest way to use a mobile phone in your vehicle?

Mark one answer
- A. Use hands-free equipment
- B. Find a suitable place to stop
- C. Drive slowly on a quiet road
- D. Direct your call through the operator

22 You are driving on a wet road. You have to stop your vehicle in an emergency. You should

Mark one answer
- A. apply the handbrake and footbrake together
- B. keep both hands on the wheel
- C. select reverse gear
- D. give an arm signal

23 When you are moving off from behind a parked car you should

Mark three answers
- A. look round before you move off
- B. use all the mirrors on the vehicle
- C. look round after moving off
- D. use the exterior mirrors only
- E. give a signal if necessary
- F. give a signal after moving off

24 You are travelling along this narrow country road. When passing the cyclist you should go

Mark one answer
- A. slowly, sounding the horn as you pass
- B. quickly, leaving plenty of room
- C. slowly, leaving plenty of room
- D. quickly, sounding the horn as you pass

25 Your vehicle is fitted with a hand-held telephone. To use the telephone you should

Mark one answer
- A. reduce your speed
- B. find a safe place to stop
- C. steer the vehicle with one hand
- D. be particularly careful at junctions

26 To answer a call on your mobile phone while travelling you should

Mark one answer
- A. reduce your speed wherever you are
- B. stop in a proper and convenient place
- C. keep the call time to a minimum
- D. slow down and allow others to overtake

27 Your mobile phone rings while you are on the motorway. Before answering you should

Mark one answer
- **A.** reduce your speed to 30mph
- **B.** pull up on the hard shoulder
- **C.** move into the left-hand lane
- **D.** stop in a safe place

28 You are turning right onto a dual carriageway. What should you do before emerging?

Mark one answer
- **A.** Stop, apply the handbrake and then select a low gear
- **B.** Position your vehicle well to the left of the side road
- **C.** Check that the central reservation is wide enough for your vehicle
- **D.** Make sure that you leave enough room for a vehicle behind

29 You lose your way on a busy road. What is the best action to take?

Mark one answer
- **A.** Stop at traffic lights and ask pedestrians
- **B.** Shout to other drivers to ask them the way
- **C.** Turn into a side road, stop and check a map
- **D.** Check a map, and keep going with the traffic flow

30 You are waiting to emerge from a junction. The windscreen pillar is restricting your view. What should you be particularly aware of?

Mark one answer
- **A.** Lorries
- **B.** Buses
- **C.** Motorcyclists
- **D.** Coaches

31 When emerging from junctions which is most likely to obstruct your view?

Mark one answer
- **A.** Windscreen pillars
- **B.** Steering wheel
- **C.** Interior mirror
- **D.** Windscreen wipers

32 Windscreen pillars can obstruct your view. You should take particular care when

Mark one answer
- **A.** driving on a motorway
- **B.** driving on a dual carriageway
- **C.** approaching a one-way street
- **D.** approaching bends and junctions

33 You cannot see clearly behind when reversing. What should you do?

Mark one answer
- **A.** Open your window to look behind
- **B.** Open the door and look behind
- **C.** Look in the nearside mirror
- **D.** Ask someone to guide you

34 When you see a hazard ahead you should use the mirrors. Why is this?

Mark one answer

A. Because you will need to accelerate out of danger

B. To assess how your actions will affect following traffic

C. Because you will need to brake sharply to a stop

D. To check what is happening on the road ahead

35 You are waiting to turn right at the end of a road. Your view is obstructed by parked vehicles. What should you do?

Mark one answer

A. Stop and then move forward slowly and carefully for a proper view

B. Move quickly to where you can see so you only block traffic from one direction

C. Wait for a pedestrian to let you know when it is safe for you to emerge

D. Turn your vehicle around immediately and find another junction to use

36 Your vehicle is fitted with a navigation system. How should you avoid letting this distract you while driving?

Mark one answer

A. Keep going and input your destination into the system

B. Keep going as the system will adjust to your route

C. Stop immediately to view and use the system

D. Stop in a safe place before using the system

37 You are driving on a motorway and want to use your mobile phone. What should you do?

Mark one answer

A. Try to find a safe place on the hard shoulder

B. Leave the motorway and stop in a safe place

C. Use the next exit and pull up on the slip road

D. Move to the left lane and reduce your speed

38 At a pelican crossing the flashing amber light means you MUST

Mark one answer

- **A.** stop and wait for the green light
- **B.** stop and wait for the red light
- **C.** give way to pedestrians waiting to cross
- **D.** give way to pedestrians already on the crossing

39 You should never wave people across at pedestrian crossings because

Mark one answer

- **A.** there may be another vehicle coming
- **B.** they may not be looking
- **C.** it is safer for you to carry on
- **D.** they may not be ready to cross

40 At a puffin crossing, which colour follows the green signal?

Mark one answer

- **A.** Steady red
- **B.** Flashing amber
- **C.** Steady amber
- **D.** Flashing green

41 The conditions are good and dry. You could use the 'two-second rule'

Mark one answer

- **A.** before restarting the engine after it has stalled
- **B.** to keep a safe gap from the vehicle in front
- **C.** before using the 'Mirror-Signal-Manoeuvre' routine
- **D.** when emerging on wet roads

42 'Tailgating' means

Mark one answer

- **A.** using the rear door of a hatchback car
- **B.** reversing into a parking space
- **C.** following another vehicle too closely
- **D.** driving with rear fog lights on

43 Following this vehicle too closely is unwise because

Mark one answer

- **A.** your brakes will overheat
- **B.** your view ahead is increased
- **C.** your engine will overheat
- **D.** your view ahead is reduced

44 You are following a vehicle on a wet road. You should leave a time gap of at least

Mark one answer

- **A.** one second
- **B.** two seconds
- **C.** three seconds
- **D.** four seconds

45 You are in a line of traffic. The driver behind you is following very closely. What action should you take?

Mark one answer

- **A.** Ignore the following driver and continue to travel within the speed limit
- **B.** Slow down, gradually increasing the gap between you and the vehicle in front
- **C.** Signal left and wave the following driver past
- **D.** Move over to a position just left of the centre line of the road

46 A long, heavily laden lorry is taking a long time to overtake you. What should you do?

Mark one answer
- A. Speed up
- B. Slow down
- C. Hold your speed
- D. Change direction

47 Which of the following vehicles will use blue flashing beacons?

Mark three answers
- A. Motorway maintenance
- B. Bomb disposal
- C. Blood transfusion
- D. Police patrol
- E. Breakdown recovery

48 Which THREE of these emergency services might have blue flashing beacons?

Mark three answers
- A. Coastguard
- B. Bomb disposal
- C. Gritting lorries
- D. Animal ambulances
- E. Mountain rescue
- F. Doctors' cars

49 When being followed by an ambulance showing a flashing blue beacon you should

Mark one answer
- A. pull over as soon as safely possible to let it pass
- B. accelerate hard to get away from it
- C. maintain your speed and course
- D. brake harshly and immediately stop in the road

50 What type of emergency vehicle is fitted with a green flashing beacon?

Mark one answer
- A. Fire engine
- B. Road gritter
- C. Ambulance
- D. Doctor's car

51 A flashing green beacon on a vehicle means

Mark one answer
- A. police on non-urgent duties
- B. doctor on an emergency call
- C. road safety patrol operating
- D. gritting in progress

52 A vehicle has a flashing green beacon. What does this mean?

Mark one answer
- A. A doctor is answering an emergency call
- B. The vehicle is slow moving
- C. It is a motorway police patrol vehicle
- D. The vehicle is carrying hazardous chemicals

53 Diamond-shaped signs give instructions to

Mark one answer
- A. tram drivers
- B. bus drivers
- C. lorry drivers
- D. taxi drivers

30

54 On a road where trams operate, which of these vehicles will be most at risk from the tram rails?

Mark one answer
- A. Cars
- B. Cycles
- C. Buses
- D. Lorries

55 What should you use your horn for?

Mark one answer

- A. To alert others to your presence
- B. To allow you right of way
- C. To greet other road users
- D. To signal your annoyance

56 You are in a one-way street and want to turn right. You should position yourself

Mark one answer

- A. in the right-hand lane
- B. in the left-hand lane
- C. in either lane, depending on the traffic
- D. just left of the centre line

57 You wish to turn right ahead. Why should you take up the correct position in good time?

Mark one answer

- A. To allow other drivers to pull out in front of you
- B. To give a better view into the road that you're joining
- C. To help other road users know what you intend to do
- D. To allow drivers to pass you on the right

58 At which type of crossing are cyclists allowed to ride across with pedestrians?

Mark one answer

- A. Toucan
- B. Puffin
- C. Pelican
- D. Zebra

59 A bus has stopped at a bus stop ahead of you. Its right-hand indicator is flashing. You should

Mark one answer

- A. flash your headlights and slow down
- B. slow down and give way if it is safe to do so
- C. sound your horn and keep going
- D. slow down and then sound your horn

60 You are travelling at the legal speed limit. A vehicle comes up quickly behind, flashing its headlights. You should

Mark one answer

- A. accelerate to make a gap behind you
- B. touch the brakes sharply to show your brake lights
- C. maintain your speed to prevent the vehicle from overtaking
- D. allow the vehicle to overtake

61 You should ONLY flash your headlights to other road users

Mark one answer

- A. to show that you are giving way
- B. to show that you are about to turn
- C. to tell them that you have right of way
- D. to let them know that you are there

62 You are approaching unmarked crossroads. How should you deal with this type of junction?

Mark one answer

- [ ] **A.** Accelerate and keep to the middle
- [ ] **B.** Slow down and keep to the right
- [ ] **C.** Accelerate looking to the left
- [ ] **D.** Slow down and look both ways

63 You are approaching a pelican crossing. The amber light is flashing. You must

Mark one answer

- [ ] **A.** give way to pedestrians who are crossing
- [ ] **B.** encourage pedestrians to cross
- [ ] **C.** not move until the green light appears
- [ ] **D.** stop even if the crossing is clear

64 At puffin crossings, which light will not show to a driver?

Mark one answer

- [ ] **A.** Flashing amber
- [ ] **B.** Red
- [ ] **C.** Steady amber
- [ ] **D.** Green

65 You should leave at least a two-second gap between your vehicle and the one in front when conditions are

Mark one answer

- [ ] **A.** wet
- [ ] **B.** good
- [ ] **C.** damp
- [ ] **D.** foggy

66 You are driving on a clear night. There is a steady stream of oncoming traffic. The national speed limit applies. Which lights should you use?

Mark one answer

- [ ] **A.** Full beam headlights
- [ ] **B.** Sidelights
- [ ] **C.** Dipped headlights
- [ ] **D.** Fog lights

67 You are driving behind a large goods vehicle. It signals left but steers to the right. You should

Mark one answer

- [ ] **A.** slow down and let the vehicle turn
- [ ] **B.** drive on, keeping to the left
- [ ] **C.** overtake on the right of it
- [ ] **D.** hold your speed and sound your horn

68 You are driving along this road. The red van cuts in close in front of you. What should you do?

Mark one answer

- [ ] **A.** Accelerate to get closer to the red van
- [ ] **B.** Give a long blast on the horn
- [ ] **C.** Drop back to leave the correct separation distance
- [ ] **D.** Flash your headlights several times

69 You are waiting in a traffic queue at night. To avoid dazzling following drivers you should

Mark one answer
- A. apply the handbrake only
- B. apply the footbrake only
- C. switch off your headlights
- D. use both the handbrake and footbrake

70 You are driving in traffic at the speed limit for the road. The driver behind is trying to overtake. You should

Mark one answer
- A. move closer to the car ahead, so the driver behind has no room to overtake
- B. wave the driver behind to overtake when it is safe
- C. keep a steady course and allow the driver behind to overtake
- D. accelerate to get away from the driver behind

71 You are driving at night on an unlit road behind another vehicle. You should

Mark one answer
- A. flash your headlights
- B. use dipped beam headlights
- C. switch off your headlights
- D. use full beam headlights

72 A bus lane on your left shows no times of operation. This means it is

Mark one answer
- A. not in operation at all
- B. only in operation at peak times
- C. in operation 24 hours a day
- D. only in operation in daylight hours

73 You are driving along a country road. A horse and rider are approaching. What should you do?

Mark two answers
- A. Increase your speed
- B. Sound your horn
- C. Flash your headlights
- D. Drive slowly past
- E. Give plenty of room
- F. Rev your engine

74 A person herding sheep asks you to stop. You should

Mark one answer

- [ ] **A.** ignore them as they have no authority
- [ ] **B.** stop and switch off your engine
- [ ] **C.** continue on but drive slowly
- [ ] **D.** try and get past quickly

75 When overtaking a horse and rider you should

Mark one answer

- [ ] **A.** sound your horn as a warning
- [ ] **B.** go past as quickly as possible
- [ ] **C.** flash your headlights as a warning
- [ ] **D.** go past slowly and carefully

76 You are approaching a zebra crossing. Pedestrians are waiting to cross. You should

Mark one answer

- [ ] **A.** give way to the elderly and infirm only
- [ ] **B.** slow down and prepare to stop
- [ ] **C.** use your headlights to indicate they can cross
- [ ] **D.** wave at them to cross the road

77 You are driving a slow-moving vehicle on a narrow winding road. You should

Mark one answer

- [ ] **A.** keep well out to stop vehicles overtaking dangerously
- [ ] **B.** wave following vehicles past you if you think they can overtake quickly
- [ ] **C.** pull in safely when you can, to let following vehicles overtake
- [ ] **D.** give a left signal when it is safe for vehicles to overtake you

78 You have a loose filler cap on your diesel fuel tank. This will

Mark two answers

- [ ] **A.** waste fuel and money
- [ ] **B.** make roads slippery for other road users
- [ ] **C.** improve your vehicle's fuel consumption
- [ ] **D.** increase the level of exhaust emissions

79 To avoid spillage after refuelling, you should make sure that

Mark one answer

- [ ] **A.** your tank is only three-quarters full
- [ ] **B.** you have used a locking filler cap
- [ ] **C.** you check your fuel gauge is working
- [ ] **D.** your filler cap is securely fastened

80 A vehicle pulls out in front of you at a junction. What should you do?

Mark one answer

- [ ] **A.** Swerve past it and sound your horn
- [ ] **B.** Flash your headlights and drive up close behind
- [ ] **C.** Slow down and be ready to stop
- [ ] **D.** Accelerate past it immediately

81 You stop for pedestrians waiting to cross at a zebra crossing. They do not start to cross. What should you do?

Mark one answer

- [ ] **A.** Be patient and wait
- [ ] **B.** Sound your horn
- [ ] **C.** Carry on
- [ ] **D.** Wave them to cross

82

You are following this lorry. You should keep well back from it to

Mark one answer
- A. give you a good view of the road ahead
- B. stop following traffic from rushing through the junction
- C. prevent traffic behind you from overtaking
- D. allow you to hurry through the traffic lights if they change

83

You are approaching a red light at a puffin crossing. Pedestrians are on the crossing. The red light will stay on until

Mark one answer
- A. you start to edge forward on to the crossing
- B. the pedestrians have reached a safe position
- C. the pedestrians are clear of the front of your vehicle
- D. a driver from the opposite direction reaches the crossing

84

Which instrument panel warning light would show that headlights are on full beam?

Mark one answer
- A.
- B.
- C.
- D.

85

If your vehicle uses diesel fuel, take extra care when refuelling. Diesel fuel when spilt is

Mark one answer
- A. sticky
- B. odourless
- C. clear
- D. slippery

86

What style of driving causes increased risk to everyone?

Mark one answer
- A. Considerate
- B. Defensive
- C. Competitive
- D. Responsible

87

Young, inexperienced and newly qualified drivers can often be involved in crashes. This is due to

Mark one answer
- A. being too cautious at junctions
- B. driving in the middle of their lane
- C. showing off and being competitive
- D. staying within the speed limit

88 Which of these, if allowed to get low, could cause you to crash?

Mark one answer
- A. Anti-freeze level
- B. Brake fluid level
- C. Battery water level
- D. Radiator coolant level

89 Which TWO are badly affected if the tyres are under-inflated?

Mark two answers
- A. Braking
- B. Steering
- C. Changing gear
- D. Parking

90 Motor vehicles can harm the environment. This has resulted in

Mark three answers
- A. air pollution
- B. damage to buildings
- C. less risk to health
- D. improved public transport
- E. less use of electrical vehicles
- F. using up of natural resources

91 Excessive or uneven tyre wear can be caused by faults in which THREE of the following?

Mark three answers
- A. The gearbox
- B. The braking system
- C. The accelerator
- D. The exhaust system
- E. Wheel alignment
- F. The suspension

92 You must NOT sound your horn

Mark one answer
- A. between 10pm and 6am in a built-up area
- B. at any time in a built-up area
- C. between 11.30pm and 7am in a built-up area
- D. between 11.30pm and 6am on any road

93 The pictured vehicle is 'environmentally friendly' because it

Mark three answers
- A. reduces noise pollution
- B. uses diesel fuel
- C. uses electricity
- D. uses unleaded fuel
- E. reduces parking spaces
- F. reduces town traffic

94 Supertrams or Light Rapid Transit (LRT) systems are environmentally friendly because

Mark one answer
- A. they use diesel power
- B. they use quieter roads
- C. they use electric power
- D. they do not operate during rush hour

95 'Red routes' in major cities have been introduced to

Mark one answer
- A. raise the speed limits
- B. help the traffic flow
- C. provide better parking
- D. allow lorries to load more freely

96 Road humps, chicanes and narrowings are

Mark one answer
- A. always at major road works
- B. used to increase traffic speed
- C. at toll-bridge approaches only
- D. traffic calming measures

97 The purpose of a catalytic converter is to reduce

Mark one answer

- [ ] **A.** fuel consumption
- [ ] **B.** the risk of fire
- [ ] **C.** toxic exhaust gases
- [ ] **D.** engine wear

98 Catalytic converters are fitted to make the

Mark one answer

- [ ] **A.** engine produce more power
- [ ] **B.** exhaust system easier to replace
- [ ] **C.** engine run quietly
- [ ] **D.** exhaust fumes cleaner

99 It is essential that tyre pressures are checked regularly. When should this be done?

Mark one answer

- [ ] **A.** After any lengthy journey
- [ ] **B.** After travelling at high speed
- [ ] **C.** When tyres are hot
- [ ] **D.** When tyres are cold

100 When should you NOT use your horn in a built-up area?

Mark one answer

- [ ] **A.** Between 8pm and 8am
- [ ] **B.** Between 9pm and dawn
- [ ] **C.** Between dusk and 8am
- [ ] **D.** Between 11.30pm and 7am

101 You will use more fuel if your tyres are

Mark one answer

- [ ] **A.** under-inflated
- [ ] **B.** of different makes
- [ ] **C.** over-inflated
- [ ] **D.** new and hardly used

102 How should you dispose of a used battery?

Mark two answers

- [ ] **A.** Take it to a local authority site
- [ ] **B.** Put it in the dustbin
- [ ] **C.** Break it up into pieces
- [ ] **D.** Leave it on waste land
- [ ] **E.** Take it to a garage
- [ ] **F.** Burn it on a fire

103 What is most likely to cause high fuel consumption?

Mark one answer

- [ ] **A.** Poor steering control
- [ ] **B.** Accelerating around bends
- [ ] **C.** Staying in high gears
- [ ] **D.** Harsh braking and accelerating

104 The fluid level in your battery is low. What should you top it up with?

Mark one answer

- [ ] **A.** Battery acid
- [ ] **B.** Distilled water
- [ ] **C.** Engine oil
- [ ] **D.** Engine coolant

105 You need to top up your battery. What level should you fill to?

Mark one answer

- [ ] **A.** The top of the battery
- [ ] **B.** Half-way up the battery
- [ ] **C.** Just below the cell plates
- [ ] **D.** Just above the cell plates

106 You have too much oil in your engine. What could this cause?

Mark one answer

- [ ] **A.** Low oil pressure
- [ ] **B.** Engine overheating
- [ ] **C.** Chain wear
- [ ] **D.** Oil leaks

107 You are parking on a two-way road at night. The speed limit is 40mph. You should park on the

Mark one answer
- A. left with parking lights on
- B. left with no lights on
- C. right with parking lights on
- D. right with dipped headlights on

108 You are parked on the road at night. Where must you use parking lights?

Mark one answer
- A. Where there are continuous white lines in the middle of the road
- B. Where the speed limit exceeds 30mph
- C. Where you are facing oncoming traffic
- D. Where you are near a bus stop

109 New petrol-engined cars must be fitted with catalytic converters. The reason for this is to

Mark one answer
- A. control exhaust noise levels
- B. prolong the life of the exhaust system
- C. allow the exhaust system to be recycled
- D. reduce harmful exhaust emissions

110 What can cause heavy steering?

Mark one answer
- A. Driving on ice
- B. Badly worn brakes
- C. Over-inflated tyres
- D. Under-inflated tyres

111 Driving with under-inflated tyres can affect

Mark two answers
- A. engine temperature
- B. fuel consumption
- C. braking
- D. oil pressure

112 Excessive or uneven tyre wear can be caused by faults in the

Mark two answers
- A. gearbox
- B. braking system
- C. suspension
- D. exhaust system

113 The main cause of brake fade is

Mark one answer
- A. the brakes overheating
- B. air in the brake fluid
- C. oil on the brakes
- D. the brakes out of adjustment

114 Your anti-lock brakes warning light stays on. You should

Mark one answer
- A. check the brake fluid level
- B. check the footbrake free play
- C. check that the handbrake is released
- D. have the brakes checked immediately

115 While driving, this warning light on your dashboard comes on. It means

Mark one answer
- A. a fault in the braking system
- B. the engine oil is low
- C. a rear light has failed
- D. your seat belt is not fastened

116 It is important to wear suitable shoes when you are driving. Why is this?

Mark one answer

- [ ] A. To prevent wear on the pedals
- [ ] B. To maintain control of the pedals
- [ ] C. To enable you to adjust your seat
- [ ] D. To enable you to walk for assistance if you break down

117 The most important reason for having a properly adjusted head restraint is to

Mark one answer

- [ ] A. make you more comfortable
- [ ] B. help you to avoid neck injury
- [ ] C. help you to relax
- [ ] D. help you to maintain your driving position

118 What will reduce the risk of neck injury resulting from a collision?

Mark one answer

- [ ] A. An air-sprung seat
- [ ] B. Anti-lock brakes
- [ ] C. A collapsible steering wheel
- [ ] D. A properly adjusted head restraint

119 You are driving the children of a friend home from school. They are both under 14 years old. Who is responsible for making sure they wear a seat belt or approved child restraint where required?

Mark one answer

- [ ] A. An adult passenger
- [ ] B. The children
- [ ] C. You, the driver
- [ ] D. Your friend

120 Car passengers MUST wear a seat belt/restraint if one is available, unless they are

Mark one answer

- [ ] A. under 14 years old
- [ ] B. under 1.5 metres (5 feet) in height
- [ ] C. sitting in the rear seat
- [ ] D. exempt for medical reasons

121 You are testing your suspension. You notice that your vehicle keeps bouncing when you press down on the front wing. What does this mean?

Mark one answer

- [ ] A. Worn tyres
- [ ] B. Tyres under-inflated
- [ ] C. Steering wheel not located centrally
- [ ] D. Worn shock absorbers

122 A roof rack fitted to your car will

Mark one answer

- [ ] A. reduce fuel consumption
- [ ] B. improve the road handling
- [ ] C. make your car go faster
- [ ] D. increase fuel consumption

123 It is illegal to drive with tyres that

Mark one answer

- [ ] A. have been bought second-hand
- [ ] B. have a large deep cut in the side wall
- [ ] C. are of different makes
- [ ] D. are of different tread patterns

124 The legal minimum depth of tread for car tyres over three quarters of the breadth is

Mark one answer

- [ ] A. 1mm
- [ ] B. 1.6mm
- [ ] C. 2.5mm
- [ ] D. 4mm

125 You are carrying two 13-year-old children and their parents in your car. Who is responsible for seeing that the children wear seat belts?

Mark one answer

- [ ] A. The children's parents
- [ ] B. You, the driver
- [ ] C. The front-seat passenger
- [ ] D. The children

126 When a roof rack is not in use it should be removed. Why is this?

Mark one answer

- A. It will affect the suspension
- B. It is illegal
- C. It will affect your braking
- D. It will waste fuel

127 How can you, as a driver, help the environment?

Mark three answers

- A. By reducing your speed
- B. By gentle acceleration
- C. By using leaded fuel
- D. By driving faster
- E. By harsh acceleration
- F. By servicing your vehicle properly

128 To help the environment, you can avoid wasting fuel by

Mark three answers

- A. having your vehicle properly serviced
- B. making sure your tyres are correctly inflated
- C. not over-revving in the lower gears
- D. driving at higher speeds where possible
- E. keeping an empty roof rack properly fitted
- F. servicing your vehicle less regularly

129 To reduce the volume of traffic on the roads you could

Mark three answers

- A. use public transport more often
- B. share a car when possible
- C. walk or cycle on short journeys
- D. travel by car at all times
- E. use a car with a smaller engine
- F. drive in a bus lane

130 Which THREE of the following are most likely to waste fuel?

Mark three answers

- A. Reducing your speed
- B. Carrying unnecessary weight
- C. Using the wrong grade of fuel
- D. Under-inflated tyres
- E. Using different brands of fuel
- F. A fitted, empty roof rack

131 Which THREE things can you, as a road user, do to help the environment?

Mark three answers

- A. Cycle when possible
- B. Drive on under-inflated tyres
- C. Use the choke for as long as possible on a cold engine
- D. Have your vehicle properly tuned and serviced
- E. Watch the traffic and plan ahead
- F. Brake as late as possible without skidding

132 As a driver you can cause more damage to the environment by

Mark two answers

- A. choosing a fuel-efficient vehicle
- B. making a lot of short journeys
- C. driving in as high a gear as possible
- D. accelerating as quickly as possible
- E. having your vehicle regularly serviced

133 To help protect the environment you should NOT

Mark one answer

- A. remove your roof rack when unloaded
- B. use your car for very short journeys
- C. walk, cycle or use public transport
- D. empty the boot of unnecessary weight

134 Which THREE does the law require you to keep in good condition?

Mark three answers

- [ ] **A.** Gears
- [ ] **B.** Transmission
- [ ] **C.** Headlights
- [ ] **D.** Windscreen
- [ ] **E.** Seat belts

135 Driving at 70mph uses more fuel than driving at 50mph by up to

Mark one answer

- [ ] **A.** 10%
- [ ] **B.** 30%
- [ ] **C.** 75%
- [ ] **D.** 100%

136 Your vehicle pulls to one side when braking. You should

Mark one answer

- [ ] **A.** change the tyres around
- [ ] **B.** consult your garage as soon as possible
- [ ] **C.** pump the pedal when braking
- [ ] **D.** use your handbrake at the same time

137 As a driver, you can help reduce pollution levels in town centres by

Mark one answer

- [ ] **A.** driving more quickly
- [ ] **B.** over-revving in a low gear
- [ ] **C.** walking or cycling
- [ ] **D.** driving short journeys

138 Unbalanced wheels on a car may cause

Mark one answer

- [ ] **A.** the steering to pull to one side
- [ ] **B.** the steering to vibrate
- [ ] **C.** the brakes to fail
- [ ] **D.** the tyres to deflate

139 Turning the steering wheel while your car is stationary can cause damage to the

Mark two answers

- [ ] **A.** gearbox
- [ ] **B.** engine
- [ ] **C.** brakes
- [ ] **D.** steering
- [ ] **E.** tyres

140 How can you reduce the chances of your car being broken into when leaving it unattended?

Mark one answer

- [ ] **A.** Take all valuables with you
- [ ] **B.** Park near a taxi rank
- [ ] **C.** Place any valuables on the floor
- [ ] **D.** Park near a fire station

141 You have to leave valuables in your car. It would be safer to

Mark one answer

- [ ] **A.** put them in a carrier bag
- [ ] **B.** park near a school entrance
- [ ] **C.** lock them out of sight
- [ ] **D.** park near a bus stop

142 How could you deter theft from your car when leaving it unattended?

Mark one answer

- [ ] **A.** Leave valuables in a carrier bag
- [ ] **B.** Lock valuables out of sight
- [ ] **C.** Put valuables on the seats
- [ ] **D.** Leave valuables on the floor

143 Which of the following may help to deter a thief from stealing your car?

Mark one answer

- [ ] **A.** Always keeping the headlights on
- [ ] **B.** Fitting reflective glass windows
- [ ] **C.** Always keeping the interior light on
- [ ] **D.** Etching the car number on the windows

144
How can you help to prevent your car radio being stolen?

Mark one answer

- A. Park in an unlit area
- B. Hide the radio with a blanket
- C. Park near a busy junction
- D. Install a security-coded radio

145
Which of the following should not be kept in your vehicle?

Mark one answer

- A. A first aid kit
- B. A road atlas
- C. The tax disc
- D. The vehicle documents

146
What should you do when leaving your vehicle?

Mark one answer

- A. Put valuable documents under the seats
- B. Remove all valuables
- C. Cover valuables with a blanket
- D. Leave the interior light on

147
You are parking your car. You have some valuables which you are unable to take with you. What should you do?

Mark one answer

- A. Park near a police station
- B. Put them under the driver's seat
- C. Lock them out of sight
- D. Park in an unlit side road

148
Which of these is most likely to deter the theft of your vehicle?

Mark one answer

- A. An immobiliser
- B. Tinted windows
- C. Locking wheel nuts
- D. A sun screen

149
Wherever possible, which one of the following should you do when parking at night?

Mark one answer

- A. Park in a quiet car park
- B. Park in a well-lit area
- C. Park facing against the flow of traffic
- D. Park next to a busy junction

150
When parking and leaving your car you should

Mark one answer

- A. park under a shady tree
- B. remove the tax disc
- C. park in a quiet road
- D. engage the steering lock

151
When leaving your vehicle parked and unattended you should

Mark one answer

- A. park near a busy junction
- B. park in a housing estate
- C. remove the key and lock it
- D. leave the left indicator on

152
How can you lessen the risk of your vehicle being broken into at night?

Mark one answer

- A. Leave it in a well-lit area
- B. Park in a quiet side road
- C. Don't engage the steering lock
- D. Park in a poorly-lit area

153
To help keep your car secure you could join a

Mark one answer

- A. vehicle breakdown organisation
- B. vehicle watch scheme
- C. advanced driver's scheme
- D. car maintenance class

154 Which TWO of the following will improve fuel consumption?

Mark two answers

- A. Reducing your road speed
- B. Planning well ahead
- C. Late and harsh braking
- D. Driving in lower gears
- E. Short journeys with a cold engine
- F. Rapid acceleration

155 You service your own vehicle. How should you get rid of the old engine oil?

Mark one answer

- A. Take it to a local authority site
- B. Pour it down a drain
- C. Tip it into a hole in the ground
- D. Put it into your dustbin

156 On a vehicle, where would you find a catalytic converter?

Mark one answer

- A. In the fuel tank
- B. In the air filter
- C. On the cooling system
- D. On the exhaust system

157 Why do MOT tests include a strict exhaust emission test?

Mark one answer

- A. To recover the cost of expensive garage equipment
- B. To help protect the environment against pollution
- C. To discover which fuel supplier is used the most
- D. To make sure diesel and petrol engines emit the same fumes

158 To reduce the damage your vehicle causes to the environment you should

Mark three answers

- A. use narrow side streets
- B. avoid harsh acceleration
- C. brake in good time
- D. anticipate well ahead
- E. use busy routes

159 Your vehicle has a catalytic converter. Its purpose is to reduce

Mark one answer

- A. exhaust noise
- B. fuel consumption
- C. exhaust emissions
- D. engine noise

160 A properly serviced vehicle will give

Mark two answers

- A. lower insurance premiums
- B. you a refund on your road tax
- C. better fuel economy
- D. cleaner exhaust emissions

161 You enter a road where there are road humps. What should you do?

Mark one answer

- A. Maintain a reduced speed throughout
- B. Accelerate quickly between each one
- C. Always keep to the maximum legal speed
- D. Drive slowly at school times only

162 When should you especially check the engine oil level?

Mark one answer

- A. Before a long journey
- B. When the engine is hot
- C. Early in the morning
- D. Every 6,000 miles

163 You are having difficulty finding a parking space in a busy town. You can see there is space on the zigzag lines of a zebra crossing. Can you park there?

Mark one answer

- A. No, unless you stay with your car
- B. Yes, in order to drop off a passenger
- C. Yes, if you do not block people from crossing
- D. No, not in any circumstances

164 When leaving your car unattended for a few minutes you should

Mark one answer

- A. leave the engine running
- B. switch the engine off but leave the key in
- C. lock it and remove the key
- D. park near a traffic warden

165 When parking and leaving your car for a few minutes you should

Mark one answer

- A. leave it unlocked
- B. lock it and remove the key
- C. leave the hazard warning lights on
- D. leave the interior light on

166 When leaving your car to help keep it secure you should

Mark one answer

- A. leave the hazard warning lights on
- B. lock it and remove the key
- C. park on a one-way street
- D. park in a residential area

167 When leaving your vehicle where should you park if possible?

Mark one answer

- A. Opposite a traffic island
- B. In a secure car park
- C. On a bend
- D. At or near a taxi rank

168 You are leaving your vehicle parked on a road unattended. When may you leave the engine running?

Mark one answer

- A. If you will be parking for less than 5 minutes
- B. If the battery keeps going flat
- C. When parked in a 20mph zone
- D. Never if you are away from the vehicle

169 In which THREE places would parking your vehicle cause danger or obstruction to other road users?

Mark three answers

- A. In front of a property entrance
- B. At or near a bus stop
- C. On your driveway
- D. In a marked parking space
- E. On the approach to a level crossing

170 In which THREE places would parking cause an obstruction to others?

Mark three answers

- A. Near the brow of a hill
- B. In a lay-by
- C. Where the kerb is raised
- D. Where the kerb has been lowered for wheelchairs
- E. At or near a bus stop

171 You are away from home and have to park your vehicle overnight. Where should you leave it?

Mark one answer

- **A.** Opposite another parked vehicle
- **B.** In a quiet road
- **C.** Opposite a traffic island
- **D.** In a secure car park

172 Before starting a journey it is wise to plan your route. How can you do this?

Mark one answer

- **A.** Look at a map
- **B.** Contact your local garage
- **C.** Look in your vehicle handbook
- **D.** Check your vehicle registration document

173 It can help to plan your route before starting a journey. You can do this by contacting

Mark one answer

- **A.** your local filling station **NI**
- **B.** a motoring organisation
- **C.** the Driver Vehicle Licensing Agency
- **D.** your vehicle manufacturer

174 How can you plan your route before starting a long journey?

Mark one answer

- **A.** Check your vehicle's workshop manual
- **B.** Ask your local garage
- **C.** Use a route planner on the internet
- **D.** Consult your travel agents

175 Planning your route before setting out can be helpful. How can you do this?

Mark one answer

- **A.** Look in a motoring magazine
- **B.** Only visit places you know
- **C.** Try to travel at busy times
- **D.** Print or write down the route

176 Why is it a good idea to plan your journey to avoid busy times?

Mark one answer

- **A.** You will have an easier journey
- **B.** You will have a more stressful journey
- **C.** Your journey time will be longer
- **D.** It will cause more traffic congestion

177 Planning your journey to avoid busy times has a number of advantages. One of these is

Mark one answer

- **A.** your journey will take longer
- **B.** you will have a more pleasant journey
- **C.** you will cause more pollution
- **D.** your stress level will be greater

178 It is a good idea to plan your journey to avoid busy times. This is because

Mark one answer

- **A.** your vehicle will use more fuel
- **B.** you will see less road works
- **C.** it will help to ease congestion
- **D.** you will travel a much shorter distance

179 By avoiding busy times when travelling

Mark one answer

- **A.** you are more likely to be held up
- **B.** your journey time will be longer
- **C.** you will travel a much shorter distance
- **D.** you are less likely to be delayed

180 It can help to plan your route before starting a journey. Why should you also plan an alternative route?

Mark one answer

- **A.** Your original route may be blocked
- **B.** Your maps may have different scales
- **C.** You may find you have to pay a congestion charge
- **D.** Because you may get held up by a tractor

181 You will find that driving smoothly can

Mark one answer
- [ ] **A.** reduce journey times by about 15%
- [ ] **B.** increase fuel consumption by about 15%
- [ ] **C.** reduce fuel consumption by about 15%
- [ ] **D.** increase journey times by about 15%

182 You can save fuel when conditions allow by

Mark one answer
- [ ] **A.** using lower gears as often as possible
- [ ] **B.** accelerating sharply in each gear
- [ ] **C.** using each gear in turn
- [ ] **D.** missing out some gears

183 As well as planning your route before starting a journey, you should also plan an alternative route. Why is this?

Mark one answer
- [ ] **A.** To let another driver overtake
- [ ] **B.** Your first route may be blocked
- [ ] **C.** To avoid a railway level crossing
- [ ] **D.** In case you have to avoid emergency vehicles

184 You are making an appointment and will have to travel a long distance. You should

Mark one answer
- [ ] **A.** allow plenty of time for your journey
- [ ] **B.** plan to go at busy times
- [ ] **C.** avoid all national speed limit roads
- [ ] **D.** prevent other drivers from overtaking

185 You are checking your trailer tyres. What is the legal minimum tread depth over the central three quarters of its breadth?

Mark one answer
- [ ] **A.** 1mm
- [ ] **B.** 1.6mm
- [ ] **C.** 2mm
- [ ] **D.** 2.6mm

186 How can driving in an Eco-safe manner help protect the environment?

Mark one answer
- [ ] **A.** Through the legal enforcement of speed regulations
- [ ] **B.** By increasing the number of cars on the road
- [ ] **C.** Through increased fuel bills
- [ ] **D.** By reducing exhaust emissions

187 What does Eco-safe driving achieve?

Mark one answer
- [ ] **A.** Increased fuel consumption
- [ ] **B.** Improved road safety
- [ ] **C.** Damage to the environment
- [ ] **D.** Increased exhaust emissions

188 How can missing out some gear changes save fuel?

Mark one answer
- [ ] **A.** By reducing the amount of time you are accelerating
- [ ] **B.** Because there is less need to use the footbrake
- [ ] **C.** By controlling the amount of steering
- [ ] **D.** Because coasting is kept to a minimum

189 Fuel consumption is at its highest when you are

Mark one answer
- [ ] **A.** braking
- [ ] **B.** coasting
- [ ] **C.** accelerating
- [ ] **D.** steering

190 Missing out some gears saves fuel by reducing the amount of time you spend

Mark one answer
- [ ] **A.** braking
- [ ] **B.** coasting
- [ ] **C.** steering
- [ ] **D.** accelerating

191 Rapid acceleration and heavy braking can lead to

Mark one answer
- [ ] A. reduced pollution
- [ ] B. increased fuel consumption
- [ ] C. reduced exhaust emissions
- [ ] D. increased road safety

192 What percentage of all emissions does road transport account for?

Mark one answer
- [ ] A. 10%
- [ ] B. 20%
- [ ] C. 30%
- [ ] D. 40%

193 Car passengers MUST wear a seat belt if one is available, unless they are

Mark one answer
- [ ] A. in a vehicle fitted with air bags
- [ ] B. travelling within a congestion charging zone
- [ ] C. sitting in the rear seat
- [ ] D. exempt for medical reasons

194 You are carrying a 5-year-old child in the back seat of your car. They are under 1.35 metres (4 feet 5 inches) in height. A correct child restraint is NOT available. They MUST

Mark one answer
- [ ] A. sit behind the passenger seat
- [ ] B. use an adult seat belt
- [ ] C. share a belt with an adult
- [ ] D. sit between two other children

195 You are carrying a child using a rear-facing baby seat. You want to put it on the front passenger seat. What MUST you do before setting off?

Mark one answer
- [ ] A. Deactivate all front and rear airbags
- [ ] B. Make sure any front passenger airbag is deactivated
- [ ] C. Make sure all the child safety locks are off
- [ ] D. Recline the front passenger seat

196 You are carrying an 11-year-old child in the back seat of your car. They are under 1.35 metres (4 feet 5 inches) in height. You MUST make sure that

Mark one answer
- [ ] A. they sit between two belted people
- [ ] B. they can fasten their own seat belt
- [ ] C. a suitable child restraint is available
- [ ] D. they can see clearly out of the front window

197 You are parked at the side of the road. You will be waiting for some time for a passenger. What should you do?

Mark one answer
- [ ] A. Switch off the engine
- [ ] B. Apply the steering lock
- [ ] C. Switch off the radio
- [ ] D. Use your headlights

198 You are using a rear-facing baby seat. You want to put it on the front passenger seat which is protected by a frontal airbag. What MUST you do before setting off?

Mark one answer
- [ ] A. Deactivate the airbag
- [ ] B. Turn the seat to face sideways
- [ ] C. Ask a passenger to hold the baby
- [ ] D. Put the child in an adult seat belt

199 You are carrying a 5-year-old child in the back seat of your car. They are under 1.35 metres (4 feet 5 inches) in height. They MUST use an adult seat belt ONLY if

Mark one answer
- [ ] A. a correct child restraint is not available
- [ ] B. it is a lap type belt
- [ ] C. they sit between two adults
- [ ] D. it can be shared with another adult

200 Braking distances on ice can be

Mark one answer

- [ ] **A.** twice the normal distance
- [ ] **B.** five times the normal distance
- [ ] **C.** seven times the normal distance
- [ ] **D.** ten times the normal distance

201 Freezing conditions will affect the distance it takes you to come to a stop. You should expect stopping distances to increase by up to

Mark one answer

- [ ] **A.** two times
- [ ] **B.** three times
- [ ] **C.** five times
- [ ] **D.** ten times

202 In very hot weather the road surface can become soft. Which TWO of the following will be most affected?

Mark two answers

- [ ] **A.** The suspension
- [ ] **B.** The grip of the tyres
- [ ] **C.** The braking
- [ ] **D.** The exhaust

203 Where are you most likely to be affected by a side wind?

Mark one answer

- [ ] **A.** On a narrow country lane
- [ ] **B.** On an open stretch of road
- [ ] **C.** On a busy stretch of road
- [ ] **D.** On a long, straight road

204 In windy conditions you need to take extra care when

Mark one answer

- [ ] **A.** using the brakes
- [ ] **B.** making a hill start
- [ ] **C.** turning into a narrow road
- [ ] **D.** passing pedal cyclists

205 In good conditions, what is the typical stopping distance at 70mph?

Mark one answer

- [ ] **A.** 53 metres (175 feet)
- [ ] **B.** 60 metres (197 feet)
- [ ] **C.** 73 metres (240 feet)
- [ ] **D.** 96 metres (315 feet)

206 What is the shortest overall stopping distance on a dry road at 60mph?

Mark one answer

- [ ] **A.** 53 metres (175 feet)
- [ ] **B.** 58 metres (190 feet)
- [ ] **C.** 73 metres (240 feet)
- [ ] **D.** 96 metres (315 feet)

207 You are following a vehicle at a safe distance on a wet road. Another driver overtakes you and pulls into the gap you have left. What should you do?

Mark one answer

- [ ] **A.** Flash your headlights as a warning
- [ ] **B.** Try to overtake safely as soon as you can
- [ ] **C.** Drop back to regain a safe distance
- [ ] **D.** Stay close to the other vehicle until it moves on

208 When approaching a right-hand bend you should keep well to the left. Why is this?

Mark one answer

- [ ] **A.** To improve your view of the road
- [ ] **B.** To overcome the effect of the road's slope
- [ ] **C.** To let faster traffic from behind overtake
- [ ] **D.** To be positioned safely if you skid

209 You have just gone through deep water. To dry off the brakes you should

Mark one answer
- A. accelerate and keep to a high speed for a short time
- B. go slowly while gently applying the brakes
- C. avoid using the brakes at all for a few miles
- D. stop for at least an hour to allow them time to dry

210 You are on a fast, open road in good conditions. For safety, the distance between you and the vehicle in front should be

Mark one answer
- A. a two-second time gap
- B. one car length
- C. 2 metres (6 feet 6 inches)
- D. two car lengths

211 What is the most common cause of skidding?

Mark one answer
- A. Worn tyres
- B. Driver error
- C. Other vehicles
- D. Pedestrians

212 You are driving on an icy road. How can you avoid wheelspin?

Mark one answer
- A. Drive at a slow speed in as high a gear as possible
- B. Use the handbrake if the wheels start to slip
- C. Brake gently and repeatedly
- D. Drive in a low gear at all times

213 Skidding is mainly caused by

Mark one answer
- A. the weather
- B. the driver
- C. the vehicle
- D. the road

214 You are driving in freezing conditions. What should you do when approaching a sharp bend?

Mark two answers
- A. Slow down before you reach the bend
- B. Gently apply your handbrake
- C. Firmly use your footbrake
- D. Coast into the bend
- E. Avoid sudden steering movements

215 You are turning left on a slippery road. The back of your vehicle slides to the right. You should

Mark one answer
- A. brake firmly and not turn the steering wheel
- B. steer carefully to the left
- C. steer carefully to the right
- D. brake firmly and steer to the left

216 Travelling for long distances in neutral (known as coasting)

Mark one answer
- A. improves the driver's control
- B. makes steering easier
- C. reduces the driver's control
- D. uses more fuel

217 Before starting a journey in freezing weather you should clear ice and snow from your vehicle's

Mark four answers

- [ ] **A.** aerial
- [ ] **B.** windows
- [ ] **C.** bumper
- [ ] **D.** lights
- [ ] **E.** mirrors
- [ ] **F.** number plates

218 You are trying to move off on snow. You should use

Mark one answer

- [ ] **A.** the lowest gear you can
- [ ] **B.** the highest gear you can
- [ ] **C.** a high engine speed
- [ ] **D.** the handbrake and footbrake together

219 When driving in falling snow you should

Mark one answer

- [ ] **A.** brake firmly and quickly
- [ ] **B.** be ready to steer sharply
- [ ] **C.** use sidelights only
- [ ] **D.** brake gently in plenty of time

220 The MAIN benefit of having four-wheel drive is to improve

Mark one answer

- [ ] **A.** road holding
- [ ] **B.** fuel consumption
- [ ] **C.** stopping distances
- [ ] **D.** passenger comfort

221 You are about to go down a steep hill. To control the speed of your vehicle you should

Mark one answer

- [ ] **A.** select a high gear and use the brakes carefully
- [ ] **B.** select a high gear and use the brakes firmly
- [ ] **C.** select a low gear and use the brakes carefully
- [ ] **D.** select a low gear and avoid using the brakes

222 How can you use your vehicle's engine as a brake?

Mark one answer

- [ ] **A.** By changing to a lower gear
- [ ] **B.** By selecting reverse gear
- [ ] **C.** By changing to a higher gear
- [ ] **D.** By selecting neutral gear

223 You wish to park facing DOWNHILL. Which TWO of the following should you do?

Mark two answers

- [ ] **A.** Turn the steering wheel towards the kerb
- [ ] **B.** Park close to the bumper of another car
- [ ] **C.** Park with two wheels on the kerb
- [ ] **D.** Put the handbrake on firmly
- [ ] **E.** Turn the steering wheel away from the kerb

224 You are driving in a built-up area. You approach a speed hump. You should

Mark one answer

- [ ] **A.** move across to the left-hand side of the road
- [ ] **B.** wait for any pedestrians to cross
- [ ] **C.** slow your vehicle right down
- [ ] **D.** stop and check both pavements

225 You are on a long, downhill slope. What should you do to help control the speed of your vehicle?

Mark one answer

- [ ] **A.** Select neutral
- [ ] **B.** Select a lower gear
- [ ] **C.** Grip the handbrake firmly
- [ ] **D.** Apply the parking brake gently

226 Your vehicle is fitted with anti-lock brakes. To stop quickly in an emergency you should

Mark one answer

- **A.** brake firmly and pump the brake pedal on and off
- **B.** brake rapidly and firmly without releasing the brake pedal
- **C.** brake gently and pump the brake pedal on and off
- **D.** brake rapidly once, and immediately release the brake pedal

227 Anti-lock brakes prevent wheels from locking. This means the tyres are less likely to

Mark one answer

- **A.** aquaplane
- **B.** skid
- **C.** puncture
- **D.** wear

228 Anti-lock brakes reduce the chances of a skid occurring particularly when

Mark one answer

- **A.** driving down steep hills
- **B.** braking during normal driving
- **C.** braking in an emergency
- **D.** driving on good road surfaces

229 Anti-lock brakes are most effective when you

Mark one answer

- **A.** keep pumping the footbrake to prevent skidding
- **B.** brake normally, but grip the steering wheel tightly
- **C.** brake promptly and firmly until you have slowed down
- **D.** apply the handbrake to reduce the stopping distance

230 Your car is fitted with anti-lock brakes. You need to stop in an emergency. You should

Mark one answer

- **A.** brake normally and avoid turning the steering wheel
- **B.** press the brake pedal promptly and firmly until you have stopped
- **C.** keep pushing and releasing the footbrake quickly to prevent skidding
- **D.** apply the handbrake to reduce the stopping distance

231 Vehicles fitted with anti-lock brakes

Mark one answer

- **A.** are impossible to skid
- **B.** can be steered while you are braking
- **C.** accelerate much faster
- **D.** are not fitted with a handbrake

232 Anti-lock brakes may not work as effectively if the road surface is

Mark two answers

- **A.** dry
- **B.** loose
- **C.** wet
- **D.** good
- **E.** firm

233 Anti-lock brakes are of most use when you are

Mark one answer

- **A.** braking gently
- **B.** driving on worn tyres
- **C.** braking excessively
- **D.** driving normally

234 Driving a vehicle fitted with anti-lock brakes allows you to

Mark one answer

- **A.** brake harder because it is impossible to skid
- **B.** drive at higher speeds
- **C.** steer and brake at the same time
- **D.** pay less attention to the road ahead

235 Anti-lock brakes can greatly assist with

Mark one answer

- **A.** a higher cruising speed
- **B.** steering control when braking
- **C.** control when accelerating
- **D.** motorway driving

236 When would an anti-lock braking system start to work?

Mark one answer

- **A.** After the parking brake has been applied
- **B.** Whenever pressure on the brake pedal is applied
- **C.** Just as the wheels are about to lock
- **D.** When the normal braking system fails to operate

237 You are driving a vehicle fitted with anti-lock brakes. You need to stop in an emergency. You should apply the footbrake

Mark one answer

- **A.** slowly and gently
- **B.** slowly but firmly
- **C.** rapidly and gently
- **D.** rapidly and firmly

238 Your vehicle has anti-lock brakes, but they may not always prevent skidding. This is most likely to happen when driving

Mark two answers

- **A.** in foggy conditions
- **B.** on surface water
- **C.** on loose road surfaces
- **D.** on dry tarmac
- **E.** at night on unlit roads

239 Anti-lock brakes will take effect when

Mark one answer

- **A.** you do not brake quickly enough
- **B.** maximum brake pressure has been applied
- **C.** you have not seen a hazard ahead
- **D.** speeding on slippery road surfaces

240 When driving in fog, which THREE of these are correct?

Mark three answers

- **A.** Use dipped headlights
- **B.** Position close to the centre line
- **C.** Allow more time for your journey
- **D.** Keep close to the car in front
- **E.** Slow down
- **F.** Use sidelights only

241 You are driving along a country road. You see this sign. AFTER dealing safely with the hazard you should always

Mark one answer

- **A.** check your tyre pressures
- **B.** switch on your hazard warning lights
- **C.** accelerate briskly
- **D.** test your brakes

242 You are driving in heavy rain. Your steering suddenly becomes very light. You should

Mark one answer
- A. steer towards the side of the road
- B. apply gentle acceleration
- C. brake firmly to reduce speed
- D. ease off the accelerator

243 How can you tell when you are driving over black ice?

Mark one answer
- A. It is easier to brake
- B. The noise from your tyres sounds louder
- C. You will see tyre tracks on the road
- D. Your steering feels light

244 The roads are icy. You should drive slowly

Mark one answer
- A. in the highest gear possible
- B. in the lowest gear possible
- C. with the handbrake partly on
- D. with your left foot on the brake

245 You are driving along a wet road. How can you tell if your vehicle is aquaplaning?

Mark one answer
- A. The engine will stall
- B. The engine noise will increase
- C. The steering will feel very heavy
- D. The steering will feel very light

246 How can you tell if you are driving on ice?

Mark two answers
- A. The tyres make a rumbling noise
- B. The tyres make hardly any noise
- C. The steering becomes heavier
- D. The steering becomes lighter

247 You are driving along a wet road. How can you tell if your vehicle's tyres are losing their grip on the surface?

Mark one answer
- A. The engine will stall
- B. The steering will feel very heavy
- C. The engine noise will increase
- D. The steering will feel very light

248 You are travelling at 50mph on a good, dry road. What is your typical overall stopping distance?

Mark one answer
- A. 36 metres (120 feet)
- B. 53 metres (175 feet)
- C. 75 metres (245 feet)
- D. 96 metres (315 feet)

249 Your overall stopping distance will be much longer when driving

Mark one answer
- A. in the rain
- B. in fog
- C. at night
- D. in strong winds

250 You have driven through a flood. What is the first thing you should do?

Mark one answer
- A. Stop and check the tyres
- B. Stop and dry the brakes
- C. Check your exhaust
- D. Test your brakes

251 Overall stopping distance is made up of thinking and braking distance. You are on a good, dry road surface with good brakes and tyres. What is a typical BRAKING distance from 50mph?

Mark one answer

- **A.** 14 metres (46 feet)
- **B.** 24 metres (80 feet)
- **C.** 38 metres (125 feet)
- **D.** 55 metres (180 feet)

252 You are on a good, dry road surface. Your brakes and tyres are good. What is the typical overall STOPPING distance at 40mph?

Mark one answer

- **A.** 23 metres (75 feet)
- **B.** 36 metres (120 feet)
- **C.** 53 metres (175 feet)
- **D.** 96 metres (315 feet)

253 You are on a wet motorway with surface spray. You should use

Mark one answer

- **A.** hazard flashers
- **B.** dipped headlights
- **C.** rear fog lights
- **D.** sidelights

254 What should you do when overtaking a motorcyclist in strong winds?

Mark one answer

- **A.** Pass close
- **B.** Pass quickly
- **C.** Pass wide
- **D.** Pass immediately

255 You are overtaking a motorcyclist in strong winds? What should you do?

Mark one answer

- **A.** Allow extra room
- **B.** Give a thank you wave
- **C.** Move back early
- **D.** Sound your horn

256 In heavy motorway traffic the vehicle behind you is following too closely. How can you lower the risk of a collision?

Mark one answer

- **A.** Increase your distance from the vehicle in front
- **B.** Operate the brakes sharply
- **C.** Switch on your hazard lights
- **D.** Move onto the hard shoulder and stop

257 You are following other vehicles in fog. You have your lights on. What else can you do to reduce the chances of being in a collision?

Mark one answer

- **A.** Keep close to the vehicle in front
- **B.** Use your main beam instead of dipped headlights
- **C.** Keep up with the faster vehicles
- **D.** Reduce your speed and increase the gap in front

258 To avoid a collision when entering a contraflow system, you should

Mark three answers

- **A.** reduce speed in good time
- **B.** switch lanes at any time to make progress
- **C.** choose an appropriate lane in good time
- **D.** keep the correct separation distance
- **E.** increase speed to pass through quickly
- **F.** follow other motorists closely to avoid long queues

259

You see this sign on the rear of a slow-moving lorry that you want to pass. It is travelling in the middle lane of a three-lane motorway. You should

Mark one answer

- **A.** cautiously approach the lorry then pass on either side
- **B.** follow the lorry until you can leave the motorway
- **C.** wait on the hard shoulder until the lorry has stopped
- **D.** approach with care and keep to the left of the lorry

260

Where would you expect to see these markers?

Mark two answers

- **A.** On a motorway sign
- **B.** At the entrance to a narrow bridge
- **C.** On a large goods vehicle
- **D.** On a builder's skip placed on the road

261

What does this signal from a police officer mean to oncoming traffic?

Mark one answer

- **A.** Go ahead
- **B.** Stop
- **C.** Turn left
- **D.** Turn right

262

What is the main hazard shown in this picture?

Mark one answer

- **A.** Vehicles turning right
- **B.** Vehicles doing U-turns
- **C.** The cyclist crossing the road
- **D.** Parked cars around the corner

263 Which road user has caused a hazard?

Mark one answer

- **A.** The parked car (arrowed A)
- **B.** The pedestrian waiting to cross (arrowed B)
- **C.** The moving car (arrowed C)
- **D.** The car turning (arrowed D)

264 What should the driver of the car approaching the crossing do?

Mark one answer

- **A.** Continue at the same speed
- **B.** Sound the horn
- **C.** Drive through quickly
- **D.** Slow down and get ready to stop

265 What THREE things should the driver of the grey car (arrowed) be especially aware of?

Mark three answers

- **A.** Pedestrians stepping out between cars
- **B.** Other cars behind the grey car
- **C.** Doors opening on parked cars
- **D.** The bumpy road surface
- **E.** Cars leaving parking spaces
- **F.** Empty parking spaces

266 You think the driver of the vehicle in front has forgotten to cancel their right indicator. You should

Mark one answer

- **A.** flash your lights to alert the driver
- **B.** sound your horn before overtaking
- **C.** overtake on the left if there is room
- **D.** stay behind and not overtake

267 What is the main hazard the driver of the red car (arrowed) should be aware of?

Mark one answer

- **A.** Glare from the sun may affect the driver's vision
- **B.** The black car may stop suddenly
- **C.** The bus may move out into the road
- **D.** Oncoming vehicles will assume the driver is turning right

268 You see this sign ahead. You should expect the road to

Mark one answer

- **A.** go steeply uphill
- **B.** go steeply downhill
- **C.** bend sharply to the left
- **D.** bend sharply to the right

269 You are approaching this cyclist. You should

Mark one answer

- **A.** overtake before the cyclist gets to the junction
- **B.** flash your headlights at the cyclist
- **C.** slow down and allow the cyclist to turn
- **D.** overtake the cyclist on the left-hand side

270 Why must you take extra care when turning right at this junction?

Mark one answer

- **A.** Road surface is poor
- **B.** Footpaths are narrow
- **C.** Road markings are faint
- **D.** There is reduced visibility

271 This yellow sign on a vehicle indicates this is

Mark one answer
- [ ] **A.** a broken-down vehicle
- [ ] **B.** a school bus
- [ ] **C.** an ice-cream van
- [ ] **D.** a private ambulance

272 When approaching this bridge you should give way to

Mark one answer
- [ ] **A.** bicycles
- [ ] **B.** buses
- [ ] **C.** motorcycles
- [ ] **D.** cars

273 What type of vehicle could you expect to meet in the middle of the road?

Mark one answer
- [ ] **A.** Lorry
- [ ] **B.** Bicycle
- [ ] **C.** Car
- [ ] **D.** Motorcycle

274 At this blind junction you must stop

Mark one answer
- [ ] **A.** behind the line, then edge forward to see clearly
- [ ] **B.** beyond the line at a point where you can see clearly
- [ ] **C.** only if there is traffic on the main road
- [ ] **D.** only if you are turning to the right

275 A driver pulls out of a side road in front of you. You have to brake hard. You should

Mark one answer

- [ ] **A.** ignore the error and stay calm
- [ ] **B.** flash your lights to show your annoyance
- [ ] **C.** sound your horn to show your annoyance
- [ ] **D.** overtake as soon as possible

276 An elderly person's driving ability could be affected because they may be unable to

Mark one answer

- [ ] **A.** obtain car insurance
- [ ] **B.** understand road signs
- [ ] **C.** react very quickly
- [ ] **D.** give signals correctly

277 You have just passed these warning lights. What hazard would you expect to see next?

Mark one answer

- [ ] **A.** A level crossing with no barrier
- [ ] **B.** An ambulance station
- [ ] **C.** A school crossing patrol
- [ ] **D.** An opening bridge

278 Why should you be especially cautious when going past this stationary bus?

Mark two answers

- [ ] **A.** There is traffic approaching in the distance
- [ ] **B.** The driver may open the door
- [ ] **C.** It may suddenly move off
- [ ] **D.** People may cross the road in front of it
- [ ] **E.** There are bicycles parked on the pavement

279 In areas where there are 'traffic calming' measures you should

Mark one answer

- [ ] **A.** travel at a reduced speed
- [ ] **B.** always travel at the speed limit
- [ ] **C.** position in the centre of the road
- [ ] **D.** only slow down if pedestrians are near

280 You are planning a long journey. Do you need to plan rest stops?

Mark one answer

- [ ] **A.** Yes, you should plan to stop every half an hour
- [ ] **B.** Yes, regular stops help concentration
- [ ] **C.** No, you will be less tired if you get there as soon as possible
- [ ] **D.** No, only fuel stops will be needed

281 A driver does something that upsets you. You should

Mark one answer

- A. try not to react
- B. let them know how you feel
- C. flash your headlights several times
- D. sound your horn

282 The red lights are flashing. What should you do when approaching this level crossing?

Mark one answer

- A. Go through quickly
- B. Go through carefully
- C. Stop before the barrier
- D. Switch on hazard warning lights

283 What TWO main hazards should you be aware of when going along this street?

Mark two answers

- A. Glare from the sun
- B. Car doors opening suddenly
- C. Lack of road markings
- D. The headlights on parked cars being switched on
- E. Large goods vehicles
- F. Children running out from between vehicles

284 What is the main hazard you should be aware of when following this cyclist?

Mark one answer

- A. The cyclist may move to the left and dismount
- B. The cyclist may swerve out into the road
- C. The contents of the cyclist's carrier may fall on to the road
- D. The cyclist may wish to turn right at the end of the road

285 When approaching this hazard why should you slow down?

Mark two answers

- **A.** Because of the bend
- **B.** Because it's hard to see to the right
- **C.** Because of approaching traffic
- **D.** Because of animals crossing
- **E.** Because of the level crossing

286 A driver's behaviour has upset you. It may help if you

Mark one answer

- **A.** stop and take a break
- **B.** shout abusive language
- **C.** gesture to them with your hand
- **D.** follow their car, flashing your headlights

287 You are on a dual carriageway. Ahead you see a vehicle with an amber flashing light. What will this be?

Mark one answer

- **A.** An ambulance
- **B.** A fire engine
- **C.** A doctor on call
- **D.** A disabled person's vehicle

288 You are approaching crossroads. The traffic lights have failed. What should you do?

Mark one answer

- **A.** Brake and stop only for large vehicles
- **B.** Brake sharply to a stop before looking
- **C.** Be prepared to brake sharply to a stop
- **D.** Be prepared to stop for any traffic

289 Why are place names painted on the road surface?

Mark one answer

- **A.** To restrict the flow of traffic
- **B.** To warn you of oncoming traffic
- **C.** To enable you to change lanes early
- **D.** To prevent you changing lanes

290 What should the driver of the red car (arrowed) do?

Mark one answer

- **A.** Wave the pedestrians who are waiting to cross
- **B.** Wait for the pedestrian in the road to cross
- **C.** Quickly drive behind the pedestrian in the road
- **D.** Tell the pedestrian in the road she should not have crossed

291
You are following a slower-moving vehicle on a narrow country road. There is a junction just ahead on the right. What should you do?

Mark one answer
- **A.** Overtake after checking your mirrors and signalling
- **B.** Stay behind until you are past the junction
- **C.** Accelerate quickly to pass before the junction
- **D.** Slow down and prepare to overtake on the left

292
What should you do as you approach this overhead bridge?

Mark one answer
- **A.** Move out to the centre of the road before going through
- **B.** Find another route, this is only for high vehicles
- **C.** Be prepared to give way to large vehicles in the middle of the road
- **D.** Move across to the right-hand side before going through

293
Why are mirrors often slightly curved (convex)?

Mark one answer
- **A.** They give a wider field of vision
- **B.** They totally cover blind spots
- **C.** They make it easier to judge the speed of following traffic
- **D.** They make following traffic look bigger

294
What does the solid white line at the side of the road indicate?

Mark one answer
- **A.** Traffic lights ahead
- **B.** Edge of the carriageway
- **C.** Footpath on the left
- **D.** Cycle path

295
You are driving towards this level crossing. What would be the first warning of an approaching train?

Mark one answer
- **A.** Both half barriers down
- **B.** A steady amber light
- **C.** One half barrier down
- **D.** Twin flashing red lights

296
You are driving along this motorway. It is raining. When following this lorry you should

Mark two answers

- A. allow at least a two-second gap
- B. move left and drive on the hard shoulder
- C. allow at least a four-second gap
- D. be aware of spray reducing your vision
- E. move right and stay in the right-hand lane

297
You are behind this cyclist. When the traffic lights change, what should you do?

Mark one answer

- A. Try to move off before the cyclist
- B. Allow the cyclist time and room
- C. Turn right but give the cyclist room
- D. Tap your horn and drive through first

298
You are driving towards this left-hand bend. What dangers should you be aware of?

Mark one answer

- A. A vehicle overtaking you
- B. No white lines in the centre of the road
- C. No sign to warn you of the bend
- D. Pedestrians walking towards you

299
While driving, you see this sign ahead. You should

Mark one answer

- A. stop at the sign
- B. slow, but continue around the bend
- C. slow to a crawl and continue
- D. stop and look for open farm gates

300 Why should the junction on the left be kept clear?

Mark one answer

- A. To allow vehicles to enter and emerge
- B. To allow the bus to reverse
- C. To allow vehicles to make a U-turn
- D. To allow vehicles to park

301 When the traffic lights change to green the white car should

Mark one answer

- A. wait for the cyclist to pull away
- B. move off quickly and turn in front of the cyclist
- C. move close up to the cyclist to beat the lights
- D. sound the horn to warn the cyclist

302 You intend to turn left at the traffic lights. Just before turning you should

Mark one answer

- A. check your right mirror
- B. move close up to the white car
- C. straddle the lanes
- D. check for bicycles on your left

303 You should reduce your speed when drving along this road because

Mark one answer

- A. there is a staggered junction ahead
- B. there is a low bridge ahead
- C. there is a change in the road surface
- D. the road ahead narrows

304 You are driving at 60mph. As you approach this hazard you should

Mark one answer

- A. maintain your speed
- B. reduce your speed
- C. take the next right turn
- D. take the next left turn

305 The traffic ahead of you in the left-hand lane is slowing. You should

Mark two answers

- A. be wary of cars on your right cutting in
- B. accelerate past the vehicles in the left-hand lane
- C. pull up on the left-hand verge
- D. move across and continue in the right-hand lane
- E. slow down, keeping a safe separation distance

306 What might you expect to happen in this situation?

Mark one answer

- A. Traffic will move into the right-hand lane
- B. Traffic speed will increase
- C. Traffic will move into the left-hand lane
- D. Traffic will not need to change position

307 You are driving on a road with several lanes. You see these signs above the lanes. What do they mean?

Mark one answer

- A. The two right lanes are open
- B. The two left lanes are open
- C. Traffic in the left lanes should stop
- D. Traffic in the right lanes should stop

308 As a provisional licence holder, you must not drive a motor car

Mark two answers
- A. at more than 40mph
- B. on your own
- C. on the motorway
- D. under the age of 18 years at night
- E. with passengers in the rear seats

309 After passing your driving test, you suffer from ill health. This affects your driving. You MUST

Mark one answer
- A. inform your local police station
- B. avoid using motorways
- C. always drive accompanied
- D. inform the licensing authority

310 You are invited to a pub lunch. You know that you will have to drive in the evening. What is your best course of action?

Mark one answer
- A. Avoid mixing your alcoholic drinks
- B. Not drink any alcohol at all
- C. Have some milk before drinking alcohol
- D. Eat a hot meal with your alcoholic drinks

311 You have been convicted of driving whilst unfit through drink or drugs. You will find this is likely to cause the cost of one of the following to rise considerably. Which one?

Mark one answer
- A. Road fund licence
- B. Insurance premiums
- C. Vehicle test certificate
- D. Driving licence

312 What advice should you give to a driver who has had a few alcoholic drinks at a party?

Mark one answer
- A. Have a strong cup of coffee and then drive home
- B. Drive home carefully and slowly
- C. Go home by public transport
- D. Wait a short while and then drive home

313 You have been taking medicine for a few days which made you feel drowsy. Today you feel better but still need to take the medicine. You should only drive

Mark one answer
- A. if your journey is necessary
- B. at night on quiet roads
- C. if someone goes with you
- D. after checking with your doctor

314

You are about to return home from holiday when you become ill. A doctor prescribes drugs which are likely to affect your driving. You should

Mark one answer

- [ ] **A.** drive only if someone is with you
- [ ] **B.** avoid driving on motorways
- [ ] **C.** not drive yourself
- [ ] **D.** never drive at more than 30mph

315

During periods of illness your ability to drive may be impaired. You MUST

Mark two answers

- [ ] **A.** see your doctor each time before you drive
- [ ] **B.** only take smaller doses of any medicines
- [ ] **C.** be medically fit to drive
- [ ] **D.** not drive after taking certain medicines
- [ ] **E.** take all your medicines with you when you drive

316

You feel drowsy when driving. You should

Mark two answers

- [ ] **A.** stop and rest as soon as possible
- [ ] **B.** turn the heater up to keep you warm and comfortable
- [ ] **C.** make sure you have a good supply of fresh air
- [ ] **D.** continue with your journey but drive more slowly
- [ ] **E.** close the car windows to help you concentrate

317

You are driving along a motorway and become tired. You should

Mark two answers

- [ ] **A.** stop at the next service area and rest
- [ ] **B.** leave the motorway at the next exit and rest
- [ ] **C.** increase your speed and turn up the radio volume
- [ ] **D.** close all your windows and set heating to warm
- [ ] **E.** pull up on the hard shoulder and change drivers

318

You are taking drugs that are likely to affect your driving. What should you do?

Mark one answer

- [ ] **A.** Seek medical advice before driving
- [ ] **B.** Limit your driving to essential journeys
- [ ] **C.** Only drive if accompanied by a full licence-holder
- [ ] **D.** Drive only for short distances

319

You are about to drive home. You feel very tired and have a severe headache. You should

Mark one answer

- [ ] **A.** wait until you are fit and well before driving
- [ ] **B.** drive home, but take a tablet for headaches
- [ ] **C.** drive home if you can stay awake for the journey
- [ ] **D.** wait for a short time, then drive home slowly

320 If you are feeling tired it is best to stop as soon as you can. Until then you should

Mark one answer

- A. increase your speed to find a stopping place quickly
- B. ensure a supply of fresh air
- C. gently tap the steering wheel
- D. keep changing speed to improve concentration

321 Your motorway journey seems boring and you feel drowsy. What should you do?

Mark one answer

- A. stop on the hard shoulder for a sleep
- B. open a window and stop as soon as it's safe and legal
- C. speed up to arrive at your destination sooner
- D. slow down and let other drivers overtake

322 Driving long distances can be tiring. You can prevent this by

Mark three answers

- A. stopping every so often for a walk
- B. opening a window for some fresh air
- C. ensuring plenty of refreshment breaks
- D. completing the journey without stopping
- E. eating a large meal before driving

323 You go to a social event and need to drive a short time after. What precaution should you take?

Mark one answer

- A. Avoid drinking alcohol on an empty stomach
- B. Drink plenty of coffee after drinking alcohol
- C. Avoid drinking alcohol completely
- D. Drink plenty of milk before drinking alcohol

324 You take some cough medicine given to you by a friend. What should you do before driving?

Mark one answer

- A. Ask your friend if taking the medicine affected their driving
- B. Drink some strong coffee one hour before driving
- C. Check the label to see if the medicine will affect your driving
- D. Drive a short distance to see if the medicine is affecting your driving

325 You take the wrong route and find you are on a one-way street. You should

Mark one answer

- A. reverse out of the road
- B. turn round in a side road
- C. continue to the end of the road
- D. reverse into a driveway

326 Which THREE are likely to make you lose concentration while driving?

Mark three answers

- A. Looking at road maps
- B. Listening to loud music
- C. Using your windscreen washers
- D. Looking in your wing mirror
- E. Using a mobile phone

327 You are driving along this road. The driver on the left is reversing from a driveway. You should

Mark one answer

- A. move to the opposite side of the road
- B. drive through as you have priority
- C. sound your horn and be prepared to stop
- D. speed up and drive through quickly

328 You have been involved in an argument before starting your journey. This has made you feel angry. You should

Mark one answer

- A. start to drive, but open a window
- B. drive slower than normal and turn your radio on
- C. have an alcoholic drink to help you relax before driving
- D. calm down before you start to drive

329 You start to feel tired while driving. What should you do?

Mark one answer

- A. Increase your speed slightly
- B. Decrease your speed slightly
- C. Find a less busy route
- D. Pull over at a safe place to rest

330 You are driving on this dual carriageway. Why may you need to slow down?

Mark one answer

- A. There is a broken white line in the centre
- B. There are solid white lines either side
- C. There are road works ahead of you
- D. There are no footpaths

331 You have just been overtaken by this motorcyclist who is cutting in sharply. You should

Mark one answer

- [ ] **A.** sound the horn
- [ ] **B.** brake firmly
- [ ] **C.** keep a safe gap
- [ ] **D.** flash your lights

332 You are about to drive home. You cannot find the glasses you need to wear. You should

Mark one answer

- [ ] **A.** drive home slowly, keeping to quiet roads
- [ ] **B.** borrow a friend's glasses and use those
- [ ] **C.** drive home at night, so that the lights will help you
- [ ] **D.** find a way of getting home without driving

333 Which THREE result from drinking alcohol?

Mark three answers

- [ ] **A.** Less control
- [ ] **B.** A false sense of confidence
- [ ] **C.** Faster reactions
- [ ] **D.** Poor judgement of speed
- [ ] **E.** Greater awareness of danger

334 Which THREE of these are likely effects of drinking alcohol?

Mark three answers

- [ ] **A.** Reduced co-ordination
- [ ] **B.** Increased confidence
- [ ] **C.** Poor judgement
- [ ] **D.** Increased concentration
- [ ] **E.** Faster reactions
- [ ] **F.** Colour blindness

335 How does alcohol affect you?

Mark one answer

- [ ] **A.** It speeds up your reactions
- [ ] **B.** It increases your awareness
- [ ] **C.** It improves your co-ordination
- [ ] **D.** It reduces your concentration

336 Your doctor has given you a course of medicine. Why should you ask how it will affect you?

Mark one answer

- [ ] **A.** Drugs make you a better driver by quickening your reactions
- [ ] **B.** You will have to let your insurance company know about the medicine
- [ ] **C.** Some types of medicine can cause your reactions to slow down
- [ ] **D.** The medicine you take may affect your hearing

337 You are not sure if your cough medicine will affect you. What TWO things should you do?

Mark two answers
- [ ] **A.** Ask your doctor
- [ ] **B.** Check the medicine label
- [ ] **C.** Drive if you feel alright
- [ ] **D.** Ask a friend or relative for advice

338 You are on a motorway. You feel tired. You should

Mark one answer
- [ ] **A.** carry on but go slowly
- [ ] **B.** leave the motorway at the next exit
- [ ] **C.** complete your journey as quickly as possible
- [ ] **D.** stop on the hard shoulder

339 You find that you need glasses to read vehicle number plates at the required distance. When MUST you wear them?

Mark one answer
- [ ] **A.** Only in bad weather conditions
- [ ] **B.** At all times when driving
- [ ] **C.** Only when you think it necessary
- [ ] **D.** Only in bad light or at night time

340 Which TWO things would help to keep you alert during a long journey?

Mark two answers
- [ ] **A.** Finishing your journey as fast as you can
- [ ] **B.** Keeping off the motorways and using country roads
- [ ] **C.** Making sure that you get plenty of fresh air
- [ ] **D.** Making regular stops for refreshments

341 Which of the following types of glasses should NOT be worn when driving at night?

Mark one answer
- [ ] **A.** Half-moon
- [ ] **B.** Round
- [ ] **C.** Bi-focal
- [ ] **D.** Tinted

342 Drinking any amount of alcohol is likely to

Mark three answers
- [ ] **A.** slow down your reactions to hazards
- [ ] **B.** increase the speed of your reactions
- [ ] **C.** worsen your judgement of speed
- [ ] **D.** improve your awareness of danger
- [ ] **E.** give a false sense of confidence

343 What else can seriously affect your concentration, other than alcoholic drinks?

Mark three answers
- [ ] **A.** Drugs
- [ ] **B.** Tiredness
- [ ] **C.** Tinted windows
- [ ] **D.** Contact lenses
- [ ] **E.** Loud music

344 As a driver you find that your eyesight has become very poor. Your optician says they cannot help you. The law says that you should tell

Mark one answer
- [ ] **A.** the licensing authority
- [ ] **B.** your own doctor
- [ ] **C.** the local police station
- [ ] **D.** another optician

345 For which of these may you use hazard warning lights?

Mark one answer

- [ ] **A.** When driving on a motorway to warn traffic behind of a hazard ahead
- [ ] **B.** When you are double parked on a two-way road
- [ ] **C.** When your direction indicators are not working
- [ ] **D.** When warning oncoming traffic that you intend to stop

346 When should you use hazard warning lights?

Mark one answer

- [ ] **A.** When you are double parked on a two-way road
- [ ] **B.** When your direction indicators are not working
- [ ] **C.** When warning oncoming traffic that you intend to stop
- [ ] **D.** When your vehicle has broken down and is causing an obstruction

347 You want to turn left at this junction. The view of the main road is restricted. What should you do?

Mark one answer

- [ ] **A.** Stay well back and wait to see if something comes
- [ ] **B.** Build up your speed so that you can emerge quickly
- [ ] **C.** Stop and apply the handbrake even if the road is clear
- [ ] **D.** Approach slowly and edge out until you can see more clearly

348 You are driving on a motorway. The traffic ahead is braking sharply because of an incident. How could you warn traffic behind you?

Mark one answer

- [ ] **A.** Briefly use the hazard warning lights
- [ ] **B.** Switch on the hazard warning lights continuously
- [ ] **C.** Briefly use the rear fog lights
- [ ] **D.** Switch on the headlights continuously

349 When may you use hazard warning lights?

Mark one answer

- [ ] **A.** To park alongside another car
- [ ] **B.** To park on double yellow lines
- [ ] **C.** When you are being towed
- [ ] **D.** When you have broken down

350 Hazard warning lights should be used when vehicles are

Mark one answer

- [ ] **A.** broken down and causing an obstruction
- [ ] **B.** faulty and moving slowly
- [ ] **C.** being towed along a road
- [ ] **D.** reversing into a side road

351 Some two-way roads are divided into three lanes. Why are these particularly dangerous?

Mark one answer

- [ ] **A.** Traffic in both directions can use the middle lane to overtake
- [ ] **B.** Traffic can travel faster in poor weather conditions
- [ ] **C.** Traffic can overtake on the left
- [ ] **D.** Traffic uses the middle lane for emergencies only

352 When driving a car fitted with automatic transmission what would you use 'kick down' for?

Mark one answer

- [ ] **A.** Cruise control
- [ ] **B.** Quick acceleration
- [ ] **C.** Slow braking
- [ ] **D.** Fuel economy

353 You are waiting to emerge at a junction. Your view is restricted by parked vehicles. What can help you to see traffic on the road you are joining?

Mark one answer

- [ ] **A.** Looking for traffic behind you
- [ ] **B.** Reflections of traffic in shop windows
- [ ] **C.** Making eye contact with other road users
- [ ] **D.** Checking for traffic in your interior mirror

354 Overtaking is a major cause of collisions. In which THREE of these situations should you NOT overtake?

Mark three answers

- [ ] **A.** If you are turning left shortly afterwards
- [ ] **B.** When you are in a one-way street
- [ ] **C.** When you are approaching a junction
- [ ] **D.** If you are travelling up a long hill
- [ ] **E.** When your view ahead is blocked

355 Which sign means that there may be people walking along the road?

Mark one answer

A.

B.

C.

D.

356 You are turning left at a junction. Pedestrians have started to cross the road. You should

Mark one answer

- A. go on, giving them plenty of room
- B. stop and wave at them to cross
- C. blow your horn and proceed
- D. give way to them

357 You are turning left from a main road into a side road. People are already crossing the road into which you are turning. You should

Mark one answer

- A. continue, as it is your right of way
- B. signal to them to continue crossing
- C. wait and allow them to cross
- D. sound your horn to warn them of your presence

358 You are at a road junction, turning into a minor road. There are pedestrians crossing the minor road. You should

Mark one answer

- A. stop and wave the pedestrians across
- B. sound your horn to let the pedestrians know that you are there
- C. give way to the pedestrians who are already crossing
- D. carry on; the pedestrians should give way to you

359
You are turning left into a side road. What hazards should you be especially aware of?

Mark one answer

- **A.** One-way street
- **B.** Pedestrians
- **C.** Traffic congestion
- **D.** Parked vehicles

360
You intend to turn right into a side road. Just before turning you should check for motorcyclists who might be

Mark one answer

- **A.** overtaking on your left
- **B.** following you closely
- **C.** emerging from the side road
- **D.** overtaking on your right

361
A toucan crossing is different from other crossings because

Mark one answer

- **A.** moped riders can use it
- **B.** it is controlled by a traffic warden
- **C.** it is controlled by two flashing lights
- **D.** cyclists can use it

362
At toucan crossings

Mark one answer

- **A.** you only stop if someone is waiting to cross
- **B.** cyclists are not permitted
- **C.** there is a continuously flashing amber beacon
- **D.** pedestrians and cyclists may cross

363
What does this sign tell you?

Mark one answer

- **A.** No cycling
- **B.** Cycle route ahead
- **C.** Cycle parking only
- **D.** End of cycle route

364
How will a school crossing patrol signal you to stop?

Mark one answer

- **A.** By pointing to children on the opposite pavement
- **B.** By displaying a red light
- **C.** By displaying a stop sign
- **D.** By giving you an arm signal

365
Where would you see this sign?

Mark one answer

- **A.** In the window of a car taking children to school
- **B.** At the side of the road
- **C.** At playground areas
- **D.** On the rear of a school bus or coach

366 Which sign tells you that pedestrians may be walking in the road as there is no pavement?

Mark one answer

A.

B.

C.

D.

367 What does this sign mean?

Mark one answer

A. No route for pedestrians and cyclists

B. A route for pedestrians only

C. A route for cyclists only

D. A route for pedestrians and cyclists

368 You see a pedestrian with a white stick and red band. This means that the person is

Mark one answer

A. physically disabled

B. deaf only

C. blind only

D. deaf and blind

369 What action would you take when elderly people are crossing the road?

Mark one answer

A. Wave them across so they know that you have seen them

B. Be patient and allow them to cross in their own time

C. Rev the engine to let them know that you are waiting

D. Tap the horn in case they are hard of hearing

370 You see two elderly pedestrians about to cross the road ahead. You should

Mark one answer

A. expect them to wait for you to pass

B. speed up to get past them quickly

C. stop and wave them across the road

D. be careful, they may misjudge your speed

371 What does this sign mean?

Mark one answer

A. Contraflow pedal cycle lane

B. With-flow pedal cycle lane

C. Pedal cycles and buses only

D. No pedal cycles or buses

372
You are coming up to a roundabout. A cyclist is signalling to turn right. What should you do?

Mark one answer

- A. Overtake on the right
- B. Give a horn warning
- C. Signal the cyclist to move across
- D. Give the cyclist plenty of room

373
You are approaching this roundabout and see the cyclist signal right. Why is the cyclist keeping to the left?

Mark one answer

- A. It is a quicker route for the cyclist
- B. The cyclist is going to turn left instead
- C. The cyclist thinks *The Highway Code* does not apply to bicycles
- D. The cyclist is slower and more vulnerable

374
When you are overtaking a cyclist you should leave as much room as you would give to a car. What is the main reason for this?

Mark one answer

- A. The cyclist might speed up
- B. The cyclist might get off the bike
- C. The cyclist might swerve
- D. The cyclist might have to make a left turn

375
Which TWO should you allow extra room when overtaking?

Mark two answers

- A. Motorcycles
- B. Tractors
- C. Bicycles
- D. Road-sweeping vehicles

376
Why should you look particularly for motorcyclists and cyclists at junctions?

Mark one answer

- A. They may want to turn into the side road
- B. They may slow down to let you turn
- C. They are harder to see
- D. They might not see you turn

377
You are waiting to come out of a side road. Why should you watch carefully for motorcycles?

Mark one answer

- A. Motorcycles are usually faster than cars
- B. Police patrols often use motorcycles
- C. Motorcycles are small and hard to see
- D. Motorcycles have right of way

378
In daylight, an approaching motorcyclist is using a dipped headlight. Why?

Mark one answer

- A. So that the rider can be seen more easily
- B. To stop the battery overcharging
- C. To improve the rider's vision
- D. The rider is inviting you to proceed

379 Motorcyclists should wear bright clothing mainly because

Mark one answer

- [ ] **A.** they must do so by law
- [ ] **B.** it helps keep them cool in summer
- [ ] **C.** the colours are popular
- [ ] **D.** drivers often do not see them

380 There is a slow-moving motorcyclist ahead of you. You are unsure what the rider is going to do. You should

Mark one answer

- [ ] **A.** pass on the left
- [ ] **B.** pass on the right
- [ ] **C.** stay behind
- [ ] **D.** move closer

381 Motorcyclists will often look round over their right shoulder just before turning right. This is because

Mark one answer

- [ ] **A.** they need to listen for following traffic
- [ ] **B.** motorcycles do not have mirrors
- [ ] **C.** looking around helps them balance as they turn
- [ ] **D.** they need to check for traffic in their blind area

382 At road junctions which of the following are most vulnerable?

Mark three answers

- [ ] **A.** Cyclists
- [ ] **B.** Motorcyclists
- [ ] **C.** Pedestrians
- [ ] **D.** Car drivers
- [ ] **E.** Lorry drivers

383 Motorcyclists are particularly vulnerable

Mark one answer

- [ ] **A.** when moving off
- [ ] **B.** on dual carriageways
- [ ] **C.** when approaching junctions
- [ ] **D.** on motorways

384 You notice horse riders in front. What should you do FIRST?

Mark one answer

- [ ] **A.** Pull out to the middle of the road
- [ ] **B.** Slow down and be ready to stop
- [ ] **C.** Accelerate around them
- [ ] **D.** Signal right

385
You are approaching a roundabout. There are horses just ahead of you. You should

Mark two answers

- [ ] **A.** be prepared to stop
- [ ] **B.** treat them like any other vehicle
- [ ] **C.** give them plenty of room
- [ ] **D.** accelerate past as quickly as possible
- [ ] **E.** sound your horn as a warning

386
Which THREE should you do when passing sheep on a road?

Mark three answers

- [ ] **A.** Allow plenty of room
- [ ] **B.** Go very slowly
- [ ] **C.** Pass quickly but quietly
- [ ] **D.** Be ready to stop
- [ ] **E.** Briefly sound your horn

387
At night you see a pedestrian wearing reflective clothing and carrying a bright red light. What does this mean?

Mark one answer

- [ ] **A.** You are approaching road works
- [ ] **B.** You are approaching an organised walk
- [ ] **C.** You are approaching a slow-moving vehicle
- [ ] **D.** You are approaching a traffic danger spot

388
As you approach a pelican crossing the lights change to green. Elderly people are half-way across. You should

Mark one answer

- [ ] **A.** wave them to cross as quickly as they can
- [ ] **B.** rev your engine to make them hurry
- [ ] **C.** flash your lights in case they have not heard you
- [ ] **D.** wait because they will take longer to cross

389
There are flashing amber lights under a school warning sign. What action should you take?

Mark one answer

- [ ] **A.** Reduce speed until you are clear of the area
- [ ] **B.** Keep up your speed and sound the horn
- [ ] **C.** Increase your speed to clear the area quickly
- [ ] **D.** Wait at the lights until they change to green

390 You are approaching this crossing. You should

Mark one answer

- **A.** prepare to slow down and stop
- **B.** stop and wave the pedestrians across
- **C.** speed up and pass by quickly
- **D.** continue unless the pedestrians step out

391 You see a pedestrian with a dog. The dog has a yellow or burgundy coat. This especially warns you that the pedestrian is

Mark one answer

- **A.** elderly
- **B.** dog training
- **C.** colour blind
- **D.** deaf

392 These road markings must be kept clear to allow

Mark one answer

- **A.** schoolchildren to be dropped off
- **B.** for teachers to park
- **C.** schoolchildren to be picked up
- **D.** a clear view of the crossing area

393 You must not stop on these road markings because you may obstruct

Mark one answer

- **A.** children's view of the crossing area
- **B.** teachers' access to the school
- **C.** delivery vehicles' access to the school
- **D.** emergency vehicles' access to the school

394 The left-hand pavement is closed due to street repairs. What should you do?

Mark one answer

- **A.** Watch out for pedestrians walking in the road
- **B.** Use your right-hand mirror more often
- **C.** Speed up to get past the road works quicker
- **D.** Position close to the left-hand kerb

395 Where would you see this sign?

Mark one answer

- **A.** Near a school crossing
- **B.** At a playground entrance
- **C.** On a school bus
- **D.** At a 'pedestrians only' area

396
You are following a motorcyclist on an uneven road. You should

Mark one answer

- A. allow less room so you can be seen in their mirrors
- B. overtake immediately
- C. allow extra room in case they swerve to avoid potholes
- D. allow the same room as normal because road surfaces do not affect motorcyclists

397
You are following two cyclists. They approach a roundabout in the left-hand lane. In which direction should you expect the cyclists to go?

Mark one answer

- A. Left
- B. Right
- C. Any direction
- D. Straight ahead

398
You are travelling behind a moped. You want to turn left just ahead. You should

Mark one answer

- A. overtake the moped before the junction
- B. pull alongside the moped and stay level until just before the junction
- C. sound your horn as a warning and pull in front of the moped
- D. stay behind until the moped has passed the junction

399
You see a horse rider as you approach a roundabout. They are signalling right but keeping well to the left. You should

Mark one answer

- A. proceed as normal
- B. keep close to them
- C. cut in front of them
- D. stay well back

400
How would you react to drivers who appear to be inexperienced?

Mark one answer

- A. Sound your horn to warn them of your presence
- B. Be patient and prepare for them to react more slowly
- C. Flash your headlights to indicate that it is safe for them to proceed
- D. Overtake them as soon as possible

401
You are following a learner driver who stalls at a junction. You should

Mark one answer

- [ ] **A.** be patient as you expect them to make mistakes
- [ ] **B.** stay very close behind and flash your headlights
- [ ] **C.** start to rev your engine if they take too long to restart
- [ ] **D.** immediately steer around them and drive on

402
You are on a country road. What should you expect to see coming towards you on YOUR side of the road?

Mark one answer

- [ ] **A.** Motorcycles
- [ ] **B.** Bicycles
- [ ] **C.** Pedestrians
- [ ] **D.** Horse riders

403
You are turning left into a side road. Pedestrians are crossing the road near the junction. You must

Mark one answer

- [ ] **A.** wave them on
- [ ] **B.** sound your horn
- [ ] **C.** switch on your hazard lights
- [ ] **D.** wait for them to cross

404
You are following a car driven by an elderly driver. You should

Mark one answer

- [ ] **A.** expect the driver to drive badly
- [ ] **B.** flash your lights and overtake
- [ ] **C.** be aware that the driver's reactions may not be as fast as yours
- [ ] **D.** stay very close behind but be careful

405
You are following a cyclist. You wish to turn left just ahead. You should

Mark one answer

- [ ] **A.** overtake the cyclist before the junction
- [ ] **B.** pull alongside the cyclist and stay level until after the junction
- [ ] **C.** hold back until the cyclist has passed the junction
- [ ] **D.** go around the cyclist on the junction

406
A horse rider is in the left-hand lane approaching a roundabout. You should expect the rider to

Mark one answer

- [ ] **A.** go in any direction
- [ ] **B.** turn right
- [ ] **C.** turn left
- [ ] **D.** go ahead

407 You have just passed your test. How can you reduce your risk of a collision?

Mark one answer

- A. By always staying close to the vehicle in front
- B. By never going over 40mph
- C. By staying only in the left-hand lane on all roads
- D. By taking further training

408 Powered vehicles used by disabled people are small and hard to see. How do they give early warning when on a dual carriageway?

Mark one answer

- A. They will have a flashing red light
- B. They will have a flashing green light
- C. They will have a flashing blue light
- D. They will have a flashing amber light

409 You should never attempt to overtake a cyclist

Mark one answer

- A. just before you turn left
- B. on a left-hand bend
- C. on a one-way street
- D. on a dual carriageway

410 Ahead of you there is a moving vehicle with a flashing amber beacon. This means it is

Mark one answer

- A. slow moving
- B. broken down
- C. a doctor's car
- D. a school crossing patrol

411 You want to reverse into a side road. You are not sure that the area behind your car is clear. What should you do?

Mark one answer

- A. Look through the rear window only
- B. Get out and check
- C. Check the mirrors only
- D. Carry on, assuming it is clear

412 You are about to reverse into a side road. A pedestrian wishes to cross behind you. You should

Mark one answer

- A. wave to the pedestrian to stop
- B. give way to the pedestrian
- C. wave to the pedestrian to cross
- D. reverse before the pedestrian starts to cross

413 Who is especially in danger of not being seen as you reverse your car?

Mark one answer

- A. Motorcyclists
- B. Car drivers
- C. Cyclists
- D. Children

414 You are reversing around a corner when you notice a pedestrian walking behind you. What should you do?

Mark one answer

- A. Slow down and wave the pedestrian across
- B. Continue reversing and steer round the pedestrian
- C. Stop and give way
- D. Continue reversing and sound your horn

415 You want to turn right from a junction but your view is restricted by parked vehicles. What should you do?

Mark one answer

- **A.** Move out quickly, but be prepared to stop
- **B.** Sound your horn and pull out if there is no reply
- **C.** Stop, then move slowly forward until you have a clear view
- **D.** Stop, get out and look along the main road to check

416 You are at the front of a queue of traffic waiting to turn right into a side road. Why is it important to check your right mirror just before turning?

Mark one answer

- **A.** To look for pedestrians about to cross
- **B.** To check for overtaking vehicles
- **C.** To make sure the side road is clear
- **D.** To check for emerging traffic

417 What must a driver do at a pelican crossing when the amber light is flashing?

Mark one answer

- **A.** Signal the pedestrian to cross
- **B.** Always wait for the green light before proceeding
- **C.** Give way to any pedestrians on the crossing
- **D.** Wait for the red-and-amber light before proceeding

418 You have stopped at a pelican crossing. A disabled person is crossing slowly in front of you. The lights have now changed to green. You should

Mark two answers

- **A.** allow the person to cross
- **B.** drive in front of the person
- **C.** drive behind the person
- **D.** sound your horn
- **E.** be patient
- **F.** edge forward slowly

419 You are driving past parked cars. You notice a bicycle wheel sticking out between them. What should you do?

Mark one answer

- **A.** Accelerate past quickly and sound your horn
- **B.** Slow down and wave the cyclist across
- **C.** Brake sharply and flash your headlights
- **D.** Slow down and be prepared to stop for a cyclist

420

You are driving past a line of parked cars. You notice a ball bouncing out into the road ahead. What should you do?

Mark one answer

A. Continue driving at the same speed and sound your horn

B. Continue driving at the same speed and flash your headlights

C. Slow down and be prepared to stop for children

D. Stop and wave the children across to fetch their ball

421

You want to turn right from a main road into a side road. Just before turning you should

Mark one answer

A. cancel your right-turn signal

B. select first gear

C. check for traffic overtaking on your right

D. stop and set the handbrake

422

You are driving in slow-moving queues of traffic. Just before changing lane you should

Mark one answer

A. sound the horn

B. look for motorcyclists filtering through the traffic

C. give a 'slowing down' arm signal

D. change down to first gear

423

You are driving in town. There is a bus at the bus stop on the other side of the road. Why should you be careful?

Mark one answer

A. The bus may have broken down

B. Pedestrians may come from behind the bus

C. The bus may move off suddenly

D. The bus may remain stationary

424

How should you overtake horse riders?

Mark one answer

A. Drive up close and overtake as soon as possible

B. Speed is not important but allow plenty of room

C. Use your horn just once to warn them

D. Drive slowly and leave plenty of room

425

You are dazzled at night by a vehicle behind you. You should

Mark one answer

A. set your mirror to anti-dazzle

B. set your mirror to dazzle the other driver

C. brake sharply to a stop

D. switch your rear lights on and off

426 Yellow zigzag lines on the road outside schools mean

Mark one answer

- [ ] **A.** sound your horn to alert other road users
- [ ] **B.** stop to allow children to cross
- [ ] **C.** you must not park or stop on these lines
- [ ] **D.** you must not drive over these lines

427 What do these road markings outside a school mean?

Mark one answer

- [ ] **A.** You may park here if you are a teacher
- [ ] **B.** Sound your horn before parking
- [ ] **C.** When parking, use your hazard warning lights
- [ ] **D.** You should not wait or park your vehicle here

428 You are driving on a main road. You intend to turn right into a side road. Just before turning you should

Mark one answer

- [ ] **A.** adjust your interior mirror
- [ ] **B.** flash your headlamps
- [ ] **C.** steer over to the left
- [ ] **D.** check for traffic overtaking on your right

429 Why should you allow extra room when overtaking a motorcyclist on a windy day?

Mark one answer

- [ ] **A.** The rider may turn off suddenly to get out of the wind
- [ ] **B.** The rider may be blown across in front of you
- [ ] **C.** The rider may stop suddenly
- [ ] **D.** The rider may be travelling faster than normal

430 You are driving towards a zebra crossing. A person in a wheelchair is waiting to cross. What should you do?

Mark one answer

- [ ] **A.** Continue on your way
- [ ] **B.** Wave to the person to cross
- [ ] **C.** Wave to the person to wait
- [ ] **D.** Be prepared to stop

431
Where in particular should you look out for motorcyclists?

Mark one answer
- A. In a filling station
- B. At a road junction
- C. Near a service area
- D. When entering a car park

432
Where should you take particular care to look out for motorcyclists and cyclists?

Mark one answer
- A. On dual carriageways
- B. At junctions
- C. At zebra crossings
- D. On one-way streets

433
The road outside this school is marked with yellow zigzag lines. What do these lines mean?

Mark one answer
- A. You may park on the lines when dropping off schoolchildren
- B. You may park on the lines when picking schoolchildren up
- C. You must not wait or park your vehicle here at all
- D. You must stay with your vehicle if you park here

434
Some junctions controlled by traffic lights have a marked area between two stop lines. What is this for?

Mark one answer
- A. To allow taxis to position in front of other traffic
- B. To allow people with disabilities to cross the road
- C. To allow cyclists and pedestrians to cross the road together
- D. To allow cyclists to position in front of other traffic

435
At some traffic lights there are advance stop lines and a marked area. What are these for?

Mark one answer
- A. To allow cyclists to position in front of other traffic
- B. To let pedestrians cross when the lights change
- C. To prevent traffic from jumping the lights
- D. To let passengers get off a bus which is queuing

436

You are about to overtake a slow-moving motorcyclist. Which one of these signs would make you take special care?

Mark one answer

A.

B.

C.

D.

437

You are waiting to emerge left from a minor road. A large vehicle is approaching from the right. You have time to turn, but you should wait. Why?

Mark one answer

A. The large vehicle can easily hide an overtaking vehicle

B. The large vehicle can turn suddenly

C. The large vehicle is difficult to steer in a straight line

D. The large vehicle can easily hide vehicles from the left

438

You are following a long vehicle. It approaches a crossroads and signals left, but moves out to the right. You should

Mark one answer

A. get closer in order to pass it quickly

B. stay well back and give it room

C. assume the signal is wrong and it is really turning right

D. overtake as it starts to slow down

439

You are following a long vehicle approaching a crossroads. The driver signals right but moves close to the left-hand kerb. What should you do?

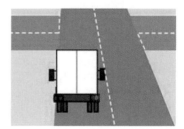

Mark one answer

A. Warn the driver of the wrong signal

B. Wait behind the long vehicle

C. Report the driver to the police

D. Overtake on the right-hand side

440

You are approaching a mini-roundabout. The long vehicle in front is signalling left but positioned over to the right. You should

Mark one answer

- A. sound your horn
- B. overtake on the left
- C. follow the same course as the lorry
- D. keep well back

441

Before overtaking a large vehicle you should keep well back. Why is this?

Mark one answer

- A. To give acceleration space to overtake quickly on blind bends
- B. To get the best view of the road ahead
- C. To leave a gap in case the vehicle stops and rolls back
- D. To offer other drivers a safe gap if they want to overtake you

442

Why is it more difficult to overtake a large vehicle than a car?

Mark one answer

- A. It takes longer to pass one
- B. They may suddenly pull up
- C. Their brakes are not as good
- D. They climb hills more slowly

443

You are travelling behind a bus that pulls up at a bus stop. What should you do?

Mark two answers

- A. Accelerate past the bus sounding your horn
- B. Watch carefully for pedestrians
- C. Be ready to give way to the bus
- D. Pull in closely behind the bus

444

When you approach a bus signalling to move off from a bus stop you should

Mark one answer

- A. get past before it moves
- B. allow it to pull away, if it is safe to do so
- C. flash your headlights as you approach
- D. signal left and wave the bus on

445 Which of these is LEAST likely to be affected by crosswinds?

Mark one answer

- [ ] A. Cyclists
- [ ] B. Motorcyclists
- [ ] C. High-sided vehicles
- [ ] D. Cars

446 You are following a large lorry on a wet road. Spray makes it difficult to see. You should

Mark one answer

- [ ] A. drop back until you can see better
- [ ] B. put your headlights on full beam
- [ ] C. keep close to the lorry, away from the spray
- [ ] D. speed up and overtake quickly

447 What should you do as you approach this lorry?

Mark one answer

- [ ] A. Slow down and be prepared to wait
- [ ] B. Make the lorry wait for you
- [ ] C. Flash your lights at the lorry
- [ ] D. Move to the right-hand side of the road

448 You are following a large articulated vehicle. It is going to turn left into a narrow road. What action should you take?

Mark one answer

- [ ] A. Move out and overtake on the right
- [ ] B. Pass on the left as the vehicle moves out
- [ ] C. Be prepared to stop behind
- [ ] D. Overtake quickly before the lorry moves out

449 You keep well back while waiting to overtake a large vehicle. A car fills the gap. You should

Mark one answer

- [ ] A. sound your horn
- [ ] B. drop back further
- [ ] C. flash your headlights
- [ ] D. start to overtake

450 You are following a large vehicle approaching crossroads. The driver signals to turn left. What should you do?

Mark one answer

- [ ] A. Overtake if you can leave plenty of room
- [ ] B. Overtake only if there are no oncoming vehicles
- [ ] C. Do not overtake until the vehicle begins to turn
- [ ] D. Do not overtake when at or approaching a junction

451 You are following a long lorry. The driver signals to turn left into a narrow road. What should you do?

Mark one answer
- **A.** Overtake on the left before the lorry reaches the junction
- **B.** Overtake on the right as soon as the lorry slows down
- **C.** Do not overtake unless you can see there is no oncoming traffic
- **D.** Do not overtake, stay well back and be prepared to stop

452 You wish to overtake a long, slow-moving vehicle on a busy road. You should

Mark one answer
- **A.** follow it closely and keep moving out to see the road ahead
- **B.** flash your headlights for the oncoming traffic to give way
- **C.** stay behind until the driver waves you past
- **D.** keep well back until you can see that it is clear

453 It is very windy. You are behind a motorcyclist who is overtaking a high-sided vehicle. What should you do?

Mark one answer
- **A.** Overtake the motorcyclist immediately
- **B.** Keep well back
- **C.** Stay level with the motorcyclist
- **D.** Keep close to the motorcyclist

454 It is very windy. You are about to overtake a motorcyclist. You should

Mark one answer
- **A.** overtake slowly
- **B.** allow extra room
- **C.** sound your horn
- **D.** keep close as you pass

455 You are towing a caravan. Which is the safest type of rear-view mirror to use?

Mark one answer
- **A.** Interior wide-angle mirror
- **B.** Extended-arm side mirrors
- **C.** Ordinary door mirrors
- **D.** Ordinary interior mirror

456 You are driving in town. Ahead of you a bus is at a bus stop. Which TWO of the following should you do?

Mark two answers
- **A.** Be prepared to give way if the bus suddenly moves off
- **B.** Continue at the same speed but sound your horn as a warning
- **C.** Watch carefully for the sudden appearance of pedestrians
- **D.** Pass the bus as quickly as you possibly can

457
You are driving in heavy traffic on a wet road. Spray makes it difficult to be seen. You should use your

Mark two answers
- [ ] A. full beam headlights
- [ ] B. rear fog lights if visibility is less than 100 metres (328 feet)
- [ ] C. rear fog lights if visibility is more than 100 metres (328 feet)
- [ ] D. dipped headlights
- [ ] E. sidelights only

458
You are driving along this road. What should you be prepared to do?

Mark one answer
- [ ] A. Sound your horn and continue
- [ ] B. Slow down and give way
- [ ] C. Report the driver to the police
- [ ] D. Squeeze through the gap

459
As a driver why should you be more careful where trams operate?

Mark one answer
- [ ] A. Because they do not have a horn
- [ ] B. Because they do not stop for cars
- [ ] C. Because they do not have lights
- [ ] D. Because they cannot steer to avoid you

460
It is a very windy day and you are about to overtake a cyclist. What should you do?

Mark one answer
- [ ] A. Overtake very closely
- [ ] B. Keep close as you pass
- [ ] C. Sound your horn repeatedly
- [ ] D. Allow extra room

461
Powered vehicles, such as wheelchairs or scooters, used by disabled people have a maximum speed of

Mark one answer
- [ ] A. 8mph
- [ ] B. 12mph
- [ ] C. 16mph
- [ ] D. 20mph

462
In front of you is a Class 3 powered vehicle (powered wheelchair) driven by a disabled person. These vehicles have a maximum speed of

Mark one answer
- [ ] A. 8mph (12km/h)
- [ ] B. 18mph (29km/h)
- [ ] C. 28mph (45km/h)
- [ ] D. 38mph (61km/h)

463 In which THREE of these situations may you overtake another vehicle on the left?

Mark three answers

- A. When you are in a one-way street
- B. When approaching a motorway slip road where you will be turning off
- C. When the vehicle in front is signalling to turn right
- D. When a slower vehicle is travelling in the right-hand lane of a dual carriageway
- E. In slow-moving traffic queues when traffic in the right-hand lane is moving more slowly

464 You are travelling in very heavy rain. Your overall stopping distance is likely to be

Mark one answer

- A. doubled
- B. halved
- C. up to ten times greater
- D. no different

465 Which TWO of the following are correct? When overtaking at night you should

Mark two answers

- A. wait until a bend so that you can see the oncoming headlights
- B. sound your horn twice before moving out
- C. be careful because you can see less
- D. beware of bends in the road ahead
- E. put headlights on full beam

466 When may you wait in a box junction?

Mark one answer

- A. When you are stationary in a queue of traffic
- B. When approaching a pelican crossing
- C. When approaching a zebra crossing
- D. When oncoming traffic prevents you turning right

467 Which of these plates normally appear with this road sign?

Mark one answer

- A. Humps for ½ mile
- B. Hump Bridge
- C. Low Bridge
- D. Soft Verge

468 Areas reserved for trams may have

Mark three answers

- [ ] **A.** metal studs around them
- [ ] **B.** white line markings
- [ ] **C.** zigzag markings
- [ ] **D.** a different coloured surface
- [ ] **E.** yellow hatch markings
- [ ] **F.** a different surface texture

469 Traffic calming measures are used to

Mark one answer

- [ ] **A.** stop road rage
- [ ] **B.** help overtaking
- [ ] **C.** slow traffic down
- [ ] **D.** help parking

470 Why should you always reduce your speed when travelling in fog?

Mark one answer

- [ ] **A.** The brakes do not work as well
- [ ] **B.** You will be dazzled by other headlights
- [ ] **C.** The engine will take longer to warm up
- [ ] **D.** It is more difficult to see events ahead

471 You are on a motorway in fog. The left-hand edge of the motorway can be identified by reflective studs. What colour are they?

Mark one answer

- [ ] **A.** Green
- [ ] **B.** Amber
- [ ] **C.** Red
- [ ] **D.** White

472 A rumble device is designed to

Mark two answers

- [ ] **A.** give directions
- [ ] **B.** prevent cattle escaping
- [ ] **C.** alert you to low tyre pressure
- [ ] **D.** alert you to a hazard
- [ ] **E.** encourage you to reduce speed

473 After this hazard you should test your brakes. Why is this?

Ford

Mark one answer

- [ ] **A.** You will be on a slippery road
- [ ] **B.** Your brakes will be soaking wet
- [ ] **C.** You will be going down a long hill
- [ ] **D.** You will have just crossed a long bridge

474 You have to make a journey in foggy conditions. You should

Mark one answer

- [ ] **A.** follow other vehicles' tail-lights closely
- [ ] **B.** avoid using dipped headlights
- [ ] **C.** leave plenty of time for your journey
- [ ] **D.** keep two seconds behind other vehicles

475 You see a vehicle coming towards you on a single-track road. You should

Mark one answer

- [ ] **A.** go back to the main road
- [ ] **B.** do an emergency stop
- [ ] **C.** stop at a passing place
- [ ] **D.** put on your hazard warning lights

476 You are overtaking a car at night. You must be sure that

Mark one answer

- [ ] **A.** you flash your headlights before overtaking
- [ ] **B.** you select a higher gear
- [ ] **C.** you have switched your lights to full beam before overtaking
- [ ] **D.** you do not dazzle other road users

477 You are on a road which has speed humps. A driver in front is travelling slower than you. You should

Mark one answer

- [ ] **A.** sound your horn
- [ ] **B.** overtake as soon as you can
- [ ] **C.** flash your headlights
- [ ] **D.** slow down and stay behind

478 You see these markings on the road. Why are they there?

Mark one answer

- [ ] **A.** To show a safe distance between vehicles
- [ ] **B.** To keep the area clear of traffic
- [ ] **C.** To make you aware of your speed
- [ ] **D.** To warn you to change direction

479 When MUST you use dipped headlights during the day?

Mark one answer

- [ ] **A.** All the time
- [ ] **B.** Along narrow streets
- [ ] **C.** In poor visibility
- [ ] **D.** When parking

480 What are TWO main reasons why coasting downhill is wrong?

Mark two answers

- [ ] **A.** Fuel consumption will be higher
- [ ] **B.** The vehicle will get faster
- [ ] **C.** It puts more wear and tear on the tyres
- [ ] **D.** You have less braking and steering control
- [ ] **E.** It damages the engine

481 Hills can affect the performance of your vehicle. Which TWO apply when driving up steep hills?

Mark two answers

- [ ] **A.** Higher gears will pull better
- [ ] **B.** You will slow down sooner
- [ ] **C.** Overtaking will be easier
- [ ] **D.** The engine will work harder
- [ ] **E.** The steering will feel heavier

482 Why is travelling in neutral for long distances (known as coasting) wrong?

Mark one answer

- [ ] **A.** It will cause the car to skid
- [ ] **B.** It will make the engine stall
- [ ] **C.** The engine will run faster
- [ ] **D.** There is no engine braking

483 You are driving on the motorway in windy conditions. When passing high-sided vehicles you should

Mark one answer

- [ ] **A.** increase your speed
- [ ] **B.** be wary of a sudden gust
- [ ] **C.** drive alongside very closely
- [ ] **D.** expect normal conditions

484 To correct a rear-wheel skid you should

Mark one answer

- [ ] **A.** not steer at all
- [ ] **B.** steer away from it
- [ ] **C.** steer into it
- [ ] **D.** apply your handbrake

485 You have to make a journey in fog. What are the TWO most important things you should do before you set out?

Mark two answers

- [ ] **A.** Top up the radiator with antifreeze
- [ ] **B.** Make sure that you have a warning triangle in the vehicle
- [ ] **C.** Check that your lights are working
- [ ] **D.** Check the battery
- [ ] **E.** Make sure that the windows are clean

486 You are driving in fog. Why should you keep well back from the vehicle in front?

Mark one answer

- [ ] **A.** In case it changes direction suddenly
- [ ] **B.** In case its fog lights dazzle you
- [ ] **C.** In case it stops suddenly
- [ ] **D.** In case its brake lights dazzle you

487 You should switch your rear fog lights on when visibility drops below

Mark one answer

- [ ] **A.** your overall stopping distance
- [ ] **B.** ten car lengths
- [ ] **C.** 200 metres (656 feet)
- [ ] **D.** 100 metres (328 feet)

488 Whilst driving, the fog clears and you can see more clearly. You must remember to

Mark one answer
- [ ] **A.** switch off the fog lights
- [ ] **B.** reduce your speed
- [ ] **C.** switch off the demister
- [ ] **D.** close any open windows

489 You have to park on the road in fog. You should

Mark one answer
- [ ] **A.** leave sidelights on
- [ ] **B.** leave dipped headlights and fog lights on
- [ ] **C.** leave dipped headlights on
- [ ] **D.** leave main beam headlights on

490 On a foggy day you unavoidably have to park your car on the road. You should

Mark one answer
- [ ] **A.** leave your headlights on
- [ ] **B.** leave your fog lights on
- [ ] **C.** leave your sidelights on
- [ ] **D.** leave your hazard lights on

491 You are travelling at night. You are dazzled by headlights coming towards you. You should

Mark one answer
- [ ] **A.** pull down your sun visor
- [ ] **B.** slow down or stop
- [ ] **C.** switch on your main beam headlights
- [ ] **D.** put your hand over your eyes

492 Which FOUR of the following may apply when dealing with this hazard?

Mark four answers
- [ ] **A.** It could be more difficult in winter
- [ ] **B.** Use a low gear and drive slowly
- [ ] **C.** Use a high gear to prevent wheelspin
- [ ] **D.** Test your brakes afterwards
- [ ] **E.** Always switch on fog lamps
- [ ] **F.** There may be a depth gauge

493 Front fog lights may be used ONLY if

Mark one answer
- [ ] **A.** visibility is seriously reduced
- [ ] **B.** they are fitted above the bumper
- [ ] **C.** they are not as bright as the headlights
- [ ] **D.** an audible warning device is used

494 Front fog lights may be used ONLY if

Mark one answer
- [ ] **A.** your headlights are not working
- [ ] **B.** they are operated with rear fog lights
- [ ] **C.** they were fitted by the vehicle manufacturer
- [ ] **D.** visibility is seriously reduced

495

You are driving with your front fog lights switched on. Earlier fog has now cleared. What should you do?

N 512 CTW

Mark one answer

- A. Leave them on if other drivers have their lights on
- B. Switch them off as long as visibility remains good
- C. Flash them to warn oncoming traffic that it is foggy
- D. Drive with them on instead of your headlights

496

Front fog lights should be used ONLY when

Mark one answer

- A. travelling in very light rain
- B. visibility is seriously reduced
- C. daylight is fading
- D. driving after midnight

497

Why is it dangerous to leave rear fog lights on when they are not needed?

Mark two answers

- A. Brake lights are less clear
- B. Following drivers can be dazzled
- C. Electrical systems could be overloaded
- D. Direction indicators may not work properly
- E. The battery could fail

498

Using rear fog lights on a clear dry night will

Mark two answers

- A. reduce glare from the road surface
- B. make your brake lights less visible
- C. give a better view of the road ahead
- D. dazzle following drivers
- E. help your indicators to be seen more clearly

499

You have just driven out of fog. Visibility is now good. You MUST

Mark one answer

- A. switch off all your fog lights
- B. keep your rear fog lights on
- C. keep your front fog lights on
- D. leave fog lights on in case fog returns

500

You forget to switch off your rear fog lights when the fog has cleared. This may

Mark three answers

- A. dazzle other road users
- B. reduce battery life
- C. cause brake lights to be less clear
- D. be breaking the law
- E. seriously affect engine power

501

You have been driving in thick fog which has now cleared. You must switch OFF your rear fog lights because

Mark one answer

- A. they use a lot of power from the battery
- B. they make your brake lights less clear
- C. they will cause dazzle in your rear-view mirrors
- D. they may not be properly adjusted

502 Front fog lights should be used

Mark one answer
- [ ] A. when visibility is reduced to 100 metres (328 feet)
- [ ] B. as a warning to oncoming traffic
- [ ] C. when driving during the hours of darkness
- [ ] D. in any conditions and at any time

503 Using rear fog lights in clear daylight will

Mark one answer
- [ ] A. be useful when towing a trailer
- [ ] B. give extra protection
- [ ] C. dazzle other drivers
- [ ] D. make following drivers keep back

504 Using front fog lights in clear daylight will

Mark one answer
- [ ] A. flatten the battery
- [ ] B. dazzle other drivers
- [ ] C. improve your visibility
- [ ] D. increase your awareness

505 You may use front fog lights with headlights ONLY when visibility is reduced to less than

Mark one answer
- [ ] A. 100 metres (328 feet)
- [ ] B. 200 metres (656 feet)
- [ ] C. 300 metres (984 feet)
- [ ] D. 400 metres (1,312 feet)

506 You may drive with front fog lights switched on

Mark one answer
- [ ] A. when visibility is less than 100 metres (328 feet)
- [ ] B. at any time to be noticed
- [ ] C. instead of headlights on high-speed roads
- [ ] D. when dazzled by the lights of oncoming vehicles

507 Chains can be fitted to your wheels to help prevent

Mark one answer
- [ ] A. damage to the road surface
- [ ] B. wear to the tyres
- [ ] C. skidding in deep snow
- [ ] D. the brakes locking

508 Holding the clutch pedal down or rolling in neutral for too long while driving will

Mark one answer
- [ ] A. use more fuel
- [ ] B. cause the engine to overheat
- [ ] C. reduce your control
- [ ] D. improve tyre wear

509 How can you use the engine of your vehicle to control your speed?

Mark one answer
- A. By changing to a lower gear
- B. By selecting reverse gear
- C. By changing to a higher gear
- D. By selecting neutral

510 You are driving down a steep hill. Why could keeping the clutch down or rolling in neutral for too long be dangerous?

Mark one answer
- A. Fuel consumption will be higher
- B. Your vehicle will pick up speed
- C. It will damage the engine
- D. It will wear tyres out more quickly

511 Why could keeping the clutch down or selecting neutral for long periods of time be dangerous?

Mark one answer
- A. Fuel spillage will occur
- B. Engine damage may be caused
- C. You will have less steering and braking control
- D. It will wear tyres out more quickly

512 You are driving on an icy road. What distance should you drive from the car in front?

Mark one answer
- A. four times the normal distance
- B. six times the normal distance
- C. eight times the normal distance
- D. ten times the normal distance

513 You are on a well-lit motorway at night. You must

Mark one answer
- A. use only your sidelights
- B. always use your headlights
- C. always use rear fog lights
- D. use headlights only in bad weather

514 You are on a motorway at night with other vehicles just ahead of you. Which lights should you have on?

Mark one answer
- A. Front fog lights
- B. Main beam headlights
- C. Sidelights only
- D. Dipped headlights

515 Which THREE of the following will affect your stopping distance?

Mark three answers
- A. How fast you are going
- B. The tyres on your vehicle
- C. The time of day
- D. The weather
- E. The street lighting

516 You are on a motorway at night. You MUST have your headlights switched on unless

Mark one answer
- A. there are vehicles close in front of you
- B. you are travelling below 50mph
- C. the motorway is lit
- D. your vehicle is broken down on the hard shoulder

517 You will feel the effects of engine braking when you

Mark one answer
- [ ] **A.** only use the handbrake
- [ ] **B.** only use neutral
- [ ] **C.** change to a lower gear
- [ ] **D.** change to a higher gear

518 Daytime visibility is poor but not seriously reduced. You should switch on

Mark one answer
- [ ] **A.** headlights and fog lights
- [ ] **B.** front fog lights
- [ ] **C.** dipped headlights
- [ ] **D.** rear fog lights

519 Why are vehicles fitted with rear fog lights?

Mark one answer
- [ ] **A.** To be seen when driving at high speed
- [ ] **B.** To use if broken down in a dangerous position
- [ ] **C.** To make them more visible in thick fog
- [ ] **D.** To warn drivers following closely to drop back

520 While you are driving in fog, it becomes necessary to use front fog lights. You should

Mark one answer
- [ ] **A.** only turn them on in heavy traffic conditions
- [ ] **B.** remember not to use them on motorways
- [ ] **C.** only use them on dual carriageways
- [ ] **D.** remember to switch them off as visibility improves

521 When snow is falling heavily you should

Mark one answer
- [ ] **A.** only drive with your hazard lights on
- [ ] **B.** not drive unless you have a mobile phone
- [ ] **C.** only drive when your journey is short
- [ ] **D.** not drive unless it is essential

522 You are driving down a long steep hill. You suddenly notice your brakes are not working as well as normal. What is the usual cause of this?

Mark one answer
- [ ] **A.** The brakes overheating
- [ ] **B.** Air in the brake fluid
- [ ] **C.** Oil on the brakes
- [ ] **D.** Badly adjusted brakes

523 The road is wet. Why might a motorcyclist steer round drain covers on a bend?

Mark one answer
- [ ] **A.** To avoid puncturing the tyres on the edge of the drain covers
- [ ] **B.** To prevent the motorcycle sliding on the metal drain covers
- [ ] **C.** To help judge the bend using the drain covers as marker points
- [ ] **D.** To avoid splashing pedestrians on the pavement

524 You are braking on a wet road. Your vehicle begins to skid. It does not have anti-lock brakes. What is the FIRST thing you should do?

Mark one answer
- [ ] **A.** Quickly pull up the handbrake
- [ ] **B.** Release the footbrake
- [ ] **C.** Push harder on the brake pedal
- [ ] **D.** Gently use the accelerator

525 Which FOUR of these must NOT use motorways?

Mark four answers
- [ ] A. Learner car drivers
- [ ] B. Motorcycles over 50cc
- [ ] C. Double-deck buses
- [ ] D. Farm tractors
- [ ] E. Horse riders
- [ ] F. Cyclists

526 Which FOUR of these must NOT use motorways?

Mark four answers
- [ ] A. Learner car drivers
- [ ] B. Motorcycles over 50cc
- [ ] C. Double-deck buses
- [ ] D. Farm tractors
- [ ] E. Learner motorcyclists
- [ ] F. Cyclists

527 Immediately after joining a motorway you should normally

Mark one answer
- [ ] A. try to overtake
- [ ] B. re-adjust your mirrors
- [ ] C. position your vehicle in the centre lane
- [ ] D. keep in the left-hand lane

528 When joining a motorway you must always

Mark one answer
- [ ] A. use the hard shoulder
- [ ] B. stop at the end of the acceleration lane
- [ ] C. come to a stop before joining the motorway
- [ ] D. give way to traffic already on the motorway

529 What is the national speed limit for cars and motorcycles in the centre lane of a three-lane motorway?

Mark one answer
- [ ] A. 40mph
- [ ] B. 50mph
- [ ] C. 60mph
- [ ] D. 70mph

530 What is the national speed limit on motorways for cars and motorcycles?

Mark one answer
- [ ] A. 30mph
- [ ] B. 50mph
- [ ] C. 60mph
- [ ] D. 70mph

531 The left-hand lane on a three-lane motorway is for use by

Mark one answer
- [ ] A. any vehicle
- [ ] B. large vehicles only
- [ ] C. emergency vehicles only
- [ ] D. slow vehicles only

532 What is the right-hand lane used for on a three-lane motorway?

Mark one answer
- [ ] A. Emergency vehicles only
- [ ] B. Overtaking
- [ ] C. Vehicles towing trailers
- [ ] D. Coaches only

533 Which of these IS NOT allowed to travel in the right-hand lane of a three-lane motorway?

Mark one answer

- A. A small delivery van
- B. A motorcycle
- C. A vehicle towing a trailer
- D. A motorcycle and sidecar

534 You are on a motorway. You become tired and decide you need to rest. What should you do?

Mark one answer

- A. Stop on the hard shoulder
- B. Pull up on a slip road
- C. Park on the central reservation
- D. Leave at the next exit

535 You break down on a motorway. You need to call for help. Why may it be better to use an emergency roadside telephone rather than a mobile phone?

Mark one answer

- A. It connects you to a local garage
- B. Using a mobile phone will distract other drivers
- C. It allows easy location by the emergency services
- D. Mobile phones do not work on motorways

536 What should you use the hard shoulder of a motorway for?

Mark one answer

- A. Stopping in an emergency
- B. Leaving the motorway
- C. Stopping when you are tired
- D. Joining the motorway

537 After a breakdown you need to rejoin the main carriageway of a motorway from the hard shoulder. You should

Mark one answer

- A. move out onto the carriageway then build up your speed
- B. move out onto the carriageway using your hazard lights
- C. gain speed on the hard shoulder before moving out onto the carriageway
- D. wait on the hard shoulder until someone flashes their headlights at you

538 A crawler lane on a motorway is found

Mark one answer

- A. on a steep gradient
- B. before a service area
- C. before a junction
- D. along the hard shoulder

539 You are on a motorway. There are red flashing lights above every lane. You must

Mark one answer
A. pull on to the hard shoulder
B. slow down and watch for further signals
C. leave at the next exit
D. stop and wait

540 You are in the right-hand lane on a motorway. You see these overhead signs. This means

Mark one answer
A. move to the left and reduce your speed to 50mph
B. there are road works 50 metres (55 yards) ahead
C. use the hard shoulder until you have passed the hazard
D. leave the motorway at the next exit

541 What do these motorway signs show?

Mark one answer
A. They are countdown markers to a bridge
B. They are distance markers to the next telephone
C. They are countdown markers to the next exit
D. They warn of a police control ahead

542 On a motorway the amber reflective studs can be found between

Mark one answer
A. the hard shoulder and the carriageway
B. the acceleration lane and the carriageway
C. the central reservation and the carriageway
D. each pair of the lanes

543 What colour are the reflective studs between the lanes on a motorway?

Mark one answer
A. Green   B. Amber
C. White   D. Red

544 What colour are the reflective studs between a motorway and its slip road?

Mark one answer
A. Amber   B. White
C. Green   D. Red

545 You are allowed to stop on a motorway when you

Mark one answer
A. need to walk and get fresh air
B. wish to pick up hitchhikers
C. are told to do so by flashing red lights
D. need to use a mobile telephone

546 You have broken down on a motorway. To find the nearest emergency telephone you should always walk

Mark one answer
- **A.** with the traffic flow
- **B.** facing oncoming traffic
- **C.** in the direction shown on the marker posts
- **D.** in the direction of the nearest exit

547 You are travelling along the left-hand lane of a three-lane motorway. Traffic is joining from a slip road. You should

Mark one answer
- **A.** race the other vehicles
- **B.** move to another lane
- **C.** maintain a steady speed
- **D.** switch on your hazard flashers

548 You are joining a motorway. Why is it important to make full use of the slip road?

Mark one answer
- **A.** Because there is space available to turn round if you need to
- **B.** To allow you direct access to the overtaking lanes
- **C.** To build up a speed similar to traffic on the motorway
- **D.** Because you can continue on the hard shoulder

549 How should you use the emergency telephone on a motorway?

Mark one answer
- **A.** Stay close to the carriageway
- **B.** Face the oncoming traffic
- **C.** Keep your back to the traffic
- **D.** Stand on the hard shoulder

550 You are on a motorway. What colour are the reflective studs on the left of the carriageway?

Mark one answer
- **A.** Green
- **B.** Red
- **C.** White
- **D.** Amber

551 On a three-lane motorway which lane should you normally use?

Mark one answer
- **A.** Left
- **B.** Right
- **C.** Centre
- **D.** Either the right or centre

552 A basic rule when on motorways is

Mark one answer
- **A.** use the lane that has least traffic
- **B.** keep to the left-hand lane unless overtaking
- **C.** overtake on the side that is clearest
- **D.** try to keep above 50mph to prevent congestion

553 When going through a contraflow system on a motorway you should

Mark one answer
- A. ensure that you do not exceed 30mph
- B. keep a good distance from the vehicle ahead
- C. switch lanes to keep the traffic flowing
- D. stay close to the vehicle ahead to reduce queues

554 You are on a three-lane motorway. There are red reflective studs on your left and white ones to your right. Where are you?

Mark one answer
- A. In the right-hand lane
- B. In the middle lane
- C. On the hard shoulder
- D. In the left-hand lane

555 When should you stop on a motorway?

Mark three answers
- A. If you have to read a map
- B. When you are tired and need a rest
- C. If red lights show above every lane
- D. When told to by the police
- E. If your mobile phone rings
- F. When signalled by a Highways Agency Traffic Officer

556 You are approaching road works on a motorway. What should you do?

Mark one answer
- A. Speed up to clear the area quickly
- B. Always use the hard shoulder
- C. Obey all speed limits
- D. Stay very close to the vehicle in front

557 On motorways you should never overtake on the left unless

Mark one answer
- A. you can see well ahead that the hard shoulder is clear
- B. the traffic in the right-hand lane is signalling right
- C. you warn drivers behind by signalling left
- D. there is a queue of slow-moving traffic to your right that is moving more slowly than you are

558 You are towing a trailer on a motorway. What is your maximum speed limit?

Mark one answer

- [ ] **A.** 40mph
- [ ] **B.** 50mph
- [ ] **C.** 60mph
- [ ] **D.** 70mph

559 The left-hand lane of a motorway should be used for

Mark one answer

- [ ] **A.** breakdowns and emergencies only
- [ ] **B.** overtaking slower traffic in the other lanes
- [ ] **C.** slow vehicles only
- [ ] **D.** normal driving

560 You are driving on a motorway. You have to slow down quickly due to a hazard. You should

Mark one answer

- [ ] **A.** switch on your hazard lights
- [ ] **B.** switch on your headlights
- [ ] **C.** sound your horn
- [ ] **D.** flash your headlights

561 You get a puncture on the motorway. You manage to get your vehicle onto the hard shoulder. You should

Mark one answer

- [ ] **A.** change the wheel yourself immediately
- [ ] **B.** use the emergency telephone and call for assistance
- [ ] **C.** try to wave down another vehicle for help
- [ ] **D.** only change the wheel if you have a passenger to help you

562 You are driving on a motorway. By mistake, you go past the exit that you wanted to take. You should

Mark one answer

- [ ] **A.** carefully reverse on the hard shoulder
- [ ] **B.** carry on to the next exit
- [ ] **C.** carefully reverse in the left-hand lane
- [ ] **D.** make a U-turn at the next gap in the central reservation

563 Your vehicle breaks down on the hard shoulder of a motorway. You decide to use your mobile phone to call for help. You should

Mark one answer

- [ ] **A.** stand at the rear of the vehicle while making the call
- [ ] **B.** try to repair the vehicle yourself
- [ ] **C.** get out of the vehicle by the right-hand door
- [ ] **D.** check your location from the marker posts on the left

564 You are travelling on a motorway. Unless signs show a lower speed limit you must NOT exceed

NI

Mark one answer

- [ ] **A.** 50mph
- [ ] **B.** 60mph
- [ ] **C.** 70mph
- [ ] **D.** 80mph

565 You are on a three-lane motorway towing a trailer. You may use the right-hand lane when

NI

Mark one answer

- [ ] **A.** there are lane closures
- [ ] **B.** there is slow-moving traffic
- [ ] **C.** you can maintain a high speed
- [ ] **D.** large vehicles are in the left and centre lanes

566
You are on a motorway. There is a contraflow system ahead. What would you expect to find?

Mark one answer

- [ ] **A.** Temporary traffic lights
- [ ] **B.** Lower speed limits
- [ ] **C.** Wider lanes than normal
- [ ] **D.** Speed humps

567
You are driving at 70mph on a three-lane motorway. There is no traffic ahead. Which lane should you use?

Mark one answer

- [ ] **A.** Any lane
- [ ] **B.** Middle lane
- [ ] **C.** Right lane
- [ ] **D.** Left lane

568
Your vehicle has broken down on a motorway. You are not able to stop on the hard shoulder. What should you do?

Mark one answer

- [ ] **A.** Switch on your hazard warning lights
- [ ] **B.** Stop following traffic and ask for help
- [ ] **C.** Attempt to repair your vehicle quickly
- [ ] **D.** Stand behind your vehicle to warn others

569
Why is it particularly important to carry out a check on your vehicle before making a long motorway journey?

Mark one answer

- [ ] **A.** You will have to do more harsh braking on motorways
- [ ] **B.** Motorway service stations do not deal with breakdowns
- [ ] **C.** The road surface will wear down the tyres faster
- [ ] **D.** Continuous high speeds may increase the risk of your vehicle breaking down

570
For what reason may you use the right-hand lane of a motorway?

Mark one answer

- [ ] **A.** For keeping out of the way of lorries
- [ ] **B.** For travelling at more than 70mph
- [ ] **C.** For turning right
- [ ] **D.** For overtaking other vehicles

571
On a motorway you may ONLY stop on the hard shoulder

Mark one answer

- [ ] **A.** in an emergency
- [ ] **B.** if you feel tired and need to rest
- [ ] **C.** if you miss the exit that you wanted
- [ ] **D.** to pick up a hitchhiker

572
You are driving on a motorway. The car ahead shows its hazard lights for a short time. This tells you that

Mark one answer
- A. the driver wants you to overtake
- B. the other car is going to change lanes
- C. traffic ahead is slowing or stopping suddenly
- D. there is a police speed check ahead

573
Motorway emergency telephones are usually linked to the police. In some areas they are now linked to

Mark one answer
- A. the local ambulance service
- B. an Highways Agency control centre
- C. the local fire brigade
- D. a breakdown service control centre

574
You are intending to leave the motorway at the next exit. Before you reach the exit you should normally position your vehicle

Mark one answer
- A. in the middle lane
- B. in the left-hand lane
- C. on the hard shoulder
- D. in any lane

575
As a provisional licence holder you should not drive a car

Mark one answer
- A. over 30mph
- B. at night
- C. on the motorway
- D. with passengers in rear seats

576
Motorway emergency telephones are usually linked to the police. In some areas they are now linked to

Mark one answer   NI
- A. the Highways Agency Control Centre
- B. the Driver Vehicle Licensing Agency
- C. the Driving Standards Agency
- D. the local Vehicle Registration Office

577
An Emergency Refuge Area is an area

Mark one answer
- A. on a motorway for use in cases of emergency or breakdown
- B. for use if you think you will be involved in a road rage incident
- C. on a motorway for a police patrol to park and watch traffic
- D. for construction and road workers to store emergency equipment

578
What is an Emergency Refuge Area on a motorway for?

Mark one answer
- A. An area to park in when you want to use a mobile phone
- B. To use in cases of emergency or breakdown
- C. For an emergency recovery vehicle to park in a contraflow system
- D. To drive in when there is queuing traffic ahead

579
Highways Agency Traffic Officers

Mark one answer   NI
- A. will not be able to assist at a breakdown or emergency
- B. are not able to stop and direct anyone on a motorway
- C. will tow a broken down vehicle and its passengers home
- D. are able to stop and direct anyone on a motorway

580

You are on a motorway. A red cross is displayed above the hard shoulder. What does this mean?

Mark one answer **NI**

A. Pull up in this lane to answer your mobile phone

B. Use this lane as a running lane

C. This lane can be used if you need a rest

D. You should not travel in this lane

581

You are on a motorway in an Active Traffic Management (ATM) area. A mandatory speed limit is displayed above the hard shoulder. What does this mean?

Mark one answer **NI**

A. You should not travel in this lane

B. The hard shoulder can be used as a running lane

C. You can park on the hard shoulder if you feel tired

D. You can pull up in this lane to answer a mobile phone

582

The aim of an Active Traffic Management scheme on a motorway is to

Mark one answer **NI**

A. prevent overtaking

B. reduce rest stops

C. prevent tailgating

D. reduce congestion

583

You are in an Active Traffic Management area on a motorway. When the Actively Managed mode is operating

Mark one answer **NI**

A. speed limits are only advisory

B. the national speed limit will apply

C. the speed limit is always 30mph

D. all speed limit signals are set

584

You are on a three-lane motorway. A red cross is shown above the hard shoulder and mandatory speed limits above all other lanes. This means

Mark one answer **NI**

A. the hard shoulder can be used as a rest area if you feel tired

B. the hard shoulder is for emergency or breakdown use only

C. the hard shoulder can be used as a normal running lane

D. the hard shoulder has a speed limit of 50mph

585 You are travelling on a motorway. A red cross is shown above the hard shoulder. What does this mean?

Mark one answer **NI**
- A. Use this lane as a rest area
- B. Use this as a normal running lane
- C. Do not use this lane to travel in
- D. National speed limit applies in this lane

586 You are on a three-lane motorway and see this sign. It means you can use

Mark one answer **NI**
- A. any lane except the hard shoulder
- B. the hard shoulder only
- C. the three right hand lanes only
- D. all the lanes including the hard shoulder

587 Why can it be an advantage for traffic speed to stay constant over a longer distance?

Mark one answer
- A. You will do more stop-start driving
- B. You will use far more fuel
- C. You will be able to use more direct routes
- D. Your overall journey time will normally improve

588 You should not normally travel on the hard shoulder of a motorway. When can you use it?

Mark one answer **NI**
- A. When taking the next exit
- B. When traffic is stopped
- C. When signs direct you to
- D. When traffic is slow moving

589 On a motorway what is used to reduce traffic bunching?

Mark one answer
- A. Variable speed limits
- B. Contraflow systems
- C. National speed limits
- D. Lane closures

590 When may you stop on a motorway?

Mark one answer
- A. If you have to read a map
- B. When you are tired and need a rest
- C. If your mobile phone rings
- D. In an emergency or breakdown

591 You are travelling on a motorway. You decide you need a rest. You should

Mark one answer
- A. stop on the hard shoulder
- B. pull in at the nearest service area
- C. pull up on a slip road
- D. park on the central reservation

592 What is the meaning of this sign?

Mark one answer

- A. Local speed limit applies
- B. No waiting on the carriageway
- C. National speed limit applies
- D. No entry to vehicular traffic

593 What is the national speed limit on a single carriageway road for cars and motorcycles?

Mark one answer

- A. 30mph
- B. 50mph
- C. 60mph
- D. 70mph

594 What is the national speed limit for cars and motorcycles on a dual carriageway?

Mark one answer

- A. 30mph
- B. 50mph
- C. 60mph
- D. 70mph

595 There are no speed limit signs on the road. How is a 30mph limit indicated?

Mark one answer

- A. By hazard warning lines
- B. By street lighting
- C. By pedestrian islands
- D. By double or single yellow lines

596 Where you see street lights but no speed limit signs the limit is usually

Mark one answer

- A. 30mph
- B. 40mph
- C. 50mph
- D. 60mph

597 What does this sign mean?

Mark one answer

- A. Minimum speed 30mph
- B. End of maximum speed
- C. End of minimum speed
- D. Maximum speed 30mph

598 There is a tractor ahead of you. You wish to overtake but you are NOT sure if it is safe to do so. You should

Mark one answer

- A. follow another overtaking vehicle through
- B. sound your horn to the slow vehicle to pull over
- C. speed through but flash your lights to oncoming traffic
- D. not overtake if you are in doubt

599 Which three of the following are most likely to take an unusual course at roundabouts?

Mark three answers

- A. Horse riders
- B. Milk floats
- C. Delivery vans
- D. Long vehicles
- E. Estate cars
- F. Cyclists

600 In which TWO places should you NOT park?

Mark two answers
- [ ] **A.** Near a school entrance
- [ ] **B.** Near a police station
- [ ] **C.** In a side road
- [ ] **D.** At a bus stop
- [ ] **E.** In a one-way street

601 On a clearway you must not stop

Mark one answer
- [ ] **A.** at any time
- [ ] **B.** when it is busy
- [ ] **C.** in the rush hour
- [ ] **D.** during daylight hours

602 What is the meaning of this sign?

Mark one answer
- [ ] **A.** No entry
- [ ] **B.** Waiting restrictions
- [ ] **C.** National speed limit
- [ ] **D.** School crossing patrol

603 You can park on the right-hand side of a road at night

Mark one answer
- [ ] **A.** in a one-way street
- [ ] **B.** with your sidelights on
- [ ] **C.** more than 10 metres (32 feet) from a junction
- [ ] **D.** under a lamp-post

604 On a three-lane dual carriageway the right-hand lane can be used for

Mark one answer
- [ ] **A.** overtaking only, never turning right
- [ ] **B.** overtaking or turning right
- [ ] **C.** fast-moving traffic only
- [ ] **D.** turning right only, never overtaking

605 You are approaching a busy junction. There are several lanes with road markings. At the last moment you realise that you are in the wrong lane. You should

Mark one answer
- [ ] **A.** continue in that lane
- [ ] **B.** force your way across
- [ ] **C.** stop until the area has cleared
- [ ] **D.** use clear arm signals to cut across

606 Where may you overtake on a one-way street?

Mark one answer
- [ ] **A.** Only on the left-hand side
- [ ] **B.** Overtaking is not allowed
- [ ] **C.** Only on the right-hand side
- [ ] **D.** Either on the right or the left

607 When going straight ahead at a roundabout you should

Mark one answer
- [ ] **A.** indicate left before leaving the roundabout
- [ ] **B.** not indicate at any time
- [ ] **C.** indicate right when approaching the roundabout
- [ ] **D.** indicate left when approaching the roundabout

608 Which vehicle might have to use a different course to normal at roundabouts?

Mark one answer

- [ ] **A.** Sports car
- [ ] **B.** Van
- [ ] **C.** Estate car
- [ ] **D.** Long vehicle

609 You are going straight ahead at a roundabout. How should you signal?

Mark one answer

- [ ] **A.** Signal right on the approach and then left to leave the roundabout
- [ ] **B.** Signal left after you leave the roundabout and enter the new road
- [ ] **C.** Signal right on the approach to the roundabout and keep the signal on
- [ ] **D.** Signal left just after you pass the exit before the one you will take

610 You may only enter a box junction when

Mark one answer

- [ ] **A.** there are less than two vehicles in front of you
- [ ] **B.** the traffic lights show green
- [ ] **C.** your exit road is clear
- [ ] **D.** you need to turn left

611 You may wait in a yellow box junction when

Mark one answer

- [ ] **A.** oncoming traffic is preventing you from turning right
- [ ] **B.** you are in a queue of traffic turning left
- [ ] **C.** you are in a queue of traffic to go ahead
- [ ] **D.** you are on a roundabout

612 You MUST stop when signalled to do so by which THREE of these?

Mark three answers

- [ ] **A.** A police officer
- [ ] **B.** A pedestrian
- [ ] **C.** A school crossing patrol
- [ ] **D.** A bus driver
- [ ] **E.** A red traffic light

613 You will see these red and white markers when approaching

Mark one answer

- [ ] **A.** the end of a motorway
- [ ] **B.** a concealed level crossing
- [ ] **C.** a concealed speed limit sign
- [ ] **D.** the end of a dual carriageway

614
Someone is waiting to cross at a zebra crossing. They are standing on the pavement. You should normally

Mark one answer
- A. go on quickly before they step on to the crossing
- B. stop before you reach the zigzag lines and let them cross
- C. stop, let them cross, wait patiently
- D. ignore them as they are still on the pavement

615
At toucan crossings, apart from pedestrians you should be aware of

Mark one answer
- A. emergency vehicles emerging
- B. buses pulling out
- C. trams crossing in front
- D. cyclists riding across

616
Who can use a toucan crossing?

Mark two answers
- A. Trains
- B. Cyclists
- C. Buses
- D. Pedestrians
- E. Trams

617
At a pelican crossing, what does a flashing amber light mean?

Mark one answer
- A. You must not move off until the lights stop flashing
- B. You must give way to pedestrians still on the crossing
- C. You can move off, even if pedestrians are still on the crossing
- D. You must stop because the lights are about to change to red

618
You are waiting at a pelican crossing. The red light changes to flashing amber. This means you must

Mark one answer
- A. wait for pedestrians on the crossing to clear
- B. move off immediately without any hesitation
- C. wait for the green light before moving off
- D. get ready and go when the continuous amber light shows

619
You are travelling on a well-lit road at night in a built-up area. By using dipped headlights you will be able to

Mark one answer
- A. see further along the road
- B. go at a much faster speed
- C. switch to main beam quickly
- D. be easily seen by others

620
When can you park on the left opposite these road markings?

Mark one answer
- A. If the line nearest to you is broken
- B. When there are no yellow lines
- C. To pick up or set down passengers
- D. During daylight hours only

621 You are intending to turn right at a crossroads. An oncoming driver is also turning right. It will normally be safer to

Mark one answer

- A. keep the other vehicle to your RIGHT and turn behind it (offside to offside)
- B. keep the other vehicle to your LEFT and turn in front of it (nearside to nearside)
- C. carry on and turn at the next junction instead
- D. hold back and wait for the other driver to turn first

622 You are on a road that has no traffic signs. There are street lights. What is the speed limit?

Mark one answer

- A. 20mph
- B. 30mph
- C. 40mph
- D. 60mph

623 You are going along a street with parked vehicles on the left-hand side. For which THREE reasons should you keep your speed down?

Mark three answers

- A. So that oncoming traffic can see you more clearly
- B. You may set off car alarms
- C. Vehicles may be pulling out
- D. Drivers' doors may open
- E. Children may run out from between the vehicles

624 You meet an obstruction on your side of the road. You should

Mark one answer

- A. carry on, you have priority
- B. give way to oncoming traffic
- C. wave oncoming vehicles through
- D. accelerate to get past first

625 You are on a two-lane dual carriageway. For which TWO of the following would you use the right-hand lane?

Mark two answers

- A. Turning right
- B. Normal progress
- C. Staying at the minimum allowed speed
- D. Constant high speed
- E. Overtaking slower traffic
- F. Mending punctures

626 Who has priority at an unmarked crossroads?

Mark one answer

- A. The larger vehicle
- B. No one has priority
- C. The faster vehicle
- D. The smaller vehicle

627 What is the nearest you may park to a junction?

Mark one answer **NI**

- A. 10 metres (32 feet)
- B. 12 metres (39 feet)
- C. 15 metres (49 feet)
- D. 20 metres (66 feet)

628 In which THREE places must you NOT park?

Mark three answers **NI**

- A. Near the brow of a hill
- B. At or near a bus stop
- C. Where there is no pavement
- D. Within 10 metres (32 feet) of a junction
- E. On a 40mph road

629 You are waiting at a level crossing. A train has passed but the lights keep flashing. You must

Mark one answer

- [ ] **A.** carry on waiting
- [ ] **B.** phone the signal operator
- [ ] **C.** edge over the stop line and look for trains
- [ ] **D.** park and investigate

630 You park at night on a road with a 40mph speed limit. You should park

Mark one answer

- [ ] **A.** facing the traffic
- [ ] **B.** with parking lights on
- [ ] **C.** with dipped headlights on
- [ ] **D.** near a street light

631 The dual carriageway you are turning right on to has a very narrow central reservation. What should you do?

Mark one answer

- [ ] **A.** Proceed to the central reservation and wait
- [ ] **B.** Wait until the road is clear in both directions
- [ ] **C.** Stop in the first lane so that other vehicles give way
- [ ] **D.** Emerge slightly to show your intentions

632 At a crossroads there are no signs or road markings. Two vehicles approach. Which has priority?

Mark one answer

- [ ] **A.** Neither of the vehicles
- [ ] **B.** The vehicle travelling the fastest
- [ ] **C.** Oncoming vehicles turning right
- [ ] **D.** Vehicles approaching from the right

633 What does this sign tell you?

Mark one answer

- [ ] **A.** That it is a no-through road
- [ ] **B.** End of traffic calming zone
- [ ] **C.** Free parking zone ends
- [ ] **D.** No waiting zone ends

634 You are entering an area of road works. There is a temporary speed limit displayed. You should

Mark one answer

- [ ] **A.** not exceed the speed limit
- [ ] **B.** obey the limit only during rush hour
- [ ] **C.** ignore the displayed limit
- [ ] **D.** obey the limit except at night

635 You may drive over a footpath

Mark one answer

- [ ] **A.** to overtake slow-moving traffic
- [ ] **B.** when the pavement is very wide
- [ ] **C.** if no pedestrians are near
- [ ] **D.** to get into a property

636 A single-carriageway road has this sign. What is the maximum permitted speed for a car towing a trailer?

Mark one answer

- [ ] A. 30mph
- [ ] B. 40mph
- [ ] C. 50mph
- [ ] D. 60mph

637 You are towing a small caravan on a dual carriageway. You must not exceed

Mark one answer

- [ ] A. 50mph
- [ ] B. 40mph
- [ ] C. 70mph
- [ ] D. 60mph

638 You want to park and you see this sign. On the days and times shown you should

Mark one answer

- [ ] A. park in a bay and not pay
- [ ] B. park on yellow lines and pay
- [ ] C. park on yellow lines and not pay
- [ ] D. park in a bay and pay

Meter ZONE

Mon - Fri
8.30 am - 6.30 pm
Saturday
8.30 am - 1.30 pm

639 You are driving along a road that has a cycle lane. The lane is marked by a solid white line. This means that during its period of operation

Mark one answer

- [ ] A. the lane may be used for parking your car
- [ ] B. you may drive in that lane at any time
- [ ] C. the lane may be used when necessary
- [ ] D. you must not drive in that lane

640 A cycle lane is marked by a solid white line. You must not drive or park in it

Mark one answer

- [ ] A. at any time
- [ ] B. during the rush hour
- [ ] C. if a cyclist is using it
- [ ] D. during its period of operation

641 While driving, you intend to turn left into a minor road. On the approach you should

Mark one answer

- [ ] A. keep just left of the middle of the road
- [ ] B. keep in the middle of the road
- [ ] C. swing out wide just before turning
- [ ] D. keep well to the left of the road

642

You are waiting at a level crossing. The red warning lights continue to flash after a train has passed by. What should you do?

Mark one answer

A. Get out and investigate
B. Telephone the signal operator
C. Continue to wait
D. Drive across carefully

643

You are driving over a level crossing. The warning lights come on and a bell rings. What should you do?

Mark one answer

A. Get everyone out of the vehicle immediately
B. Stop and reverse back to clear the crossing
C. Keep going and clear the crossing
D. Stop immediately and use your hazard warning lights

644

You are on a busy main road and find that you are travelling in the wrong direction. What should you do?

Mark one answer

A. Turn into a side road on the right and reverse into the main road
B. Make a U-turn in the main road
C. Make a 'three-point' turn in the main road
D. Turn round in a side road

645

You may remove your seat belt when carrying out a manoeuvre that involves

Mark one answer

A. reversing
B. a hill start
C. an emergency stop
D. driving slowly

646

You must not reverse

Mark one answer

A. for longer than necessary
B. for more than a car's length
C. into a side road
D. in a built-up area

647

You are parked in a busy high street. What is the safest way to turn your vehicle around so you can go the opposite way?

Mark one answer

A. Find a quiet side road to turn round in
B. Drive into a side road and reverse into the main road
C. Get someone to stop the traffic
D. Do a U-turn

648 When you are NOT sure that it is safe to reverse your vehicle you should

Mark one answer

- A. use your horn
- B. rev your engine
- C. get out and check
- D. reverse slowly

649 When may you reverse from a side road into a main road?

Mark one answer

- A. Only if both roads are clear of traffic
- B. Not at any time
- C. At any time
- D. Only if the main road is clear of traffic

650 You want to turn right at a box junction. There is oncoming traffic. You should

Mark one answer

- A. wait in the box junction if your exit is clear
- B. wait before the junction until it is clear of all traffic
- C. drive on, you cannot turn right at a box junction
- D. drive slowly into the box junction when signalled by oncoming traffic

651 You are reversing your vehicle into a side road. When would the greatest hazard to passing traffic occur?

Mark one answer

- A. After you've completed the manoeuvre
- B. Just before you actually begin to manoeuvre
- C. After you've entered the side road
- D. When the front of your vehicle swings out

652 You are driving on a road that has a cycle lane. The lane is marked by a broken white line. This means that

Mark two answers

- A. you should not drive in the lane unless it is unavoidable
- B. you should not park in the lane unless it is unavoidable
- C. cyclists can travel in both directions in that lane
- D. the lane must be used by motorcyclists in heavy traffic

653 Where is the safest place to park your vehicle at night?

Mark one answer

- A. In a garage
- B. On a busy road
- C. In a quiet car park
- D. Near a red route

654 To help keep your vehicle secure at night where should you park?

Mark one answer

- A. Near a police station
- B. In a quiet road
- C. On a red route
- D. In a well-lit area

655

You are in the right-hand lane of a dual carriageway. You see signs showing that the right-hand lane is closed 800 yards ahead. You should

GET IN LANE

800 yards

Mark one answer

- A. keep in that lane until you reach the queue
- B. move to the left immediately
- C. wait and see which lane is moving faster
- D. move to the left in good time

656

You are driving on an urban clearway. You may stop only to

Mark one answer

- A. set down and pick up passengers
- B. use a mobile telephone
- C. ask for directions
- D. load or unload goods

657

You are looking for somewhere to park your vehicle. The area is full EXCEPT for spaces marked 'disabled use'. You can

Mark one answer

- A. use these spaces when elsewhere is full
- B. park if you stay with your vehicle
- C. use these spaces, disabled or not
- D. not park there unless permitted

658

Your vehicle is parked on the road at night. When must you use sidelights?

Mark one answer

- A. Where there are continuous white lines in the middle of the road
- B. Where the speed limit exceeds 30mph
- C. Where you are facing oncoming traffic
- D. Where you are near a bus stop

659

On which THREE occasions MUST you stop your vehicle?

Mark three answers

- A. When in an accident where damage or injury is caused
- B. At a red traffic light
- C. When signalled to do so by a police or traffic officer
- D. At a junction with double broken white lines
- E. At a pelican crossing when the amber light is flashing and no pedestrians are crossing

660

You are on a road that is only wide enough for one vehicle. There is a car coming towards you. What should you do?

Mark one answer

- A. Pull into a passing place on your right
- B. Force the other driver to reverse
- C. Pull into a passing place if your vehicle is wider
- D. Pull into a passing place on your left

661 What MUST you have to park in a disabled space?

Mark one answer
- [ ] **A.** A Blue Badge
- [ ] **B.** A wheelchair
- [ ] **C.** An advanced driver certificate
- [ ] **D.** An adapted vehicle

DISABLED

662 You are driving at night with full beam headlights on. A vehicle is overtaking you. You should dip your lights

Mark one answer
- [ ] **A.** some time after the vehicle has passed you
- [ ] **B.** before the vehicle starts to pass you
- [ ] **C.** only if the other driver dips their headlights
- [ ] **D.** as soon as the vehicle passes you

663 When may you drive a motor car in this bus lane?

local taxi
**Mon - Fri
7 - 10 am
4.00 - 6.30 pm**

Mark one answer
- [ ] **A.** Outside its hours of operation
- [ ] **B.** To get to the front of a traffic queue
- [ ] **C.** You may not use it at any time
- [ ] **D.** To overtake slow-moving traffic

664 Signals are normally given by direction indicators and

Mark one answer
- [ ] **A.** brake lights
- [ ] **B.** sidelights
- [ ] **C.** fog lights
- [ ] **D.** interior lights

665 You are travelling on a motorway. You MUST stop when signalled to do so by which of these?

Mark one answer **NI**
- [ ] **A.** Flashing amber lights above your lane
- [ ] **B.** A Highways Agency Traffic Officer
- [ ] **C.** Pedestrians on the hard shoulder
- [ ] **D.** A driver who has broken down

666 At a busy unmarked crossroads, which of the following has priority?

Mark one answer
- [ ] **A.** Vehicles going straight ahead
- [ ] **B.** Vehicles turning right
- [ ] **C.** None of the vehicles
- [ ] **D.** The vehicles that arrived first

667 You MUST obey signs giving orders. These signs are mostly in

Mark one answer
- [ ] **A.** green rectangles
- [ ] **B.** red triangles
- [ ] **C.** blue rectangles
- [ ] **D.** red circles

668 Traffic signs giving orders are generally which shape?

Mark one answer
- [ ] **A.**
- [ ] **B.**
- [ ] **C.**
- [ ] **D.**

669 Which type of sign tells you NOT to do something?

Mark one answer
- [ ] **A.**
- [ ] **B.**
- [ ] **C.**
- [ ] **D.**

670 What does this sign mean?

Mark one answer
- [ ] **A.** Maximum speed limit with traffic calming
- [ ] **B.** Minimum speed limit with traffic calming
- [ ] **C.** '20 cars only' parking zone
- [ ] **D.** Only 20 cars allowed at any one time

671 Which sign means no motor vehicles are allowed?

Mark one answer
- [ ] **A.**
- [ ] **B.**
- [ ] **C.**
- [ ] **D.**

672 Which of these signs means no motor vehicles?

Mark one answer
- [ ] **A.**
- [ ] **B.**
- [ ] **C.**
- [ ] **D.**

673 What does this sign mean?

Mark one answer
- A. New speed limit 20mph
- B. No vehicles over 30 tonnes
- C. Minimum speed limit 30mph
- D. End of 20mph zone

674 What does this sign mean?

Mark one answer
- A. No overtaking
- B. No motor vehicles
- C. Clearway (no stopping)
- D. Cars and motorcycles only

675 What does this sign mean?

Mark one answer
- A. No parking
- B. No road markings
- C. No through road
- D. No entry

676 What does this sign mean?

Mark one answer
- A. Bend to the right
- B. Road on the right closed
- C. No traffic from the right
- D. No right turn

677 Which sign means 'no entry'?

Mark one answer
- A.
- B.

- C.
- D.

678 What does this sign mean?

Mark one answer
- A. Route for trams only
- B. Route for buses only
- C. Parking for buses only
- D. Parking for trams only

679 Which type of vehicle does this sign apply to?

Mark one answer
- **A.** Wide vehicles
- **B.** Long vehicles
- **C.** High vehicles
- **D.** Heavy vehicles

680 Which sign means NO motor vehicles allowed?

Mark one answer
- **A.**
- **B.**
- **C.**
- **D.**

681 What does this sign mean?

Mark one answer
- **A.** You have priority
- **B.** No motor vehicles
- **C.** Two-way traffic
- **D.** No overtaking

682 What does this sign mean?

Mark one answer
- **A.** Keep in one lane
- **B.** Give way to oncoming traffic
- **C.** Do not overtake
- **D.** Form two lanes

683 Which sign means no overtaking?

Mark one answer
- **A.**
- **B.**
- **C.**
- **D.**

684 What does this sign mean?

Mark one answer
- **A.** Waiting restrictions apply
- **B.** Waiting permitted
- **C.** National speed limit applies
- **D.** Clearway (no stopping)

685 What does this sign mean?

Mark one answer
- [ ] A. End of restricted speed area
- [ ] B. End of restricted parking area
- [ ] C. End of clearway
- [ ] D. End of cycle route

686 Which sign means 'no stopping'?

Mark one answer
- [ ] A.
- [ ] B.
- [ ] C.
- [ ] D.

687 What does this sign mean?

Mark one answer
- [ ] A. Roundabout
- [ ] B. Crossroads
- [ ] C. No stopping
- [ ] D. No entry

688 You see this sign ahead. It means

Mark one answer
- [ ] A. national speed limit applies
- [ ] B. waiting restrictions apply
- [ ] C. no stopping
- [ ] D. no entry

689 What does this sign mean?

Mark one answer
- [ ] A. Distance to parking place ahead
- [ ] B. Distance to public telephone ahead
- [ ] C. Distance to public house ahead
- [ ] D. Distance to passing place ahead

690 What does this sign mean?

Mark one answer
- [ ] A. Vehicles may not park on the verge or footway
- [ ] B. Vehicles may park on the left-hand side of the road only
- [ ] C. Vehicles may park fully on the verge or footway
- [ ] D. Vehicles may park on the right-hand side of the road only

691 What does this traffic sign mean?

Mark one answer
- [ ] **A.** No overtaking allowed
- [ ] **B.** Give priority to oncoming traffic
- [ ] **C.** Two-way traffic
- [ ] **D.** One-way traffic only

692 What is the meaning of this traffic sign?

Mark one answer
- [ ] **A.** End of two-way road
- [ ] **B.** Give priority to vehicles coming towards you
- [ ] **C.** You have priority over vehicles coming towards you
- [ ] **D.** Bus lane ahead

693 What MUST you do when you see this sign?

Mark one answer
- [ ] **A.** Stop, only if traffic is approaching
- [ ] **B.** Stop, even if the road is clear
- [ ] **C.** Stop, only if children are waiting to cross
- [ ] **D.** Stop, only if a red light is showing

694 What does this sign mean?

Mark one answer
- [ ] **A.** No overtaking
- [ ] **B.** You are entering a one-way street
- [ ] **C.** Two-way traffic ahead
- [ ] **D.** You have priority over vehicles from the opposite direction

695 What shape is a STOP sign at a junction?

Mark one answer
- [ ] **A.**
- [ ] **B.**
- [ ] **C.**
- [ ] **D.**

696 At a junction you see this sign partly covered by snow. What does it mean?

Mark one answer
- [ ] **A.** Crossroads
- [ ] **B.** Give way
- [ ] **C.** Stop
- [ ] **D.** Turn right

697 Which shape is used for a 'give way' sign?

Mark one answer

A. (triangle)

B. (circle)

C. (octagon)

D. (inverted triangle)

698 What does this sign mean?

Mark one answer

A. Service area 30 miles ahead

B. Maximum speed 30mph

C. Minimum speed 30mph

D. Lay-by 30 miles ahead

699 Which of these signs means turn left ahead?

Mark one answer

A.

B.

C.

D.

700 What does this sign mean?

Mark one answer

A. Buses turning

B. Ring road

C. Mini-roundabout

D. Keep right

701 What does this sign mean?

Mark one answer

A. Give way to oncoming vehicles

B. Approaching traffic passes you on both sides

C. Turn off at the next available junction

D. Pass either side to get to the same destination

702 What does this sign mean?

Mark one answer

A. Route for trams

B. Give way to trams

C. Route for buses

D. Give way to buses

703 What does a circular traffic sign with a blue background do?

Mark one answer

- [ ] A. Give warning of a motorway ahead
- [ ] B. Give directions to a car park
- [ ] C. Give motorway information
- [ ] D. Give an instruction

704 Which sign shows that traffic can only travel in one direction on the road you're on?

Mark one answer

- [ ] A.
- [ ] B.
- [ ] C.
- [ ] D.

705 Where would you see a contraflow bus and cycle lane?

Mark one answer

- [ ] A. On a dual carriageway
- [ ] B. On a roundabout
- [ ] C. On an urban motorway
- [ ] D. On a one-way street

706 What does this sign mean?

Mark one answer

- [ ] A. Bus station on the right
- [ ] B. Contraflow bus lane
- [ ] C. With-flow bus lane
- [ ] D. Give way to buses

707 What does this sign mean?

Mark one answer

- [ ] A. With-flow bus and cycle lane
- [ ] B. Contraflow bus and cycle lane
- [ ] C. No buses and cycles allowed
- [ ] D. No waiting for buses and cycles

708 What does a sign with a brown background show?

Mark one answer

- [ ] A. Tourist directions
- [ ] B. Primary roads
- [ ] C. Motorway routes
- [ ] D. Minor routes

709 This sign means

Mark one answer
- **A.** tourist attraction
- **B.** beware of trains
- **C.** level crossing
- **D.** beware of trams

710 What are triangular signs for?

Mark one answer
- **A.** To give warnings
- **B.** To give information
- **C.** To give orders
- **D.** To give directions

711 What does this sign mean?

Mark one answer
- **A.** Turn left ahead
- **B.** T-junction
- **C.** No through road
- **D.** Give way

712 What does this sign mean?

Mark one answer
- **A.** Multi-exit roundabout
- **B.** Risk of ice
- **C.** Six roads converge
- **D.** Place of historical interest

713 What does this sign mean?

Mark one answer
- **A.** Crossroads
- **B.** Level crossing with gate
- **C.** Level crossing without gate
- **D.** Ahead only

714 What does this sign mean?

Mark one answer
- **A.** Ring road
- **B.** Mini-roundabout
- **C.** No vehicles
- **D.** Roundabout

715 Which FOUR of these would be indicated by a triangular road sign?

Mark four answers

- [ ] **A.** Road narrows
- [ ] **B.** Ahead only
- [ ] **C.** Low bridge
- [ ] **D.** Minimum speed
- [ ] **E.** Children crossing
- [ ] **F.** T-junction

716 What does this sign mean?

Mark one answer

- [ ] **A.** Cyclists must dismount
- [ ] **B.** Cycles are not allowed
- [ ] **C.** Cycle route ahead
- [ ] **D.** Cycle in single file

717 Which sign means that pedestrians may be walking along the road?

Mark one answer

- [ ] **A.**
- [ ] **B.**
- [ ] **C.**
- [ ] **D.**

718 Which of these signs warn you of a zebra crossing?

Mark one answer

- [ ] **A.**
- [ ] **B.**
- [ ] **C.**
- [ ] **D.**

719 What does this sign mean?

Mark one answer

- [ ] **A.** No footpath ahead
- [ ] **B.** Pedestrians only ahead
- [ ] **C.** Pedestrian crossing ahead
- [ ] **D.** School crossing ahead

720 What does this sign mean?

Mark one answer

- [ ] **A.** School crossing patrol
- [ ] **B.** No pedestrians allowed
- [ ] **C.** Pedestrian zone – no vehicles
- [ ] **D.** Zebra crossing ahead

721 Which of these signs means there is a double bend ahead?

Mark one answer

A.

B.

C.

D.

722 What does this sign mean?

Mark one answer

A. Wait at the barriers
B. Wait at the crossroads
C. Give way to trams
D. Give way to farm vehicles

GIVE WAY

723 What does this sign mean?

Mark one answer

A. Humpback bridge
B. Humps in the road
C. Entrance to tunnel
D. Soft verges

724 What does this sign mean?

Mark one answer

A. Low bridge ahead
B. Tunnel ahead
C. Ancient monument ahead
D. Traffic danger spot ahead

725 What does this sign mean?

Mark one answer

A. Two-way traffic straight ahead
B. Two-way traffic crosses a one-way road
C. Two-way traffic over a bridge
D. Two-way traffic crosses a two-way road

726 Which sign means there will be two-way traffic crossing your route ahead?

Mark one answer

A.

B.

C.

D.

727 Which of these signs means the end of a dual carriageway?

Mark one answer

- [ ] A.
- [ ] B.
- [ ] C.
- [ ] D.

728 What does this sign mean?

Mark one answer

- [ ] A. End of dual carriageway
- [ ] B. Tall bridge
- [ ] C. Road narrows
- [ ] D. End of narrow bridge

729 What does this sign mean?

Mark one answer

- [ ] A. Two-way traffic ahead across a one-way road
- [ ] B. Traffic approaching you has priority
- [ ] C. Two-way traffic straight ahead
- [ ] D. Motorway contraflow system ahead

730 What does this sign mean?

Mark one answer

- [ ] A. Crosswinds
- [ ] B. Road noise
- [ ] C. Airport
- [ ] D. Adverse camber

731 What does this traffic sign mean?

Mark one answer

- [ ] A. Slippery road ahead
- [ ] B. Tyres liable to punctures ahead
- [ ] C. Danger ahead
- [ ] D. Service area ahead

732 You are about to overtake when you see this sign. You should

Mark one answer

- [ ] A. overtake the other driver as quickly as possible
- [ ] B. move to the right to get a better view
- [ ] C. switch your headlights on before overtaking
- [ ] D. hold back until you can see clearly ahead

Hidden dip

733 What does this sign mean?

Mark one answer

- **A.** Level crossing with gate or barrier
- **B.** Gated road ahead
- **C.** Level crossing without gate or barrier
- **D.** Cattle grid ahead

734 What does this sign mean?

Mark one answer

- **A.** No trams ahead
- **B.** Oncoming trams
- **C.** Trams crossing ahead
- **D.** Trams only

735 What does this sign mean?

Mark one answer

- **A.** Adverse camber
- **B.** Steep hill downwards
- **C.** Uneven road
- **D.** Steep hill upwards

736 What does this sign mean?

Mark one answer

- **A.** Uneven road surface
- **B.** Bridge over the road
- **C.** Road ahead ends
- **D.** Water across the road

737 What does this sign mean?

Mark one answer

- **A.** Humpback bridge
- **B.** Traffic calming hump
- **C.** Low bridge
- **D.** Uneven road

738 What does this sign mean?

Mark one answer

- **A.** Turn left for parking area
- **B.** No through road on the left
- **C.** No entry for traffic turning left
- **D.** Turn left for ferry terminal

739 What does this sign mean?

Mark one answer
- A. T-junction
- B. No through road
- C. Telephone box ahead
- D. Toilet ahead

740 Which sign means 'no through road'?

Mark one answer
- A.
- B.
- C.
- D.

741 Which of the following signs informs you that you are coming to a 'no through road'?

Mark one answer
- A.
- B.
- C.
- D.

742 What does this sign mean?

Mark one answer
- A. Direction to park-and-ride car park
- B. No parking for buses or coaches
- C. Directions to bus and coach park
- D. Parking area for cars and coaches

743 You are in a tunnel and you see this sign. What does it mean?

Mark one answer
- A. Direction to emergency pedestrian exit
- B. Beware of pedestrians, no footpath ahead
- C. No access for pedestrians
- D. Beware of pedestrians crossing ahead

744 Which is the sign for a ring road?

Mark one answer
- A.
- B.
- C.
- D.

745 At a railway level crossing the red light signal continues to flash after a train has gone by. What should you do?

Mark one answer
- [ ] **A.** Phone the signal operator
- [ ] **B.** Alert drivers behind you
- [ ] **C.** Wait
- [ ] **D.** Proceed with caution

746 At a junction you see this signal. It means

Mark one answer
- [ ] **A.** cars must stop
- [ ] **B.** trams must stop
- [ ] **C.** both trams and cars must stop
- [ ] **D.** both trams and cars can continue

747 What does this sign mean?

Mark one answer
- [ ] **A.** The right-hand lane ahead is narrow
- [ ] **B.** Right-hand lane for buses only
- [ ] **C.** Right-hand lane for turning right
- [ ] **D.** The right-hand lane is closed

748 What does this sign mean?

Mark one answer
- [ ] **A.** Change to the left lane
- [ ] **B.** Leave at the next exit
- [ ] **C.** Contraflow system
- [ ] **D.** One-way street

749 What does this sign mean?

Mark one answer
- [ ] **A.** Leave motorway at next exit
- [ ] **B.** Lane for heavy and slow vehicles
- [ ] **C.** All lorries use the hard shoulder
- [ ] **D.** Rest area for lorries

750 You are approaching a red traffic light. What will the signal show next?

Mark one answer
- [ ] **A.** Red and amber
- [ ] **B.** Green alone
- [ ] **C.** Amber alone
- [ ] **D.** Green and amber

751 A red traffic light means

Mark one answer
- [ ] **A.** you should stop unless turning left
- [ ] **B.** stop, if you are able to brake safely
- [ ] **C.** you must stop and wait behind the stop line
- [ ] **D.** proceed with caution

752 At traffic lights, amber on its own means

Mark one answer
- [ ] **A.** prepare to go
- [ ] **B.** go if the way is clear
- [ ] **C.** go if no pedestrians are crossing
- [ ] **D.** stop at the stop line

753 You are approaching traffic lights. Red and amber are showing. This means

Mark one answer
- [ ] **A.** pass the lights if the road is clear
- [ ] **B.** there is a fault with the lights – take care
- [ ] **C.** wait for the green light before you cross the stop line
- [ ] **D.** the lights are about to change to red

754 You are at a junction controlled by traffic lights. When should you NOT proceed at green?

Mark one answer
- [ ] **A.** When pedestrians are waiting to cross
- [ ] **B.** When your exit from the junction is blocked
- [ ] **C.** When you think the lights may be about to change
- [ ] **D.** When you intend to turn right

755 You are in the left-hand lane at traffic lights. You are waiting to turn left. At which of these traffic lights must you NOT move on?

Mark one answer
- [ ] **A.**
- [ ] **B.**
- [ ] **C.**
- [ ] **D.**

756 What does this sign mean?

Mark one answer
- [ ] **A.** Traffic lights out of order
- [ ] **B.** Amber signal out of order
- [ ] **C.** Temporary traffic lights ahead
- [ ] **D.** New traffic lights ahead

757 When traffic lights are out of order, who has priority?

Mark one answer
- A. Traffic going straight on
- B. Traffic turning right
- C. Nobody
- D. Traffic turning left

758 These flashing red lights mean STOP. In which THREE of the following places could you find them?

Mark three answers
- A. Pelican crossings
- B. Lifting bridges
- C. Zebra crossings
- D. Level crossings
- E. Motorway exits
- F. Fire stations

759 What do these zigzag lines at pedestrian crossings mean?

Mark one answer
- A. No parking at any time
- B. Parking allowed only for a short time
- C. Slow down to 20mph
- D. Sounding horns is not allowed

760 When may you cross a double solid white line in the middle of the road?

Mark one answer
- A. To pass traffic that is queuing back at a junction
- B. To pass a car signalling to turn left ahead
- C. To pass a road maintenance vehicle travelling at 10mph or less
- D. To pass a vehicle that is towing a trailer

761 What does this road marking mean?

Mark one answer
- A. Do not cross the line
- B. No stopping allowed
- C. You are approaching a hazard
- D. No overtaking allowed

762 This marking appears on the road just before a

Mark one answer
- [ ] A. 'no entry' sign
- [ ] B. 'give way' sign
- [ ] C. 'stop' sign
- [ ] D. 'no through road' sign

763 Where would you see this road marking?

Mark one answer
- [ ] A. At traffic lights
- [ ] B. On road humps
- [ ] C. Near a level crossing
- [ ] D. At a box junction

764 Which is a hazard warning line?

Mark one answer
- [ ] A.

- [ ] B.

- [ ] C.

- [ ] D.

765 At this junction there is a stop sign with a solid white line on the road surface. Why is there a stop sign here?

Mark one answer
- [ ] A. Speed on the major road is de-restricted
- [ ] B. It is a busy junction
- [ ] C. Visibility along the major road is restricted
- [ ] D. There are hazard warning lines in the centre of the road

766 You see this line across the road at the entrance to a roundabout. What does it mean?

Mark one answer
- [ ] A. Give way to traffic from the right
- [ ] B. Traffic from the left has right of way
- [ ] C. You have right of way
- [ ] D. Stop at the line

767 Where would you find these road markings?

Mark one answer

- [ ] **A.** At a railway crossing
- [ ] **B.** At a junction
- [ ] **C.** On a motorway
- [ ] **D.** On a pedestrian crossing

768 How will a police officer in a patrol vehicle normally get you to stop?

Mark one answer

- [ ] **A.** Flash the headlights, indicate left and point to the left
- [ ] **B.** Wait until you stop, then approach you
- [ ] **C.** Use the siren, overtake, cut in front and stop
- [ ] **D.** Pull alongside you, use the siren and wave you to stop

769 There is a police car following you. The police officer flashes the headlights and points to the left. What should you do?

Mark one answer

- [ ] **A.** Turn left at the next junction
- [ ] **B.** Pull up on the left
- [ ] **C.** Stop immediately
- [ ] **D.** Move over to the left

770 The driver of the car in front is giving this arm signal. What does it mean?

Mark one answer

- [ ] **A.** The driver is slowing down
- [ ] **B.** The driver intends to turn right
- [ ] **C.** The driver wishes to overtake
- [ ] **D.** The driver intends to turn left

771 Where would you see these road markings?

Mark one answer

- [ ] **A.** At a level crossing
- [ ] **B.** On a motorway slip road
- [ ] **C.** At a pedestrian crossing
- [ ] **D.** On a single-track road

772 What does this motorway sign mean?

Mark one answer

- [ ] **A.** Change to the lane on your left
- [ ] **B.** Leave the motorway at the next exit
- [ ] **C.** Change to the opposite carriageway
- [ ] **D.** Pull up on the hard shoulder

773 What does this motorway sign mean?

Mark one answer

- [ ] **A.** Temporary minimum speed 50mph
- [ ] **B.** No services for 50 miles
- [ ] **C.** Obstruction 50 metres (164 feet) ahead
- [ ] **D.** Temporary maximum speed 50mph

774 What does this sign mean?

Mark one answer

- [ ] **A.** Through traffic to use left lane
- [ ] **B.** Right-hand lane T-junction only
- [ ] **C.** Right-hand lane closed ahead
- [ ] **D.** 11 tonne weight limit

775 On a motorway this sign means

Mark one answer

- [ ] **A.** move over on to the hard shoulder
- [ ] **B.** overtaking on the left only
- [ ] **C.** leave the motorway at the next exit
- [ ] **D.** move to the lane on your left

776 What does '25' mean on this motorway sign?

Mark one answer

- [ ] **A.** The distance to the nearest town
- [ ] **B.** The route number of the road
- [ ] **C.** The number of the next junction
- [ ] **D.** The speed limit on the slip road

777 The right-hand lane of a three-lane motorway is

Mark one answer

- [ ] **A.** for lorries only
- [ ] **B.** an overtaking lane
- [ ] **C.** the right-turn lane
- [ ] **D.** an acceleration lane

778 Where can you find reflective amber studs on a motorway?

Mark one answer

- [ ] **A.** Separating the slip road from the motorway
- [ ] **B.** On the left-hand edge of the road
- [ ] **C.** On the right-hand edge of the road
- [ ] **D.** Separating the lanes

779 Where on a motorway would you find green reflective studs?

Mark one answer

- **A.** Separating driving lanes
- **B.** Between the hard shoulder and the carriageway
- **C.** At slip road entrances and exits
- **D.** Between the carriageway and the central reservation

780 You are travelling along a motorway. You see this sign. You should

Mark one answer

- **A.** leave the motorway at the next exit
- **B.** turn left immediately
- **C.** change lane
- **D.** move on to the hard shoulder

781 What does this sign mean?

Mark one answer

- **A.** No motor vehicles
- **B.** End of motorway
- **C.** No through road
- **D.** End of bus lane

782 Which of these signs means that the national speed limit applies?

Mark one answer

- **A.**
- **B.**
- **C.**
- **D.**

783 What is the maximum speed on a single carriageway road?

Mark one answer

- **A.** 50mph
- **B.** 60mph
- **C.** 40mph
- **D.** 70mph

784 What does this sign mean?

Mark one answer

- **A.** End of motorway
- **B.** End of restriction
- **C.** Lane ends ahead
- **D.** Free recovery ends

785 This sign is advising you to

Mark one answer

- A. follow the route diversion
- B. follow the signs to the picnic area
- C. give way to pedestrians
- D. give way to cyclists

786 Why would this temporary speed limit sign be shown?

Mark one answer

- A. To warn of the end of the motorway
- B. To warn you of a low bridge
- C. To warn you of a junction ahead
- D. To warn of road works ahead

50 ¾ mile ahead

787 This traffic sign means there is

Mark one answer

- A. a compulsory maximum speed limit
- B. an advisory maximum speed limit
- C. a compulsory minimum speed limit
- D. an advised separation distance

788 You see this sign at a crossroads. You should

Mark one answer

- A. maintain the same speed
- B. carry on with great care
- C. find another route
- D. telephone the police

789 You are signalling to turn right in busy traffic. How would you confirm your intention safely?

Mark one answer

- A. Sound the horn
- B. Give an arm signal
- C. Flash your headlights
- D. Position over the centre line

790 What does this sign mean?

Mark one answer

- A. Motorcycles only
- B. No cars
- C. Cars only
- D. No motorcycles

791 You are on a motorway. You see this sign on a lorry that has stopped in the right-hand lane. You should

Mark one answer
- [ ] **A.** move into the right-hand lane
- [ ] **B.** stop behind the flashing lights
- [ ] **C.** pass the lorry on the left
- [ ] **D.** leave the motorway at the next exit

792 You are on a motorway. Red flashing lights appear above your lane only. What should you do?

Mark one answer
- [ ] **A.** Continue in that lane and look for further information
- [ ] **B.** Move into another lane in good time
- [ ] **C.** Pull on to the hard shoulder
- [ ] **D.** Stop and wait for an instruction to proceed

793 A red traffic light means

Mark one answer
- [ ] **A.** you must stop behind the white stop line
- [ ] **B.** you may go straight on if there is no other traffic
- [ ] **C.** you may turn left if it is safe to do so
- [ ] **D.** you must slow down and prepare to stop if traffic has started to cross

794 The driver of this car is giving an arm signal. What are they about to do?

Mark one answer
- [ ] **A.** Turn to the right
- [ ] **B.** Turn to the left
- [ ] **C.** Go straight ahead
- [ ] **D.** Let pedestrians cross

795 Which arm signal tells you that the car you are following is going to pull up?

Mark one answer
- [ ] **A.**
- [ ] **B.**
- [ ] **C.**
- [ ] **D.**

796 When may you sound the horn?

Mark one answer
- [ ] **A.** To give you right of way
- [ ] **B.** To attract a friend's attention
- [ ] **C.** To warn others of your presence
- [ ] **D.** To make slower drivers move over

797 You must not use your horn when you are stationary

Mark one answer

- [ ] **A.** unless a moving vehicle may cause you danger
- [ ] **B.** at any time whatsoever
- [ ] **C.** unless it is used only briefly
- [ ] **D.** except for signalling that you have just arrived

798 What does this sign mean?

URBAN CLEARWAY
Monday to Friday

am	pm
8.00 - 9.30	4.30 - 6.30

Mark one answer

- [ ] **A.** You can park on the days and times shown
- [ ] **B.** No parking on the days and times shown
- [ ] **C.** No parking at all from Monday to Friday
- [ ] **D.** End of the urban clearway restrictions

799 What does this sign mean?

Mark one answer

- [ ] **A.** Quayside or river bank
- [ ] **B.** Steep hill downwards
- [ ] **C.** Uneven road surface
- [ ] **D.** Road liable to flooding

800 You see this amber traffic light ahead. Which light or lights will come on next?

Mark one answer

- [ ] **A.** Red alone
- [ ] **B.** Red and amber together
- [ ] **C.** Green and amber together
- [ ] **D.** Green alone

801 This broken white line painted in the centre of the road means

Mark one answer

- [ ] **A.** oncoming vehicles have priority over you
- [ ] **B.** you should give priority to oncoming vehicles
- [ ] **C.** there is a hazard ahead of you
- [ ] **D.** the area is a national speed limit zone

802 Which sign means you have priority over oncoming vehicles?

Mark one answer

- [ ] **A.**
- [ ] **B.**
- [ ] **C.**
- [ ] **D.**

803

You see this signal overhead on the motorway. What does it mean?

Mark one answer

- A. Leave the motorway at the next exit
- B. All vehicles use the hard shoulder
- C. Sharp bend to the left ahead
- D. Stop, all lanes ahead closed

804

A white line like this along the centre of the road is a

Mark one answer

- A. bus lane marking
- B. hazard warning
- C. give way marking
- D. lane marking

805

What is the purpose of these yellow criss-cross lines on the road?

Mark one answer

- A. To make you more aware of the traffic lights
- B. To guide you into position as you turn
- C. To prevent the junction becoming blocked
- D. To show you where to stop when the lights change

806

What is the reason for the yellow criss-cross lines painted on the road here?

Mark one answer

- A. To mark out an area for trams only
- B. To prevent queuing traffic from blocking the junction on the left
- C. To mark the entrance lane to a car park
- D. To warn you of the tram lines crossing the road

807
What is the reason for the area marked in red and white along the centre of this road?

Mark one answer

- [ ] **A.** It is to separate traffic flowing in opposite directions
- [ ] **B.** It marks an area to be used by overtaking motorcyclists
- [ ] **C.** It is a temporary marking to warn of the roadworks
- [ ] **D.** It is separating the two sides of the dual carriageway

808
Other drivers may sometimes flash their headlights at you. In which situation are they allowed to do this?

Mark one answer

- [ ] **A.** To warn of a radar speed trap ahead
- [ ] **B.** To show that they are giving way to you
- [ ] **C.** To warn you of their presence
- [ ] **D.** To let you know there is a fault with your vehicle

809
You are approaching a zebra crossing where pedestrians are waiting. Which arm signal might you give?

Mark one answer

- [ ] **A.**
- [ ] **B.**
- [ ] **C.**
- [ ] **D.**

810
The white line along the side of the road

Mark one answer

- [ ] **A.** shows the edge of the carriageway
- [ ] **B.** shows the approach to a hazard
- [ ] **C.** means no parking
- [ ] **D.** means no overtaking

811
You see this white arrow on the road ahead. It means

Mark one answer

- [ ] **A.** entrance on the left
- [ ] **B.** all vehicles turn left
- [ ] **C.** keep left of the hatched markings
- [ ] **D.** road bending to the left

812
How should you give an arm signal to turn left?

Mark one answer

- [ ] **A.**
- [ ] **B.**
- [ ] **C.**
- [ ] **D.**

813
You are waiting at a T-junction. A vehicle is coming from the right with the left signal flashing. What should you do?

Mark one answer
- [ ] **A.** Move out and accelerate hard
- [ ] **B.** Wait until the vehicle starts to turn in
- [ ] **C.** Pull out before the vehicle reaches the junction
- [ ] **D.** Move out slowly

814
When may you use hazard warning lights when driving?

Mark one answer
- [ ] **A.** Instead of sounding the horn in a built-up area between 11.30pm and 7am
- [ ] **B.** On a motorway or unrestricted dual carriageway, to warn of a hazard ahead
- [ ] **C.** On rural routes, after a warning sign of animals
- [ ] **D.** On the approach to toucan crossings where cyclists are waiting to cross

815
You are driving on a motorway. There is a slow-moving vehicle ahead. On the back you see this sign. You should

Mark one answer
- [ ] **A.** pass on the right
- [ ] **B.** pass on the left
- [ ] **C.** leave at the next exit
- [ ] **D.** drive no further

816
In some narrow residential streets you may find a speed limit of

Mark one answer
- [ ] **A.** 20mph
- [ ] **B.** 25mph
- [ ] **C.** 35mph
- [ ] **D.** 40mph

817
You should NOT normally stop on these markings near schools

Mark one answer
- [ ] **A.** except when picking up children
- [ ] **B.** under any circumstances
- [ ] **C.** unless there is nowhere else available
- [ ] **D.** except to set down children

818

Why should you make sure that your indicators are cancelled after turning?

Mark one answer

- A. To avoid flattening the battery
- B. To avoid misleading other road users
- C. To avoid dazzling other road users
- D. To avoid damage to the indicator relay

819

You are driving in busy traffic. You want to pull up on the left just after a junction on the left. When should you signal?

Mark one answer

- A. As you are passing or just after the junction
- B. Just before you reach the junction
- C. Well before you reach the junction
- D. It would be better not to signal at all

820

You have just driven past this sign. You should be aware that

Mark one answer

- A. it is a single track road
- B. you cannot stop on this road
- C. there is only one lane in use
- D. all traffic is going one way

821

Which of these signs shows that you are entering a one-way system?

Mark one answer

- A.
- B.
- C.
- D.

822

You approach a junction. The traffic lights are not working. A police officer gives this signal. You should

Mark one answer

- A. turn left only
- B. turn right only
- C. stop level with the officer's arm
- D. stop at the stop line

823 An MOT certificate is normally valid for

Mark one answer

- [ ] **A.** three years after the date it was issued
- [ ] **B.** 10,000 miles
- [ ] **C.** one year after the date it was issued
- [ ] **D.** 30,000 miles

824 A cover note is a document issued before you receive your

Mark one answer

- [ ] **A.** driving licence
- [ ] **B.** insurance certificate
- [ ] **C.** registration document
- [ ] **D.** MOT certificate

825 A police officer asks to see your documents. You do not have them with you. You may be asked to take them to a police station within

Mark one answer

- [ ] **A.** 5 days
- [ ] **B.** 7 days
- [ ] **C.** 14 days
- [ ] **D.** 21 days

826 You have just passed your practical test. You do not hold a full licence in another category. Within two years you get six penalty points on your licence. What will you have to do?

Mark two answers

- [ ] **A.** Retake only your theory test
- [ ] **B.** Retake your theory and practical tests
- [ ] **C.** Retake only your practical test
- [ ] **D.** Reapply for your full licence immediately
- [ ] **E.** Reapply for your provisional licence

827 To drive on the road learners MUST

Mark one answer

- [ ] **A.** have NO penalty points on their licence
- [ ] **B.** have taken professional instruction
- [ ] **C.** have a signed, valid provisional licence
- [ ] **D.** apply for a driving test within 12 months

828 Before driving anyone else's motor vehicle you should make sure that

Mark one answer

- [ ] **A.** the vehicle owner has third party insurance cover
- [ ] **B.** your own vehicle has insurance cover
- [ ] **C.** the vehicle is insured for your use
- [ ] **D.** the owner has left the insurance documents in the vehicle

829 Your car needs an MOT certificate. If you drive without one this could invalidate your

Mark one answer

- [ ] **A.** vehicle service record
- [ ] **B.** insurance
- [ ] **C.** road tax disc
- [ ] **D.** vehicle registration document

830 When is it legal to drive a car over three years old without an MOT certificate?

NI

Mark one answer

- [ ] **A.** Up to seven days after the old certificate has run out
- [ ] **B.** When driving to an MOT centre to arrange an appointment
- [ ] **C.** Just after buying a second-hand car with no MOT
- [ ] **D.** When driving to an appointment at an MOT centre

831 To supervise a learner driver you must

Mark two answers

- [ ] **A.** have held a full licence for at least 3 years
- [ ] **B.** be at least 21 years old
- [ ] **C.** be an approved driving instructor
- [ ] **D.** hold an advanced driving certificate

832 How old must you be to supervise a learner driver?

Mark one answer

- [ ] **A.** 18 years old
- [ ] **B.** 19 years old
- [ ] **C.** 20 years old
- [ ] **D.** 21 years old

833 A newly qualified driver must

Mark one answer

- [ ] **A.** display green 'L' plates
- [ ] **B.** not exceed 40mph for 12 months
- [ ] **C.** be accompanied on a motorway
- [ ] **D.** have valid motor insurance

834 You have third party insurance. What does this cover?

Mark three answers

- [ ] **A.** Damage to your own vehicle
- [ ] **B.** Damage to your vehicle by fire
- [ ] **C.** Injury to another person
- [ ] **D.** Damage to someone's property
- [ ] **E.** Damage to other vehicles
- [ ] **F.** Injury to yourself

835 For which of these MUST you show your insurance certificate?

Mark one answer

- [ ] **A.** When making a SORN declaration
- [ ] **B.** When buying or selling a vehicle
- [ ] **C.** When a police officer asks you for it
- [ ] **D.** When having an MOT inspection

836 Vehicle excise duty is often called 'Road Tax' or 'The Tax Disc'. You must

Mark one answer

- [ ] **A.** keep it with your registration document
- [ ] **B.** display it clearly on your vehicle
- [ ] **C.** keep it concealed safely in your vehicle
- [ ] **D.** carry it on you at all times

837 Motor cars must first have an MOT test certificate when they are

NI

Mark one answer

- [ ] **A.** one year old
- [ ] **B.** three years old
- [ ] **C.** five years old
- [ ] **D.** seven years old

838 Your vehicle needs a current MOT certificate. Until you have one you will NOT be able to

Mark one answer

- [ ] **A.** renew your driving licence
- [ ] **B.** change your insurance company
- [ ] **C.** renew your road tax disc
- [ ] **D.** notify a change of address

839 Which THREE pieces of information are found on a vehicle registration document?

Mark three answers

- [ ] **A.** Registered keeper
- [ ] **B.** Make of the vehicle
- [ ] **C.** Service history details
- [ ] **D.** Date of the MOT
- [ ] **E.** Type of insurance cover
- [ ] **F.** Engine size

840
You have a duty to contact the licensing authority when

Mark three answers
- [ ] **A.** you go abroad on holiday
- [ ] **B.** you change your vehicle
- [ ] **C.** you change your name
- [ ] **D.** your job status is changed
- [ ] **E.** your permanent address changes
- [ ] **F.** your job involves travelling abroad

841
You must notify the licensing authority when

Mark three answers
- [ ] **A.** your health affects your driving
- [ ] **B.** your eyesight does not meet a set standard
- [ ] **C.** you intend lending your vehicle
- [ ] **D.** your vehicle requires an MOT certificate
- [ ] **E.** you change your vehicle

842
Your vehicle is insured third party only. This covers

Mark two answers
- [ ] **A.** damage to your vehicle
- [ ] **B.** damage to other vehicles
- [ ] **C.** injury to yourself
- [ ] **D.** injury to others
- [ ] **E.** all damage and injury

843
Your motor insurance policy has an excess of £100. What does this mean?

Mark one answer
- [ ] **A.** The insurance company will pay the first £100 of any claim
- [ ] **B.** You will be paid £100 if you do not have a crash
- [ ] **C.** Your vehicle is insured for a value of £100 if it is stolen
- [ ] **D.** You will have to pay the first £100 of any claim

844
When you apply to renew your vehicle excise licence (tax disc) what must you have?

Mark one answer
- [ ] **A.** Valid insurance
- [ ] **B.** The old tax disc
- [ ] **C.** The vehicle handbook
- [ ] **D.** A valid driving licence

845
What is the legal minimum insurance cover you must have to drive on public roads?

Mark one answer
- [ ] **A.** Third party, fire and theft
- [ ] **B.** Comprehensive
- [ ] **C.** Third party only
- [ ] **D.** Personal injury cover

846
Which THREE of these do you need before you can drive legally?

Mark three answers
- [ ] **A.** A valid driving licence
- [ ] **B.** A valid tax disc displayed on your vehicle
- [ ] **C.** A vehicle service record
- [ ] **D.** Proper insurance cover
- [ ] **E.** Breakdown cover
- [ ] **F.** A vehicle handbook

847
The cost of your insurance may reduce if you   NI

Mark one answer
- [ ] **A.** are under 25 years old
- [ ] **B.** do not wear glasses
- [ ] **C.** pass the driving test first time
- [ ] **D.** take the Pass Plus scheme

848
Which of the following may reduce the cost of your insurance?   NI

Mark one answer
- [ ] **A.** Having a valid MOT certificate
- [ ] **B.** Taking a Pass Plus course
- [ ] **C.** Driving a powerful car
- [ ] **D.** Having penalty points on your licence

849
The Pass Plus scheme has been created for new drivers. What is its main purpose?

Mark one answer **NI**

- [ ] A. To allow you to drive faster
- [ ] B. To allow you to carry passengers
- [ ] C. To improve your basic skills
- [ ] D. To let you drive on motorways

850
How long will a Statutory Off Road Notification (SORN) last for?

Mark one answer

- [ ] A. 12 months
- [ ] B. 24 months
- [ ] C. 3 years
- [ ] D. 10 years

851
What is a Statutory Off Road Notification (SORN) declaration?

Mark one answer **NI**

- [ ] A. A notification to tell VOSA that a vehicle does not have a current MOT
- [ ] B. Information kept by the police about the owner of the vehicle
- [ ] C. A notification to tell DVLA that a vehicle is not being used on the road
- [ ] D. Information held by insurance companies to check the vehicle is insured

852
A Statutory Off Road Notification (SORN) declaration is

Mark one answer **NI**

- [ ] A. to tell DVLA that your vehicle is being used on the road but the MOT has expired
- [ ] B. to tell DVLA that you no longer own the vehicle
- [ ] C. to tell DVLA that your vehicle is not being used on the road
- [ ] D. to tell DVLA that you are buying a personal number plate

853
You claim on your insurance to have your car repaired. Your policy has an excess of £100. What does this mean?

Mark one answer

- [ ] A. The insurance company will pay the first £100 of any claim
- [ ] B. You will be paid £100 if you do not claim within one year
- [ ] C. Your vehicle is insured for a value of £100 if it is stolen
- [ ] D. You will have to pay the first £100 of the cost of repair to your car

854
A Statutory Off Road Notification (SORN) is valid

Mark one answer

- [ ] A. for as long as the vehicle has an MOT
- [ ] B. for 12 months only
- [ ] C. only if the vehicle is more than 3 years old
- [ ] D. provided the vehicle is insured

855
A Statutory Off Road Notification (SORN) will last

Mark one answer

- [ ] A. for the life of the vehicle
- [ ] B. for as long as you own the vehicle
- [ ] C. for 12 months only
- [ ] D. until the vehicle warranty expires

856
What is the maximum specified fine for driving without insurance?

Mark one answer **NI**

- [ ] A. £50
- [ ] B. £500
- [ ] C. £1,000
- [ ] D. £5,000

857 When should you update your Vehicle Registration Certificate?

Mark one answer
- [ ] **A.** When you pass your driving test
- [ ] **B.** When you move house
- [ ] **C.** When your vehicle needs an MOT
- [ ] **D.** When you have a collision

858 Who is legally responsible for ensuring that a Vehicle Registration Certificate (V5C) is updated?

Mark one answer
- [ ] **A.** The registered vehicle keeper
- [ ] **B.** The vehicle manufacturer
- [ ] **C.** Your insurance company
- [ ] **D.** The licensing authority

859 The Pass Plus scheme is designed to

Mark one answer **NI**
- [ ] **A.** give you a discount on your MOT
- [ ] **B.** improve your basic driving skills
- [ ] **C.** increase your mechanical knowledge
- [ ] **D.** allow you to drive anyone else's vehicle

860 By taking part in the Pass Plus scheme you will

Mark one answer **NI**
- [ ] **A.** never get any points on your licence
- [ ] **B.** be able to service your own car
- [ ] **C.** allow you to drive anyone else's vehicle
- [ ] **D.** improve your basic driving skills

861 The Pass Plus scheme is aimed at all newly qualified drivers. It enables them to

Mark one answer **NI**
- [ ] **A.** widen their driving experience
- [ ] **B.** supervise a learner driver
- [ ] **C.** increase their insurance premiums
- [ ] **D.** avoid mechanical breakdowns

862 New drivers can take further training after passing the practical test. A Pass Plus course will help to

Mark two answers **NI**
- [ ] **A.** improve your basic skills
- [ ] **B.** widen your experience
- [ ] **C.** increase your insurance premiums
- [ ] **D.** get cheaper road tax

863 The Pass Plus scheme is operated by DSA for newly qualified drivers. It is intended to

Mark one answer **NI**
- [ ] **A.** improve your basic skills
- [ ] **B.** reduce the cost of your driving licence
- [ ] **C.** prevent you from paying congestion charges
- [ ] **D.** allow you to supervise a learner driver

864 You must have valid insurance before you can

Mark one answer **NI**
- [ ] **A.** make a SORN declaration
- [ ] **B.** buy or sell a vehicle
- [ ] **C.** apply for a driving licence
- [ ] **D.** obtain a tax disc

865 A friend wants to help you learn to drive. They must be

Mark one answer **NI**
- [ ] **A.** at least 21 and have held a full licence for at least one year
- [ ] **B.** over 18 and hold an advanced driver's certificate
- [ ] **C.** over 18 and have fully comprehensive insurance
- [ ] **D.** at least 21 and have held a full licence for at least three years

866
Which THREE of these do you need before you can use a vehicle on the road legally?

Mark three answers

A. A valid driving licence

B. A valid tax disc clearly displayed

C. Proof of your identity

D. Proper insurance cover

E. Breakdown cover

F. A vehicle handbook

867
When you apply to renew your Vehicle Excise Duty (tax disc) you must have

Mark one answer

A. valid insurance

B. the old tax disc

C. the handbook

D. a valid driving licence

868
Your vehicle needs a current MOT certificate. You do not have one. Until you do have one you will not be able to renew your

Mark one answer

A. driving licence

B. vehicle insurance

C. road tax disc

D. vehicle registration document

869
For which of these must you show your motor insurance certificate?

Mark one answer

A. When you are taking your driving test

B. When buying or selling a vehicle

C. When a police officer asks you for it

D. When having an MOT inspection

870 At the scene of a traffic accident you should

Mark one answer
- [ ] **A.** not put yourself at risk
- [ ] **B.** go to those casualties who are screaming
- [ ] **C.** pull everybody out of their vehicles
- [ ] **D.** leave vehicle engines switched on

871 You are the first to arrive at the scene of a crash. Which TWO of these should you do?

Mark two answers
- [ ] **A.** Leave as soon as another motorist arrives
- [ ] **B.** Make sure engines are switched off
- [ ] **C.** Drag all casualties away from the vehicle
- [ ] **D.** Call the emergency services promptly

872 A collision has just happened. An injured person is lying in a busy road. What is the FIRST thing you should do to help?

Mark two answers
- [ ] **A.** Treat the person for shock
- [ ] **B.** Warn other traffic
- [ ] **C.** Place them in the recovery position
- [ ] **D.** Make sure the injured person is kept warm

873 You are the first person to arrive at an incident where people are badly injured. Which THREE should you do?

Mark three answers
- [ ] **A.** Switch on your own hazard warning lights
- [ ] **B.** Make sure that someone telephones for an ambulance
- [ ] **C.** Try and get people who are injured to drink something
- [ ] **D.** Move the people who are injured clear of their vehicles
- [ ] **E.** Get people who are not injured clear of the scene

874 You arrive at the scene of a motorcycle crash. The rider is injured. When should the helmet be removed?

Mark one answer
- [ ] **A.** Only when it is essential
- [ ] **B.** Always straight away
- [ ] **C.** Only when the motorcyclist asks
- [ ] **D.** Always, unless they are in shock

875 You arrive at a serious motorcycle crash. The motorcyclist is unconscious and bleeding. Your THREE main priorities should be to

Mark three answers
- [ ] **A.** try to stop the bleeding
- [ ] **B.** make a list of witnesses
- [ ] **C.** check their breathing
- [ ] **D.** take the numbers of other vehicles
- [ ] **E.** sweep up any loose debris
- [ ] **F.** check their airways

876 You arrive at an incident. A motorcyclist is unconscious. Your FIRST priority is the casualty's

Mark one answer
- [ ] **A.** breathing
- [ ] **B.** bleeding
- [ ] **C.** broken bones
- [ ] **D.** bruising

877 At an incident a casualty is unconscious. Which THREE of these should you check urgently?

Mark three answers
- [ ] **A.** Circulation
- [ ] **B.** Airway
- [ ] **C.** Shock
- [ ] **D.** Breathing
- [ ] **E.** Broken bones

878

You arrive at the scene of an incident. It has just happened and someone is unconscious. Which THREE of these should be given urgent priority to help them?

Mark three answers

- A. Clear the airway and keep it open
- B. Try to get them to drink water
- C. Check that they are breathing
- D. Look for any witnesses
- E. Stop any heavy bleeding
- F. Take the numbers of vehicles involved

879

At an incident someone is unconscious. Your THREE main priorities should be to

Mark three answers

- A. sweep up the broken glass
- B. take the names of witnesses
- C. count the number of vehicles involved
- D. check the airway is clear
- E. make sure they are breathing
- F. stop any heavy bleeding

880

You have stopped at an incident to give help. Which THREE things should you do?

Mark three answers

- A. Keep injured people warm and comfortable
- B. Keep injured people calm by talking to them reassuringly
- C. Keep injured people on the move by walking them around
- D. Give injured people a warm drink
- E. Make sure that injured people are not left alone

881

You arrive at an incident. It has just happened and someone is injured. Which THREE should be given urgent priority?

Mark three answers

- A. Stop any severe bleeding
- B. Give them a warm drink
- C. Check they are breathing
- D. Take numbers of vehicles involved
- E. Look for witnesses
- F. Clear their airway and keep it open

882

At an incident a casualty has stopped breathing. You should

Mark two answers

- A. remove anything that is blocking the mouth
- B. keep the head tilted forwards as far as possible
- C. raise the legs to help with circulation
- D. try to give the casualty something to drink
- E. tilt the head back gently to clear the airway

883

You are at the scene of an incident. Someone is suffering from shock. You should

Mark four answers

- A. reassure them constantly
- B. offer them a cigarette
- C. keep them warm
- D. avoid moving them if possible
- E. avoid leaving them alone
- F. give them a warm drink

884

Which of the following should you NOT do at the scene of a collision?

Mark one answer

- A. Warn other traffic by switching on your hazard warning lights
- B. Call the emergency services immediately
- C. Offer someone a cigarette to calm them down
- D. Ask drivers to switch off their engines

885 There has been a collision. A driver is suffering from shock. What TWO of these should you do?

Mark two answers
- [ ] **A.** Give them a drink
- [ ] **B.** Reassure them
- [ ] **C.** Not leave them alone
- [ ] **D.** Offer them a cigarette
- [ ] **E.** Ask who caused the incident

886 You have to treat someone for shock at the scene of an incident. You should

Mark one answer
- [ ] **A.** reassure them constantly
- [ ] **B.** walk them around to calm them down
- [ ] **C.** give them something cold to drink
- [ ] **D.** cool them down as soon as possible

887 You arrive at the scene of a motorcycle crash. No other vehicle is involved. The rider is unconscious and lying in the middle of the road. The FIRST thing you should do is

Mark one answer
- [ ] **A.** move the rider out of the road
- [ ] **B.** warn other traffic
- [ ] **C.** clear the road of debris
- [ ] **D.** give the rider reassurance

888 At an incident a small child is not breathing. To restore normal breathing you should breathe into their mouth

Mark one answer
- [ ] **A.** sharply
- [ ] **B.** gently
- [ ] **C.** heavily
- [ ] **D.** rapidly

889 At an incident a casualty is not breathing. To start the process to restore normal breathing you should

Mark three answers
- [ ] **A.** tilt their head forward
- [ ] **B.** clear the airway
- [ ] **C.** turn them on their side
- [ ] **D.** tilt their head back gently
- [ ] **E.** pinch the nostrils together
- [ ] **F.** put their arms across their chest

890 You arrive at the scene of an incident. There has been an engine fire and someone's hands and arms have been burnt. You should NOT

Mark one answer
- [ ] **A.** douse the burn thoroughly with clean cool non-toxic liquid
- [ ] **B.** lay the casualty down on the ground
- [ ] **C.** remove anything sticking to the burn
- [ ] **D.** reassure them confidently and repeatedly

891 You arrive at an incident where someone is suffering from severe burns. You should

Mark one answer
- [ ] **A.** apply lotions to the injury
- [ ] **B.** burst any blisters
- [ ] **C.** remove anything stuck to the burns
- [ ] **D.** douse the burns with clean cool non-toxic liquid

892 You arrive at an incident. A pedestrian has a severe bleeding leg wound. It is not broken and there is nothing in the wound. What TWO of these should you do?

Mark two answers

A. Dab the wound to stop bleeding
B. Keep both legs flat on the ground
C. Apply firm pressure to the wound
D. Raise the leg to lessen bleeding
E. Fetch them a warm drink

893 You arrive at the scene of a crash. Someone is bleeding badly from an arm wound. There is nothing embedded in it. What should you do?

Mark one answer

A. Apply pressure over the wound and keep the arm down
B. Dab the wound
C. Get them a drink
D. Apply pressure over the wound and raise the arm

894 At an incident a casualty is unconscious but still breathing. You should only move them if

Mark one answer

A. an ambulance is on its way
B. bystanders advise you to
C. there is further danger
D. bystanders will help you to

895 At a collision you suspect a casualty has back injuries. The area is safe. You should

Mark one answer

A. offer them a drink
B. not move them
C. raise their legs
D. not call an ambulance

896 At an incident it is important to look after the casualty. When the area is safe, you should

Mark one answer

A. get them out of the vehicle
B. give them a drink
C. give them something to eat
D. keep them in the vehicle

897 A tanker is involved in a collision. Which sign shows that it is carrying dangerous goods?

Mark one answer

A.
LONG VEHICLE

B.
2YE
1089

C.

D.

898 You are involved in a collision. Because of this which THREE of these documents may the police ask you to produce?

Mark three answers

A. Vehicle registration document
B. Driving licence
C. Theory test certificate
D. Insurance certificate
E. MOT test certificate
F. Vehicle service record

899 You see a car on the hard shoulder of a motorway with a HELP pennant displayed. This means the driver is most likely to be

Mark one answer

A. a disabled person
B. first aid trained
C. a foreign visitor
D. a rescue patrol person

900
On the motorway, the hard shoulder should be used

Mark one answer

- A. to answer a mobile phone
- B. when an emergency arises
- C. for a short rest when tired
- D. to check a road atlas

901
For which TWO should you use hazard warning lights?

Mark two answers

- A. When you slow down quickly on a motorway because of a hazard ahead
- B. When you have broken down
- C. When you wish to stop on double yellow lines
- D. When you need to park on the pavement

902
When are you allowed to use hazard warning lights?

Mark one answer

- A. When stopped and temporarily obstructing traffic
- B. When travelling during darkness without headlights
- C. When parked for shopping on double yellow lines
- D. When travelling slowly because you are lost

903
You are on a motorway. A large box falls onto the road from a lorry. The lorry does not stop. You should

Mark one answer

- A. go to the next emergency telephone and inform the police
- B. catch up with the lorry and try to get the driver's attention
- C. stop close to the box until the police arrive
- D. pull over to the hard shoulder, then remove the box

904
There has been a collision. A motorcyclist is lying injured and unconscious. Unless it is essential, why should you usually NOT attempt to remove their helmet?

Mark one answer

- A. Because they may not want you to
- B. This could result in more serious injury
- C. They will get too cold if you do this
- D. Because you could scratch the helmet

905
After a collision, someone is unconscious in their vehicle. When should you call the emergency services?

Mark one answer

- A. Only as a last resort
- B. As soon as possible
- C. After you have woken them up
- D. After checking for broken bones

906
A casualty has an injured arm. They can move it freely, but it is bleeding. Why should you get them to keep it in a raised position?

Mark one answer

- A. Because it will ease the pain
- B. It will help them to be seen more easily
- C. To stop them touching other people
- D. It will help to reduce the blood flow

907
You are going through a congested tunnel and have to stop. What should you do?

Mark one answer

- A. Pull up very close to the vehicle in front to save space
- B. Ignore any message signs as they are never up to date
- C. Keep a safe distance from the vehicle in front
- D. Make a U-turn and find another route

908

You are going through a long tunnel. What will warn you of congestion or an incident ahead?

Mark one answer

- A. Hazard warning lines
- B. Other drivers flashing their lights
- C. Variable message signs
- D. Areas marked with hatch markings

909

You are going through a tunnel. What systems are provided to warn of any incidents, collisions or congestion?

Mark one answer

- A. Double white centre lines
- B. Variable message signs
- C. Chevron 'distance markers'
- D. Rumble strips

910

While driving, a warning light on your vehicle's instrument panel comes on. You should

Mark one answer

- A. continue if the engine sounds alright
- B. hope that it is just a temporary electrical fault
- C. deal with the problem when there is more time
- D. check out the problem quickly and safely

911

You have broken down on a two-way road. You have a warning triangle. You should place the warning triangle at least how far from your vehicle?

Mark one answer

- A. 5 metres (16 feet)
- B. 25 metres (82 feet)
- C. 45 metres (147 feet)
- D. 100 metres (328 feet)

912

You break down on a level crossing. The lights have not yet begun to flash. Which THREE things should you do?

Mark three answers

- A. Telephone the signal operator
- B. Leave your vehicle and get everyone clear
- C. Walk down the track and signal the next train
- D. Move the vehicle if a signal operator tells you to
- E. Tell drivers behind what has happened

913

Your vehicle has broken down on an automatic railway level crossing. What should you do FIRST?

Mark one answer

- A. Get everyone out of the vehicle and clear of the crossing
- B. Telephone your vehicle recovery service to move it
- C. Walk along the track to give warning to any approaching trains
- D. Try to push the vehicle clear of the crossing as soon as possible

914

Your tyre bursts while you are driving. Which TWO things should you do?

Mark two answers

- A. Pull on the handbrake
- B. Brake as quickly as possible
- C. Pull up slowly at the side of the road
- D. Hold the steering wheel firmly to keep control
- E. Continue on at a normal speed

915

Which TWO things should you do when a front tyre bursts?

Mark two answers

- A. Apply the handbrake to stop the vehicle
- B. Brake firmly and quickly
- C. Let the vehicle roll to a stop
- D. Hold the steering wheel lightly
- E. Grip the steering wheel firmly

916 Your vehicle has a puncture on a motorway. What should you do?

Mark one answer

- [ ] **A.** Drive slowly to the next service area to get assistance
- [ ] **B.** Pull up on the hard shoulder. Change the wheel as quickly as possible
- [ ] **C.** Pull up on the hard shoulder. Use the emergency phone to get assistance
- [ ] **D.** Switch on your hazard lights. Stop in your lane

917 Which THREE of these items should you carry for use in the event of a collision?

Mark three answers

- [ ] **A.** Road map
- [ ] **B.** Can of petrol
- [ ] **C.** Jump leads
- [ ] **D.** Fire extinguisher
- [ ] **E.** First aid kit
- [ ] **F.** Warning triangle

918 You are in a collision on a two-way road. You have a warning triangle with you. At what distance before the obstruction should you place the warning triangle?

Mark one answer

- [ ] **A.** 25 metres (82 feet)
- [ ] **B.** 45 metres (147 feet)
- [ ] **C.** 100 metres (328 feet)
- [ ] **D.** 150 metres (492 feet)

919 You have broken down on a two-way road. You have a warning triangle. It should be displayed

Mark one answer

- [ ] **A.** on the roof of your vehicle
- [ ] **B.** at least 150 metres (492 feet) behind your vehicle
- [ ] **C.** at least 45 metres (147 feet) behind your vehicle
- [ ] **D.** just behind your vehicle

920 You have stalled in the middle of a level crossing and cannot restart the engine. The warning bell starts to ring. You should

Mark one answer

- [ ] **A.** get out and clear of the crossing
- [ ] **B.** run down the track to warn the signal operator
- [ ] **C.** carry on trying to restart the engine
- [ ] **D.** push the vehicle clear of the crossing

921 You are on the motorway. Luggage falls from your vehicle. What should you do?

Mark one answer

- [ ] **A.** Stop at the next emergency telephone and contact the police
- [ ] **B.** Stop on the motorway and put on hazard lights while you pick it up
- [ ] **C.** Walk back up the motorway to pick it up
- [ ] **D.** Pull up on the hard shoulder and wave traffic down

922 You are on a motorway. When can you use hazard warning lights?

Mark two answers

- [ ] **A.** When a vehicle is following too closely
- [ ] **B.** When you slow down quickly because of danger ahead
- [ ] **C.** When you are towing another vehicle
- [ ] **D.** When driving on the hard shoulder
- [ ] **E.** When you have broken down on the hard shoulder

923

You are in collision with another moving vehicle. Someone is injured and your vehicle is damaged. Which FOUR of the following should you find out?

Mark four answers

- A. Whether the driver owns the other vehicle involved
- B. The other driver's name, address and telephone number
- C. The make and registration number of the other vehicle
- D. The occupation of the other driver
- E. The details of the other driver's vehicle insurance
- F. Whether the other driver is licensed to drive

924

You have broken down on a motorway. When you use the emergency telephone you will be asked

Mark three answers

- A. for the number on the telephone that you are using
- B. for your driving licence details
- C. for the name of your vehicle insurance company
- D. for details of yourself and your vehicle
- E. whether you belong to a motoring organisation

925

You lose control of your car and damage a garden wall. No one is around. What must you do?

Mark one answer   **NI**

- A. Report the incident to the police within 24 hours
- B. Go back to tell the house owner the next day
- C. Report the incident to your insurance company when you get home
- D. Find someone in the area to tell them about it immediately

926

Your engine catches fire. What should you do first?

Mark one answer

- A. Lift the bonnet and disconnect the battery
- B. Lift the bonnet and warn other traffic
- C. Call a breakdown service
- D. Call the fire brigade

927

Before driving through a tunnel what should you do?

Mark one answer

- A. Switch your radio off
- B. Remove any sunglasses
- C. Close your sunroof
- D. Switch on windscreen wipers

928

You are driving through a tunnel and the traffic is flowing normally. What should you do?

Mark one answer

- A. Use parking lights
- B. Use front spot lights
- C. Use dipped headlights
- D. Use rear fog lights

929

When approaching a tunnel it is good advice to

Mark one answer

- A. put on your sunglasses and use the sun visor
- B. check your tyre pressures
- C. change down to a lower gear
- D. make sure your radio is tuned to the frequency shown

930

You are driving through a tunnel. Your vehicle breaks down. What should you do?

Mark one answer

- A. Switch on hazard warning lights
- B. Remain in your vehicle
- C. Wait for the police to find you
- D. Rely on CCTV cameras seeing you

931 Your vehicle breaks down in a tunnel. What should you do?

Mark one answer

- A. Stay in your vehicle and wait for the police
- B. Stand in the lane behind your vehicle to warn others
- C. Stand in front of your vehicle to warn oncoming drivers
- D. Switch on hazard lights then go and call for help immediately

932 You have a collision while driving through a tunnel. You are not injured but your vehicle cannot be driven. What should you do FIRST?

Mark one answer

- A. Rely on other drivers phoning for the police
- B. Switch off the engine and switch on hazard lights
- C. Take the names of witnesses and other drivers
- D. Sweep up any debris that is in the road

933 When driving through a tunnel you should

Mark one answer

- A. Look out for variable message signs
- B. Use your air conditioning system
- C. Switch on your rear fog lights
- D. Always use your windscreen wipers

934 What TWO safeguards could you take against fire risk to your vehicle?

Mark two answers

- A. Keep water levels above maximum
- B. Carry a fire extinguisher
- C. Avoid driving with a full tank of petrol
- D. Use unleaded petrol
- E. Check out any strong smell of petrol
- F. Use low octane fuel

935 Your vehicle catches fire while driving through a tunnel. It is still driveable. What should you do?

Mark one answer

- A. Leave it where it is with the engine running
- B. Pull up, then walk to an emergency telephone point
- C. Park it away from the carriageway
- D. Drive it out of the tunnel if you can do so

936 You are driving through a tunnel. Your vehicle catches fire. What should you do?

Mark one answer

- A. Continue through the tunnel if you can
- B. Turn your vehicle around immediately
- C. Reverse out of the tunnel
- D. Carry out an emergency stop

937 You are in a tunnel. Your vehicle is on fire and you CANNOT drive it. What should you do?

Mark two answers

- A. Stay in the vehicle and close the windows
- B. Switch on hazard warning lights
- C. Leave the engine running
- D. Try and put out the fire
- E. Switch off all of your lights
- F. Wait for other people to phone for help

938 You are driving through a tunnel. There has been a collision and the car in front is on fire and blocking the road. What should you do?

Mark one answer

- A. Overtake and continue as quickly as you can
- B. Lock all the doors and windows
- C. Switch on hazard warning lights
- D. Stop, then reverse out of the tunnel

939 You are at an incident where a casualty is unconscious. Their breathing should be checked. This should be done for at least

Mark one answer

- [ ] **A.** 2 seconds
- [ ] **B.** 10 seconds
- [ ] **C.** 1 minute
- [ ] **D.** 2 minutes

940 Following a collision someone has suffered a burn. The burn needs to be cooled. What is the shortest time it should be cooled for?

Mark one answer

- [ ] **A.** 5 minutes
- [ ] **B.** 10 minutes
- [ ] **C.** 15 minutes
- [ ] **D.** 20 minutes

941 After a collision someone has suffered a burn. The burn needs to be cooled. What is the shortest time it should be cooled for?

Mark one answer

- [ ] **A.** 30 seconds
- [ ] **B.** 60 seconds
- [ ] **C.** 5 minutes
- [ ] **D.** 10 minutes

942 A casualty is not breathing normally. Chest compressions should be given. At what rate?

Mark one answer

- [ ] **A.** 50 per minute
- [ ] **B.** 100 per minute
- [ ] **C.** 200 per minute
- [ ] **D.** 250 per minute

943 An adult casualty is not breathing. To maintain circulation, compressions should be given. What is the correct depth to press?

Mark one answer

- [ ] **A.** 1 to 2 centimetres
- [ ] **B.** 4 to 5 centimetres
- [ ] **C.** 10 to 15 centimetres
- [ ] **D.** 15 to 20 centimetres

944 A person has been injured. They may be suffering from shock. What are the warning signs to look for?

Mark one answer

- [ ] **A.** Flushed complexion
- [ ] **B.** Warm dry skin
- [ ] **C.** Slow pulse
- [ ] **D.** Pale grey skin

945 You suspect that an injured person may be suffering from shock. What are the warning signs to look for?

Mark one answer

- [ ] **A.** Warm dry skin
- [ ] **B.** Sweating
- [ ] **C.** Slow pulse
- [ ] **D.** Skin rash

946 An injured person has been placed in the recovery position. They are unconscious but breathing normally. What else should be done?

Mark one answer

- [ ] **A.** Press firmly between the shoulders
- [ ] **B.** Place their arms by their side
- [ ] **C.** Give them a hot sweet drink
- [ ] **D.** Check the airway is clear

947 An injured motorcyclist is lying unconscious in the road. You should always

Mark one answer

- [ ] **A.** remove the safey helmet
- [ ] **B.** seek medical assistance
- [ ] **C.** move the person off the road
- [ ] **D.** remove the leather jacket

948 You have a collision whilst your car is moving. What is the FIRST thing you must do?

Mark one answer

- [ ] **A.** Stop only if someone waves at you
- [ ] **B.** Call the emergency services
- [ ] **C.** Stop at the scene of the incident
- [ ] **D.** Call your insurance company

949

You are towing a small trailer on a busy three-lane motorway. All the lanes are open. You must

Mark two answers

- [ ] **A.** not exceed 60mph
- [ ] **B.** not overtake
- [ ] **C.** have a stabiliser fitted
- [ ] **D.** use only the left and centre lanes

950

Any load that is carried on a roof rack should be

Mark one answer

- [ ] **A.** securely fastened when driving
- [ ] **B.** loaded towards the rear of the vehicle
- [ ] **C.** visible in your exterior mirror
- [ ] **D.** covered with plastic sheeting

951

You are planning to tow a caravan. Which of these will mostly help to aid the vehicle handling?

Mark one answer

- [ ] **A.** A jockey wheel fitted to the tow bar
- [ ] **B.** Power steering fitted to the towing vehicle
- [ ] **C.** Anti-lock brakes fitted to the towing vehicle
- [ ] **D.** A stabiliser fitted to the tow bar

952

If a trailer swerves or snakes when you are towing it you should

Mark one answer

- [ ] **A.** ease off the accelerator and reduce your speed
- [ ] **B.** let go of the steering wheel and let it correct itself
- [ ] **C.** brake hard and hold the pedal down
- [ ] **D.** increase your speed as quickly as possible

953

How can you stop a caravan snaking from side to side?

Mark one answer

- [ ] **A.** Turn the steering wheel slowly to each side
- [ ] **B.** Accelerate to increase your speed
- [ ] **C.** Stop as quickly as you can
- [ ] **D.** Slow down very gradually

954

On which TWO occasions might you inflate your tyres to more than the recommended normal pressure?

Mark two answers

- [ ] **A.** When the roads are slippery
- [ ] **B.** When driving fast for a long distance
- [ ] **C.** When the tyre tread is worn below 2mm
- [ ] **D.** When carrying a heavy load
- [ ] **E.** When the weather is cold
- [ ] **F.** When the vehicle is fitted with anti-lock brakes

955

A heavy load on your roof rack will

Mark one answer

- [ ] **A.** improve the road holding
- [ ] **B.** reduce the stopping distance
- [ ] **C.** make the steering lighter
- [ ] **D.** reduce stability

956

Are passengers allowed to ride in a caravan that is being towed?

Mark one answer

- [ ] **A.** Yes, if they are over 14
- [ ] **B.** No, not at any time
- [ ] **C.** Only if all the seats in the towing vehicle are full
- [ ] **D.** Only if a stabiliser is fitted

957 You are towing a caravan along a motorway. The caravan begins to swerve from side to side. What should you do?

Mark one answer

- [ ] **A.** Ease off the accelerator slowly
- [ ] **B.** Steer sharply from side to side
- [ ] **C.** Do an emergency stop
- [ ] **D.** Speed up very quickly

958 A trailer must stay securely hitched up to the towing vehicle. What additional safety device can be fitted to the trailer braking system?

Mark one answer

- [ ] **A.** Stabiliser
- [ ] **B.** Jockey wheel
- [ ] **C.** Corner steadies
- [ ] **D.** Breakaway cable

959 Overloading your vehicle can seriously affect the

Mark two answers

- [ ] **A.** gearbox
- [ ] **B.** steering
- [ ] **C.** handling
- [ ] **D.** battery life
- [ ] **E.** journey time

960 Who is responsible for making sure that a vehicle is not overloaded?

Mark one answer

- [ ] **A.** The driver of the vehicle
- [ ] **B.** The owner of the items being carried
- [ ] **C.** The person who loaded the vehicle
- [ ] **D.** The licensing authority

961 You are carrying a child in your car. They are under three years of age. Which of these is a suitable restraint?

Mark one answer

- [ ] **A.** A child seat
- [ ] **B.** An adult holding a child
- [ ] **C.** An adult seat belt
- [ ] **D.** An adult lap belt

962 Why would you fit a stabiliser before towing a caravan?

Mark one answer

- [ ] **A.** It will help with stability when driving in crosswinds
- [ ] **B.** It will allow heavy items to be loaded behind the axle
- [ ] **C.** It will help you to raise and lower the jockey wheel
- [ ] **D.** It will allow you to tow without the breakaway cable

963 You wish to tow a trailer. Where would you find the maximum noseweight of your vehicle's tow ball?

Mark one answer

- [ ] **A.** In the vehicle handbook
- [ ] **B.** In The Highway Code
- [ ] **C.** In your vehicle registration certificate
- [ ] **D.** In your licence documents

Part 4
The Highway Code

Contents

Introduction

This Highway Code applies to England, Scotland and Wales. *The Highway Code* is essential reading for everyone.

The most vulnerable road users are pedestrians, particularly children, older or disabled people, cyclists, motorcyclists and horse riders. It is important that all road users are aware of The Code and are considerate towards each other. This applies to pedestrians as much as to drivers and riders.

Many of the rules in the Code are legal requirements, and if you disobey these rules you are committing a criminal offence. You may be fined, given penalty points on your licence or be disqualified from driving. In the most serious cases you may be sent to prison. Such rules are identified by the use of the words **'MUST/MUST NOT'**. In addition, the rule includes an abbreviated reference to the legislation which creates the offence. An explanation of the abbreviations is given in Annexe 4 – The road user and the law.

Although failure to comply with the other rules of the Code will not, in itself, cause a person to be prosecuted, *The Highway Code* may be used in evidence in any court proceedings under the Traffic Acts (see Annexe 4 – The road user and the law) to establish liability. This includes rules which use advisory wording such as 'should/should not' or 'do/do not'.

Knowing and applying the rules contained in *The Highway Code* could significantly reduce road casualties. Cutting the number of deaths and injuries that occur on our roads every day is a responsibility we all share. *The Highway Code* can help us discharge that responsibility. Further information on driving/riding techniques can be found in 'The Official DSA Guide to Driving – the essential skills' and 'The Official DSA Guide to Riding – the essential skills'.

Rules for pedestrians

General guidance

1. Pavements (including any path along the side of a road) should be used if provided. Where possible, avoid being next to the kerb with your back to the traffic. If you have to step into the road, look both ways first. Always show due care and consideration for others.

2. If there is no pavement keep to the right-hand side of the road so that you can see oncoming traffic. You should take extra care and
• be prepared to walk in single file, especially on narrow roads or in poor light
• keep close to the side of the road.
It may be safer to cross the road well before a sharp right-hand bend so that oncoming traffic has a better chance of seeing you. Cross back after the bend.

3. Help other road users to see you. Wear or carry something light-coloured, bright or fluorescent in poor daylight conditions. When it is dark, use reflective materials (e.g. armbands, sashes, waistcoats, jackets, footwear), which can be seen by drivers using headlights up to three times as far away as non-reflective materials.

Help yourself to be seen

4. Young children should not be out alone on the pavement or road (see Rule 7). When taking children out, keep between them and the traffic and hold their hands firmly. Strap very young children into push-chairs or use reins. When pushing a young child in a buggy, do not push the buggy into the road when checking to see if it is clear to cross, particularly from between parked vehicles.

5. Organised walks. Large groups of people walking together should use a pavement if available; if one is not, they should keep to the left. Look-outs should be positioned at the front and back of the group, and they should wear fluorescent clothes in daylight and reflective clothes in the dark. At night, the look-out in front should show a white light and the one at the back a red light. People on the outside of large groups should also carry lights and wear reflective clothing.

6. Motorways. Pedestrians **MUST NOT** be on motorways or slip roads except in an emergency (see Rules 271 and 275).
Laws RTRA sect 17, MT(E&W)R 1982 as amended, reg 15(1)(b) & MT(S)R reg 13

Crossing the road

7. The Green Cross Code. The advice given below on crossing the road is for all pedestrians. Children should be taught the Code and should not be allowed out alone until they can understand and use it properly. The age when they can do this is different for each child. Many children cannot judge how fast vehicles are going or how far away they are. Children learn by example, so parents and carers should always use the Code in full when out with their children. They are responsible for deciding at what age children can use it safely by themselves.

a. First find a safe place to cross and where there is space to reach the pavement on the other side. Where there is a crossing nearby, use it. It is safer to cross using a subway, a footbridge, an island, a zebra, pelican, toucan or puffin crossing, or where there is a crossing point controlled by a police officer, a school crossing patrol or a traffic warden. Otherwise choose a place where you can see clearly in all directions. Try to avoid crossing between parked cars (see Rule 14), on a blind bend, or close to the brow of a hill. Move to a space where drivers and riders can see you clearly. Do not cross the road diagonally.

Look all around and listen for traffic before crossing

b. Stop just before you get to the kerb, where you can see if anything is coming. Do not get too close to the traffic. If there's no pavement, keep back from the edge of the road but make sure you can still see approaching traffic.

c. Look all around for traffic and listen. Traffic could come from any direction. Listen as well, because you can sometimes hear traffic before you see it.

d. If traffic is coming, let it pass. Look all around again and listen. Do not cross until there is a safe gap in the traffic and you are certain that there is plenty of time. Remember, even if traffic is a long way off, it may be approaching very quickly.

e. When it is safe, go straight across the road – do not run. Keep looking and listening for traffic while you cross, in case there is any traffic you did not see, or in case other traffic appears suddenly. Look out for cyclists and motorcyclists travelling between lanes of traffic. Do not walk diagonally across the road.

8. At a junction. When crossing the road, look out for traffic turning into the road, especially from behind you. If you have started crossing and traffic wants to turn into the road, you have priority and they should give way (see Rule 170).

9. Pedestrian Safety Barriers. Where there are barriers, cross the road only at the gaps provided for pedestrians. Do not climb over the barriers or walk between them and the road.

10. Tactile paving. Raised surfaces that can be felt underfoot provide warning and guidance to blind or partially sighted people. The most common surfaces are a series of raised studs, which are used at crossing points with a dropped kerb, or a series of rounded raised bars which are used at level crossings, at the top and bottom of steps and at some other hazards.

11. One-way streets. Check which way the traffic is moving. Do not cross until it is safe to do so without stopping. Bus and cycle lanes may operate in the opposite direction to the rest of the traffic.

12. Bus and cycle lanes. Take care when crossing these lanes as traffic may be moving faster than in the other lanes, or against the flow of traffic.

13. Routes shared with cyclists. Some cycle tracks run alongside footpaths or pavements, using a segregating feature to separate cyclists from people on foot. Segregated routes may also incorporate short lengths of tactile paving to help visually impaired people stay on the correct side. On the pedestrian side this will comprise a series of flat-topped bars running across the direction of travel (ladder pattern). On the cyclist side the same bars are orientated in the direction of travel (tramline pattern). Not all routes which are shared with cyclists are segregated. Take extra care where this is so (see Rule 62).

14. Parked vehicles. If you have to cross between parked vehicles, use the outside edges of the vehicles as if they were the kerb. Stop there and make sure you can see all around and that the traffic can see you. Make sure there is a gap between any parked vehicles on the other side, so you can reach the pavement. Never cross the road in front of, or behind, any vehicle with its engine running, especially a large vehicle, as the driver may not be able to see you.

15. Reversing vehicles. Never cross behind a vehicle which is reversing, showing white reversing lights or sounding a warning.

16. Moving vehicles. You **MUST NOT** get onto or hold onto a moving vehicle.
Law RTA 1988 sect 26

17. At night. Wear something reflective to make it easier for others to see you (see Rule 3). If there is no pedestrian crossing nearby, cross the road near a street light so that traffic can see you more easily.

Crossings
18. At all crossings. When using any type of crossing you should
- always check that the traffic has stopped before you start to cross or push a pram onto a crossing
- always cross between the studs or over the zebra markings. Do not cross at the side of the crossing or on the zig-zag lines, as it can be dangerous.

You **MUST NOT** loiter on any type of crossing.
Laws ZPPPCRGD reg 19 & RTRA sect 25(5)

19. Zebra crossings. Give traffic plenty of time to see you and to stop before you start to cross. Vehicles will need more time when the road is slippery. Wait until traffic has stopped from both directions or the road is clear before crossing. Remember that traffic does not have to stop until someone has moved onto the crossing. Keep looking both ways, and listening, in case a driver or rider has not seen you and attempts to overtake a vehicle that has stopped.

Zebra crossings have flashing beacons

20. Where there is an island in the middle of a zebra crossing, wait on the island and follow Rule 19 before you cross the second half of the road – it is a separate crossing.

Zebra crossings with a central island are two separate crossings

21. At traffic lights. There may be special signals for pedestrians. You should only start to cross the road when the green figure shows. If you have started to cross the road and the green figure goes out, you should still have time to reach the other side, but do not delay. If no pedestrian signals have been provided, watch carefully and do not cross until the traffic lights are red and the traffic has stopped. Keep looking and check for traffic that may be turning the corner. Remember that traffic lights may let traffic move in some lanes while traffic in other lanes has stopped.

At traffic lights, puffin and pelican crossings
*At pelican crossings only

22. Pelican crossings. These are signal-controlled crossings operated by pedestrians. Push the control button to activate the traffic signals. When the red figure shows, do not cross. When a steady green figure shows, check the traffic has stopped then cross with care. When the green figure begins to flash you should not start to cross. If you have already started you should have time to finish crossing safely.

23. Puffin crossings differ from pelican crossings as the red and green figures are above the control box on your side of the road and there is no flashing green figure phase. Press the button and wait for the green figure to show.

24. When the road is congested, traffic on your side of the road may be forced to stop even though their lights are green. Traffic may still be moving on the other side of the road, so press the button and wait for the signal to cross.

25. Toucan crossings are light-controlled crossings which allow cyclists and pedestrians to share crossing space and cross at the same time. They are push-button operated. Pedestrians and cyclists will see the green signal together. Cyclists are permitted to ride across.

Toucan crossings can be used by both cyclists and pedestrians

26. At some crossings there is a bleeping sound or voice signal to indicate to blind or partially sighted people when the steady green figure is showing, and there may be a tactile signal to help deafblind people.

27. Equestrian crossings are for horse riders. They have pavement barriers, wider crossing spaces, horse and rider figures in the light panels and either two sets of controls (one higher), or just one higher control panel.

Equestrian crossings are used by horse riders
There is often a parallel crossing

28. 'Staggered' pelican or puffin crossings. When the crossings on each side of the central refuge are not in line they are two separate crossings. On reaching the central island, press the button again and wait for a steady green figure.

Staggered crossings (with an island in the middle)
are two separate crossings

29. Crossings controlled by an authorised person. Do not cross the road unless you are signalled to do so by a police officer, traffic warden or school crossing patrol. Always cross in front of them.

30. Where there are no controlled crossing points available it is advisable to cross where there is an island in the middle of the road. Use the Green Cross Code (see Rule 7) to cross to the island and then stop and use it again to cross the second half of the road.

Situations needing extra care

31. Emergency vehicles. If an ambulance, fire engine, police or other emergency vehicle approaches using flashing blue lights, headlights and/or sirens, keep off the road.

32. Buses. Get on or off a bus only when it has stopped to allow you to do so. Watch out for cyclists when you are getting off. Never cross the road directly behind or in front of a bus. Wait until it has moved off and you can see clearly in both directions.

33. Tramways. These may run through pedestrian areas. Their path will be marked out by shallow kerbs, changes in the paving or other road surface, white lines or yellow dots. Cross at designated crossings where provided. Elsewhere treat trams as you would other road vehicles and look both ways along the track before crossing. Do not walk along the track as trams may come up behind you. Trams move quietly and cannot steer to avoid you.

34. Railway level crossings. You **MUST NOT** cross or pass a stop line when the red lights show, (including a red pedestrian figure). Also do not cross if an alarm is sounding or the barriers are being lowered. The tone of the alarm may change if another train is approaching. If there are no lights, alarms or barriers, stop, look both ways and listen before crossing. A tactile surface comprising rounded bars running across the direction of pedestrian travel may be installed on the footpath approaching a level crossing to warn visually impaired people of its presence. The tactile surface should extend across the full width of the footway and should be located at an appropriate distance from the barrier or projected line of the barrier.

Law TSRGD, reg 52

35. Street and pavement repairs. A pavement may be closed temporarily because it is not safe to use. Take extra care if you are directed to walk in or to cross the road.

Rules for users of powered wheelchairs and powered mobility scooters

(Called Invalid Carriages in law)

36. There is one class of manual wheelchair (called a Class 1 invalid carriage) and two classes of powered wheelchairs and powered mobility scooters. Manual wheelchairs and Class 2 vehicles are those with an upper speed limit of 4mph (6km/h) and are designed to be used on pavements. Class 3 vehicles are those with an upper speed limit of 8mph (12km/h) and are equipped to be used on the road as well as the pavement.

37. When you are on the road you should obey the guidance and rules for other vehicles; when on the pavement you should follow the guidance and rules for pedestrians.

On pavements

38. Pavements are safer than roads and should be used when available. You should give pedestrians priority and show consideration for other pavement users, particularly those with a hearing or visual impairment who may not be aware that you are there.

39. Powered wheelchairs and scooters **MUST NOT** travel faster than 4mph (6km/h) on pavements or in pedestrian areas. You may need to reduce your speed to adjust to other pavement users who may not be able to move out of your way quickly enough or where the pavement is too narrow.
Law UICHR 1988 reg 4

40. When moving off the pavement onto the road, you should take special care. Before moving off, always look round and make sure it's safe to join the traffic. Always try to use dropped kerbs when moving off the pavement, even if this means travelling further to locate one. If you have to climb or descend a kerb, always approach it at right angles and don't try to negotiate a kerb higher than the vehicle manufacturer's recommendations.

On the road

41. You should take care when travelling on the road as you may be travelling more slowly than other traffic (your machine is restricted to 8mph (12km/h) and may be less visible).

42. When on the road, Class 3 vehicles should travel in the direction of the traffic. Class 2 users should always use the pavement when it is available. When there is no pavement, you should use caution when on the road. Class 2 users should, where possible, travel in the direction of the traffic. If you are travelling at night when lights **MUST** be used, you should travel in the direction of the traffic to avoid confusing other road users.

Law UICHR 1988 reg 9

43. You **MUST** follow the same rules about using lights, indicators and horns as for other road vehicles, if your vehicle is fitted with them. At night, lights **MUST** be used. Be aware that other road users may not see you and you should make yourself more visible – even in the daytime and also at dusk – by, for instance, wearing a reflective jacket or reflective strips on the back of the vehicle.

Law UICHR 1988 reg 9

44. Take extra care at road junctions. When going straight ahead, check to make sure there are no vehicles about to cross your path from the left, the right, or overtaking you and turning left. There are several options for dealing with right turns, especially turning from a major road. If moving into the middle of the road is difficult or dangerous, you can

- stop on the left-hand side of the road and wait for a safe gap in the traffic
- negotiate the turn as a pedestrian, i.e. travel along the pavement and cross the road between pavements where it is safe to do so. Class 3 users should switch the vehicle to the lower speed limit when on pavements.

If the junction is too hazardous, it may be worth considering an alternative route. Similarly, when negotiating major roundabouts (i.e. with two or more lanes) it may be safer for you to use the pavement or find a route which avoids the roundabout altogether.

45. All normal parking restrictions should be observed. Your vehicle should not be left unattended if it causes an obstruction to other pedestrians – especially those in wheelchairs. Parking concessions provided under the Blue Badge scheme (see Further reading) will apply to those vehicles displaying a valid badge.

46. These vehicles **MUST NOT** be used on motorways (see Rule 253). They should not be used on unrestricted dual carriageways where the speed limit exceeds 50mph (80km/h) but if they are used on these dual carriageways, they **MUST** have a flashing amber beacon. A flashing amber beacon should be used on all other dual carriageways (see Rule 220).

Laws RTRA sect 17(2) & (3), & RVLR reg 17(1) & 26

Rules about animals

Horse-Drawn Vehicles

47. Horse-drawn vehicles used on the highway should be operated and maintained in accordance with standards set out in the Department for Transport's Code of Practice for Horse-Drawn Vehicles. This Code lays down the requirements for a road driving assessment and includes a comprehensive list of safety checks to ensure that a carriage and its fittings are safe and in good working order. The standards set out in the Road Driving Assessment may be required to be met by a Local Authority if an operator wishes to obtain a local authority licence to operate a passenger-carrying service (see Further reading).

48. Safety equipment and clothing. All horse-drawn vehicles should have two red rear reflectors. It is safer not to drive at night but if you do, a light showing white to the front and red to the rear **MUST** be fitted.
Law RVLR 1989 reg 4

Horse riders

49. Safety equipment. Children under the age of 14 **MUST** wear a helmet which complies with the Regulations. It **MUST** be fastened securely. Other riders should also follow these requirements. These requirements do not apply to a child who is a follower of the Sikh religion while wearing a turban.
Laws H(PHYR) Act 1990, sect 1 & H(PHYR) Regulations 1992, reg 3

50. Other clothing. You should wear
- boots or shoes with hard soles and heels
- light-coloured or fluorescent clothing in daylight
- reflective clothing if you have to ride at night or in poor visibility.

Help yourself to be seen

51. At night. It is safer not to ride on the road at night or in poor visibility, but if you do, make sure you wear reflective clothing and your horse has reflective bands above the fetlock joints. A light which shows white to the front and red to the rear should be fitted, with a band, to the rider's right arm and/or leg/riding boot. If you are leading a horse at night, carry a light in your right hand, showing white to the front and red to the rear, and wear reflective clothing on both you and your horse. It is strongly recommended that a fluorescent/reflective tail guard is also worn by your horse.

Riding

52. Before you take a horse on to a road, you should
- ensure all tack fits well and is in good condition
- make sure you can control the horse.

Always ride with other, less nervous horses if you think that your horse will be nervous of traffic. Never ride a horse without both a saddle and bridle.

53. Before riding off or turning, look behind you to make sure it is safe, then give a clear arm signal.

When riding on the road you should
- keep to the left
- keep both hands on the reins unless you are signalling
- keep both feet in the stirrups
- not carry another person
- not carry anything which might affect your balance or get tangled up with the reins
- keep a horse you are leading to your left
- move in the direction of the traffic flow in a one-way street
- never ride more than two abreast, and ride in single file on narrow or busy roads and when riding round bends.

54. You **MUST NOT** take a horse onto a footpath or pavement, and you should not take a horse onto a cycle track. Use a bridleway where possible. Equestrian crossings may be provided for horse riders to cross the road and you should use these where available (see Rule 27). You should dismount at level crossings where a 'horse rider dismount' sign is displayed.

Laws HA 1835 sect 72, R(S)A 1984, sect 129(5)

55. Avoid roundabouts wherever possible. If you use them you should
* keep to the left and watch out for vehicles crossing your path to leave or join the roundabout
* signal right when riding across exits to show you are not leaving
* signal left just before you leave the roundabout.

Other animals

56. Dogs. Do not let a dog out on the road on its own. Keep it on a short lead when walking on the pavement, road or path shared with cyclists or horse riders.

57. When in a vehicle make sure dogs or other animals are suitably restrained so they cannot distract you while you are driving or injure you, or themselves, if you stop quickly. A seat belt harness, pet carrier, dog cage or dog guard are ways of restraining animals in cars.

58. Animals being herded. These should be kept under control at all times. You should, if possible, send another person along the road in front to warn other road users, especially at a bend or the brow of a hill. It is safer not to move animals after dark, but if you do, then wear reflective clothing and ensure that lights are carried (white at the front and red at the rear of the herd).

Rules for cyclists

These rules are in addition to those in the following sections, which apply to all vehicles (except the Motorway section). See also Annexe 1 – You and your bicycle.

59. Clothing. You should wear
- a cycle helmet which conforms to current regulations, is the correct size and securely fastened
- appropriate clothes for cycling. Avoid clothes that may get tangled in the chain, or in a wheel or may obscure your lights
- light-coloured or fluorescent clothing which helps other road users to see you in daylight and poor light
- reflective clothing and/or accessories (belt, arm or ankle bands) in the dark.

Help yourself to be seen

60. At night your cycle **MUST** have white front and red rear lights lit. It **MUST** also be fitted with a red rear reflector (and amber pedal reflectors, if manufactured after 1/10/85). White front reflectors and spoke reflectors will also help you to be seen. Flashing lights are permitted but it is recommended that cyclists who are riding in areas without street lighting use a steady front lamp.
Law RVLR regs 13, 18 & 24

61. Cycle Routes and Other Facilities. Use cycle routes, advanced stop lines, cycle boxes and toucan crossings unless at the time it is unsafe to do so. Use of these facilities is not compulsory and will depend on your experience and skills, but they can make your journey safer.

62. Cycle Tracks. These are normally located away from the road, but may occasionally be found alongside footpaths or pavements. Cyclists and pedestrians may be segregated or they may share the same space (unsegregated). When using segregated tracks you **MUST** keep to the side intended for cyclists as the pedestrian side remains a pavement or footpath. Take care when passing pedestrians, especially children, older or disabled people, and allow them plenty of room. Always be prepared to slow down and stop if necessary. Take care near road junctions as you may have difficulty seeing other road users, who might not notice you.
Law HA 1835 sect 72

63. Cycle Lanes. These are marked by a white line (which may be broken) along the carriageway (see Rule 140). Keep within the lane when practicable. When leaving a cycle lane check before pulling out that it is safe to do so and signal your intention clearly to other road users. Use of cycle lanes is not compulsory and will depend on your experience and skills, but they can make your journey safer.

64. You **MUST NOT** cycle on a pavement.
Laws HA 1835 sect 72 & R(S)A 1984, sect 129

65. Bus Lanes. Most bus lanes may be used by cyclists as indicated on signs. Watch out for people getting on or off a bus. Be very careful when overtaking a bus or leaving a bus lane as you will be entering a busier traffic flow. Do not pass between the kerb and a bus when it is at a stop.

66. You should
- keep both hands on the handlebars except when signalling or changing gear
- keep both feet on the pedals
- never ride more than two abreast, and ride in single file on narrow or busy roads and when riding round bends
- not ride close behind another vehicle
- not carry anything which will affect your balance or may get tangled up with your wheels or chain
- be considerate of other road users, particularly blind and partially sighted pedestrians. Let them know you are there when necessary, for example, by ringing your bell if you have one. It is recommended that a bell be fitted.

67. You should
- look all around before moving away from the kerb, turning or manoeuvring, to make sure it is safe to do so. Give a clear signal to show other road users what you intend to do (see Signals to other road users)
- look well ahead for obstructions in the road, such as drains, pot-holes and parked vehicles so that you do not have to swerve suddenly to avoid them. Leave plenty of room when passing parked vehicles and watch out for doors being opened or pedestrians stepping into your path
- be aware of traffic coming up behind you
- take extra care near road humps, narrowings and other traffic calming features
- take care when overtaking (see Rules 162–169).

68. You **MUST NOT**
- carry a passenger unless your cycle has been built or adapted to carry one
- hold onto a moving vehicle or trailer
- ride in a dangerous, careless or inconsiderate manner
- ride when under the influence of drink or drugs, including medicine.

Law RTA 1988 sects 24, 26, 28, 29 & 30 as amended by RTA 1991

69. You **MUST** obey all traffic signs and traffic light signals.

Laws RTA 1988 sect 36 & TSRGD reg 10(1)

70. When parking your cycle
- find a conspicuous location where it can be seen by passers-by
- use cycle stands or other cycle parking facilities wherever possible
- do not leave it where it would cause an obstruction or hazard to other road users
- secure it well so that it will not fall over and become an obstruction or hazard.

71. You **MUST NOT** cross the stop line when the traffic lights are red. Some junctions have an advanced stop line to enable you to wait and position yourself ahead of other traffic (see Rule 178).

Laws RTA 1988 sect 36 & TSRGD regs 10 & 36(1)

Road junctions

72. On the left. When approaching a junction on the left, watch out for vehicles turning in front of you, out of or into the side road. Just before you turn, check for undertaking cyclists or motorcyclists. Do not ride on the inside of vehicles signalling or slowing down to turn left.

73. Pay particular attention to long vehicles which need a lot of room to manoeuvre at corners. Be aware that drivers may not see you. They may have to move over to the right before turning left. Wait until they have completed the manoeuvre because the rear wheels come very close to the kerb while turning. Do not be tempted to ride in the space between them and the kerb.

74. On the right. If you are turning right, check the traffic to ensure it is safe, then signal and move to the centre of the road. Wait until there is a safe gap in the oncoming traffic and give a final look before completing the turn. It may be safer to wait on the left until there is a safe gap or to dismount and push your cycle across the road.

75. Dual carriageways. Remember that traffic on most dual carriageways moves quickly. When crossing wait for a safe gap and cross each carriageway in turn. Take extra care when crossing slip roads.

Roundabouts

76. Full details about the correct procedure at roundabouts are contained in Rules 184–190. Roundabouts can be hazardous and should be approached with care.

77. You may feel safer walking your cycle round on the pavement or verge. If you decide to ride round keeping to the left-hand lane you should
- be aware that drivers may not easily see you
- take extra care when cycling across exits. You may need to signal right to show you are not leaving the roundabout
- watch out for vehicles crossing your path to leave or join the roundabout.

78. Give plenty of room to long vehicles on the roundabout as they need more space to manoeuvre. Do not ride in the space they need to get round the roundabout. It may be safer to wait until they have cleared the roundabout.

Crossing the road

79. Do not ride across equestrian crossings, as they are for horse riders only. Do not ride across a pelican, puffin or zebra crossing. Dismount and wheel your cycle across.

80. Toucan crossings. These are light-controlled crossings which allow cyclists and pedestrians to share crossing space and cross at the same time. They are push-button operated. Pedestrians and cyclists will see the green signal together. Cyclists are permitted to ride across.

81. Cycle-only crossings. Cycle tracks on opposite sides of the road may be linked by signalled crossings. You may ride across but you **MUST NOT** cross until the green cycle symbol is showing.
Law TSRGD regs 33(2) & 36(1)

82. Level crossings/Tramways. Take extra care when crossing the tracks (see Rule 306). You should dismount at level crossings where a 'cyclist dismount' sign is displayed.

Rules for motorcyclists

These Rules are in addition to those in the following sections which apply to all vehicles. For motorcycle licence requirements see Annexe 2.

General

83. On all journeys, the rider and pillion passenger on a motorcycle, scooter or moped **MUST** wear a protective helmet. This does not apply to a follower of the Sikh religion while wearing a turban. Helmets **MUST** comply with the Regulations and they **MUST** be fastened securely. Riders and passengers of motor tricycles and quadricycles, also called quadbikes, should also wear a protective helmet. Before each journey check that your helmet visor is clean and in good condition.

Laws RTA 1988 sects 16 & 17 & MC(PH)R as amended reg 4

84. It is also advisable to wear eye protectors, which **MUST** comply with the Regulations. Scratched or poorly fitting eye protectors can limit your view when riding, particularly in bright sunshine and the hours of darkness. Consider wearing ear protection. Strong boots, gloves and suitable clothing may help to protect you if you are involved in a collision.

Laws RTA sect 18 & MC(EP)R as amended reg 4

85. You **MUST NOT** carry more than one pillion passenger who **MUST** sit astride the machine on a proper seat. They should face forward with both feet on the footrests. You **MUST NOT** carry a pillion passenger unless your motorcycle is designed to do so. Provisional licence holders **MUST NOT** carry a pillion passenger.

Laws RTA 1988 sect 23, MV(DL)R 1999 reg 16(6) & CUR 1986 reg 102

86. Daylight riding. Make yourself as visible as possible from the side as well as the front and rear. You could wear a light or brightly coloured helmet and fluorescent clothing or strips. Dipped headlights, even in good daylight, may also make you more conspicuous. However, be aware that other vehicle drivers may still not have seen you, or judged your distance or speed correctly, especially at junctions.

Help yourself to be seen

87. Riding in the dark. Wear reflective clothing or strips to improve your visibility in the dark. These reflect light from the headlamps of other vehicles, making you visible from a longer distance. See Rules 113–116 for lighting requirements.

88. Manoeuvring. You should be aware of what is behind and to the sides before manoeuvring. Look behind you; use mirrors if they are fitted. When in traffic queues look out for pedestrians crossing between vehicles and vehicles emerging from junctions or changing lanes. Position yourself so that drivers in front can see you in their mirrors. Additionally, when filtering in slow-moving traffic, take care and keep your speed low.
Remember: Observation – Signal – Manoeuvre.

Rules for drivers and motorcyclists

89. Vehicle condition. You **MUST** ensure your vehicle and trailer comply with the full requirements of the Road Vehicles (Construction and Use) Regulations and Road Vehicles Lighting Regulations (see Annexe 4 – The road user and the law).

Fitness to drive

90. Make sure that you are fit to drive. You **MUST** report to the Driver and Vehicle Licensing Agency (DVLA) any health condition likely to affect your driving.
Law RTA 1988 sect 94

91. Driving when you are tired greatly increases your risk of collision. To minimise this risk
- make sure you are fit to drive. Do not begin a journey if you are tired. Get a good night's sleep before embarking on a long journey
- avoid undertaking long journeys between midnight and 6am, when natural alertness is at a minimum
- plan your journey to take sufficient breaks. A minimum break of at least 15 minutes after every two hours of driving is recommended
- if you feel at all sleepy, stop in a safe place. Do not stop on the hard shoulder of a motorway
- the most effective ways to counter sleepiness are to drink, for example, two cups of caffeinated coffee and to take a short nap (at least 15 minutes).

92. Vision. You **MUST** be able to read a vehicle number plate, in good daylight, from a distance of 20 metres (or 20.5 metres where the old style number plate is used). If you need to wear glasses (or contact lenses) to do this, you **MUST** wear them at all times while driving. The police have the power to require a driver to undertake an eyesight test.
Laws RTA 1988 sect 96 & MV(DL)R reg 40 & sch 8

93. Slow down, and if necessary stop, if you are dazzled by bright sunlight.

94. At night or in poor visibility, do not use tinted glasses, lenses or visors if they restrict your vision.

Alcohol and drugs

95. Do not drink and drive as it will seriously affect your judgement and abilities. You **MUST NOT** drive with a breath alcohol level higher than 35 microgrammes/100 millilitres of breath or a blood alcohol level of more than 80 milligrammes/100 millilitres of blood. Alcohol will

- give a false sense of confidence
- reduce co-ordination and slow down reactions
- affect judgement of speed, distance and risk
- reduce your driving ability, even if you're below the legal limit
- take time to leave your body; you may be unfit to drive in the evening after drinking at lunchtime, or in the morning after drinking the previous evening.

The best solution is not to drink at all when planning to drive because any amount of alcohol affects your ability to drive safely. If you are going to drink, arrange another means of transport.

Law RTA 1988 sects 4, 5 & 11(2)

96. You **MUST NOT** drive under the influence of drugs or medicine. Check the instructions or ask your doctor or pharmacist. Using illegal drugs is highly dangerous. Never take them if you intend to drive; the effects are unpredictable, but can be even more severe than alcohol and may result in fatal or serious road crashes.

Law RTA 1988 sect 4

97. Before setting off. You should ensure that

- you have planned your route and allowed sufficient time
- clothing and footwear do not prevent you using the controls in the correct manner
- you know where all the controls are and how to use them before you need them. Not all vehicles are the same; do not wait until it is too late to find out
- your mirrors and seat are adjusted correctly to ensure comfort, full control and maximum vision
- head restraints are properly adjusted to reduce the risk of neck and spine injuries in the event of a collision
- you have sufficient fuel before commencing your journey, especially if it includes motorway driving. It can be dangerous to lose power when driving in traffic
- ensure your vehicle is legal and roadworthy
- switch off your mobile phone.

Make sure head restraints are properly adjusted

98. Vehicle towing and loading. As a driver

- you **MUST NOT** tow more than your licence permits. If you passed a car test after 1 January 1997 you are restricted on the weight of trailer you can tow
- you **MUST NOT** overload your vehicle or trailer. You should not tow a weight greater than that recommended by the manufacturer of your vehicle
- you **MUST** secure your load and it **MUST NOT** stick out dangerously. Make sure any heavy or sharp objects and any animals are secured safely. If there is a collision, they might hit someone inside the vehicle and cause serious injury
- you should properly distribute the weight in your caravan or trailer with heavy items mainly over the axle(s) and ensure a downward load on the tow ball. Manufacturer's recommended weight and tow ball load should not be exceeded. This should avoid the possibility of swerving or snaking and going out of control. If this does happen, ease off the accelerator and reduce speed gently to regain control
- carrying a load or pulling a trailer may require you to adjust the headlights.

In the event of a breakdown, be aware that towing a vehicle on a tow rope is potentially dangerous. You should consider professional recovery.

Laws CUR reg 100 & MV(DL)R reg 43

Seat belts and child restraints

99. You **MUST** wear a seat belt in cars, vans and other goods vehicles if one is fitted (see table below). Adults, and children aged 14 years and over, **MUST** use a seat belt or child restraint, where fitted, when seated in minibuses, buses and coaches. Exemptions are allowed for the holders of medical exemption certificates and those making deliveries or collections in goods vehicles when travelling less than 50 metres (approx 162 feet).

Laws RTA 1988 sects 14 & 15, MV(WSB)R, MV(WSBCFS)R & MV(WSB)(A)R

Seat Belt Requirements.

This table summarises the main legal requirements for wearing seat belts in cars, vans and other goods vehicles

	Front seat	Rear seat	Who is responsible?
Driver	Seat belt **MUST** be worn if fitted		**Driver**
Child under 3 years of age	Correct child restraint **MUST** be used	Correct child restraint **MUST** be used. If one is not available in a taxi, may travel unrestrained.	**Driver**
Child from 3rd birthday up to 1.35 metres (approx 4ft 5ins) in height (or 12th birthday, whichever they reach first)	Correct child restraint **MUST** be used	Correct child restraint **MUST** be used where seat belts fitted. **MUST** use adult belt if correct child restraint is not available in a licensed taxi or private hire vehicle, or for reasons of unexpected necessity over a short distance, or if two occupied restraints prevent fitment of a third.	**Driver**
Child over 1.35 metres (approx 4ft 5ins) in height or 12 or 13 years	Adult seat belt **MUST** be worn if available	Adult seat belt **MUST** be worn if available	**Driver**
Adult passengers aged 14 and over	Seat belt **MUST** be worn if available	Seat belt **MUST** be worn if available	**Passenger**

100. The driver **MUST** ensure that all children under 14 years of age in cars, vans and other goods vehicles wear seat belts or sit in an approved child restraint where required (see table opposite). If a child is under 1.35 metres (approx 4 feet 5 ins) tall, a baby seat, child seat, booster seat or booster cushion **MUST** be used suitable for the child's weight and fitted to the manufacturer's instructions.

Laws RTA 1988 sects 14 & 15, MV(WSB)R, MV(WSBCFS)R & MV(WSB)(A)R

Make sure that a child uses a suitable restraint which is correctly adjusted

101. A rear-facing baby seat **MUST NOT** be fitted into a seat protected by an active frontal airbag, as in a crash it can cause serious injury or death to the child.

Laws RTA 1988 sects 14 & 15, MV(WSB)R, MV(WSBCFS)R & MV(WSB)(A)R

102. Children in cars, vans and other goods vehicles. Drivers who are carrying children in cars, vans and other goods vehicles should also ensure that

- children should get into the vehicle through the door nearest the kerb
- child restraints are properly fitted to manufacturer's instructions
- children do not sit behind the rear seats in an estate car or hatchback, unless a special child seat has been fitted
- the child safety door locks, where fitted, are used when children are in the vehicle
- children are kept under control.

General rules, techniques and advice for all drivers and riders

This section should be read by all drivers, motorcyclists, cyclists and horse riders. The rules in *The Highway Code* do not give you the right of way in any circumstance, but they advise you when you should give way to others. Always give way if it can help to avoid an incident.

Signals

103. Signals warn and inform other road users, including pedestrians (see Signals to other road users), of your intended actions. You should always

- give clear signals in plenty of time, having checked it is not misleading to signal at that time
- use them to advise other road users before changing course or direction, stopping or moving off
- cancel them after use
- make sure your signals will not confuse others. If, for instance, you want to stop after a side road, do not signal until you are passing the road. If you signal earlier it may give the impression that you intend to turn into the road. Your brake lights will warn traffic behind you that you are slowing down
- use an arm signal to emphasise or reinforce your signal if necessary. Remember that signalling does not give you priority.

104. You should also

- watch out for signals given by other road users and proceed only when you are satisfied that it is safe
- be aware that an indicator on another vehicle may not have been cancelled.

105. You **MUST** obey signals given by police officers, traffic officers, traffic wardens (see Signals by authorised persons) and signs used by school crossing patrols.
Laws RTRA sect 28, RTA 1988 sect 35, TMA 2004 sect 6, & FTWO art 3

106. Police stopping procedures. If the police want to stop your vehicle they will, where possible, attract your attention by

- flashing blue lights, headlights or sounding their siren or horn, usually from behind
- directing you to pull over to the side by pointing and/or using the left indicator.

You **MUST** then pull over and stop as soon as it is safe to do so. Then switch off your engine.
Law RTA 1988 sect 163

Other stopping procedures

107. Vehicle & Operator Services Agency Officers have powers to stop vehicles on all roads, including motorways and trunk roads, in England and Wales. They will attract your attention by flashing amber lights

- either from the front requesting you to follow them to a safe place to stop
- or from behind directing you to pull over to the side by pointing and/or using the left indicator.

It is an offence not to comply with their directions. You **MUST** obey any signals given (see Signals by authorised persons).
Laws RTA 1988, sect 67, & PRA 2002, sect 41 & sched 5(8)

108. Highways Agency Traffic Officers have powers to stop vehicles on most motorways and some 'A' class roads, in England only. If HA traffic officers in uniform want to stop your vehicle on safety grounds (e.g. an insecure load) they will, where possible, attract your attention by

- flashing amber lights, usually from behind
- directing you to pull over to the side by pointing and/or using the left indicator.

You **MUST** then pull over and stop as soon as it is safe to do so. Then switch off your engine. It is an offence not to comply with their directions (see Signals by authorised persons).
Law RTA1988, sects 35 & 163 as amended by TMA 2004, sect 6

Traffic light signals and traffic signs
109. You **MUST** obey all traffic light signals (see Light signals controlling traffic) and traffic signs giving orders, including temporary signals & signs (see Signs giving orders, Warning signs and Direction signs). Make sure you know, understand and act on all other traffic and information signs and road markings (see Signs giving orders, Warning signs, Direction signs, Information signs, Road markings and Vehicle markings).
Laws RTA 1988 sect 36 & TSRGD regs 10, 15, 16, 25, 26, 27, 28, 29, 36, 38 & 40

110. Flashing headlights. Only flash your headlights to let other road users know that you are there. Do not flash your headlights to convey any other message or intimidate other road users.

111. Never assume that flashing headlights is a signal inviting you to proceed. Use your own judgement and proceed carefully.

112. The horn. Use only while your vehicle is moving and you need to warn other road users of your presence. Never sound your horn aggressively. You **MUST NOT** use your horn
- while stationary on the road
- when driving in a built-up area between the hours of 11.30pm and 7am

except when another road user poses a danger.

Law CUR reg 99

Lighting requirements

113. You **MUST**
- ensure all sidelights and rear registration plate lights are lit between sunset and sunrise
- use headlights at night, except on a road which has lit street lighting. These roads are generally restricted to a speed limit of 30mph (48km/h) unless otherwise specified
- use headlights when visibility is seriously reduced (see Rule 226).

Night (the hours of darkness) is defined as the period between half an hour after sunset and half an hour before sunrise).

Laws RVLR regs 3, 24, & 25, (In Scotland – RTRA 1984 sect 82 (as amended by NRSWA, para 59 of sched 8))

114. You **MUST NOT**
- use any lights in a way that would dazzle or cause discomfort to other road users, including pedestrians, cyclists and horse riders
- use front or rear fog lights unless visibility is seriously reduced. You **MUST** switch them off when visibility improves to avoid dazzling other road users (see Rule 226).

In stationary queues of traffic, drivers should apply the parking brake and, once the following traffic has stopped, take their foot off the footbrake to deactivate the vehicle brake lights. This will minimise glare to road users behind until the traffic moves again.

Law RVLR reg 27

115. You should also
- use dipped headlights, or dim-dip if fitted, at night in built-up areas and in dull daytime weather, to ensure that you can be seen
- keep your headlights dipped when overtaking until you are level with the other vehicle and then change to main beam if necessary, unless this would dazzle oncoming road users
- slow down, and if necessary stop, if you are dazzled by oncoming headlights.

116. Hazard warning lights. These may be used when your vehicle is stationary, to warn that it is temporarily obstructing traffic. Never use them as an excuse for dangerous or illegal parking. You **MUST NOT** use hazard warning lights while driving or being towed unless you are on a motorway or unrestricted dual carriageway and you need to warn drivers behind you of a hazard or obstruction ahead. Only use them for long enough to ensure that your warning has been observed.
Law RVLR reg 27

Control of the vehicle

Braking
117. In normal circumstances. The safest way to brake is to do so early and lightly. Brake more firmly as you begin to stop. Ease the pressure off just before the vehicle comes to rest to avoid a jerky stop.

118. In an emergency. Brake immediately. Try to avoid braking so harshly that you lock your wheels. Locked wheels can lead to loss of control.

119. Skids. Skidding is usually caused by the driver braking, accelerating or steering too harshly or driving too fast for the road conditions. If skidding occurs, remove the cause by releasing the brake pedal fully or easing off the accelerator. Turn the steering wheel in the direction of the skid. For example, if the rear of the vehicle skids to the right, steer immediately to the right to recover.

Rear of the car skids to the right. Driver steers to the right.

120. ABS. If your vehicle is fitted with anti-lock brakes, you should follow the advice given in the vehicle handbook. However, in the case of an emergency, apply the footbrake firmly; do not release the pressure until the vehicle has slowed to the desired speed. The ABS should ensure that steering control will be retained, but do not assume that a vehicle with ABS will stop in a shorter distance.

121. Brakes affected by water. If you have driven through deep water your brakes may be less effective. Test them at the first safe opportunity by pushing gently on the brake pedal to make sure that they work. If they are not fully effective, gently apply light pressure while driving slowly. This will help to dry them out.

122. Coasting. This term describes a vehicle travelling in neutral or with the clutch pressed down. It can reduce driver control because
- engine braking is eliminated
- vehicle speed downhill will increase quickly
- increased use of the footbrake can reduce its effectiveness
- steering response will be affected, particularly on bends and corners
- it may be more difficult to select the appropriate gear when needed.

The Driver and the Environment
123. You **MUST NOT** leave a parked vehicle unattended with the engine running or leave a vehicle engine running unnecessarily while that vehicle is stationary on a public road. Generally, if the vehicle is stationary and is likely to remain so for more than a couple of minutes, you should apply the parking brake and switch off the engine to reduce emissions and noise pollution. However it is permissible to leave the engine running if the vehicle is stationary in traffic or for diagnosing faults.
Law CUR regs 98 & 107

Speed limits

124. You **MUST NOT** exceed the maximum speed limits for the road and for your vehicle (see the table opposite). The presence of street lights generally means that there is a 30mph (48km/h) speed limit unless otherwise specified.
Law RTRA sects 81, 86, 89 & sch 6

125. The speed limit is the absolute maximum and does not mean it is safe to drive at that speed irrespective of conditions. Driving at speeds too fast for the road and traffic conditions is dangerous. You should always reduce your speed when
- the road layout or condition presents hazards, such as bends
- sharing the road with pedestrians, cyclists and horse riders, particularly children, and motorcyclists
- weather conditions make it safer to do so
- driving at night as it is more difficult to see other road users.

Speed Limits

Types of vehicle	Built up areas* MPH (km/h)	Single carriageways MPH (km/h)	Dual carriageways MPH (km/h)	Motorways MPH (km/h)
Cars & motorcycles (including car derived vans up to 2 tonnes maximum laden weight)	30 (48)	60 (96)	70 (112)	70 (112)
Cars towing caravans or trailers (including car derived vans and motorcycles)	30 (48)	50 (80)	60 (96)	60 (96)
Buses, coaches and minibuses (not exceeding 12 metres (39 feet) in overall length)	30 (48)	50 (80)	60 (96)	70 (112)
Goods vehicles (not exceeding 7.5 tonnes maximum laden weight)	30 (48)	50 (80)	60 (96)	70† (112)
Goods vehicles (exceeding 7.5 tonnes maximum laden weight)	30 (48)	40 (64)	50 (80)	60 (96)

* The 30mph (48km/h) limit usually applies to all traffic on all roads with street lighting unless signs show otherwise.

† 60mph (96km/h) if articulated or towing a trailer.

126. Stopping Distances. Drive at a speed that will allow you to stop well within the distance you can see to be clear. You should

- leave enough space between you and the vehicle in front so that you can pull up safely if it suddenly slows down or stops. The safe rule is never to get closer than the overall stopping distance (see Typical Stopping Distances diagram, opposite)
- allow at least a two-second gap between you and the vehicle in front on roads carrying faster-moving traffic and in tunnels where visibility is reduced. The gap should be at least doubled on wet roads and increased still further on icy roads
- remember, large vehicles and motorcycles need a greater distance to stop. If driving a large vehicle in a tunnel, you should allow a four-second gap between you and the vehicle in front.

If you have to stop in a tunnel, leave at least a 5-metre (16 feet) gap between you and the vehicle in front.

Use a fixed point to help measure a two-second gap

Typical Stopping distances

The distances below are a general guide. The distance will depend on your attention (thinking distance), the road surface, the weather and the condition of your vehicle at the time.

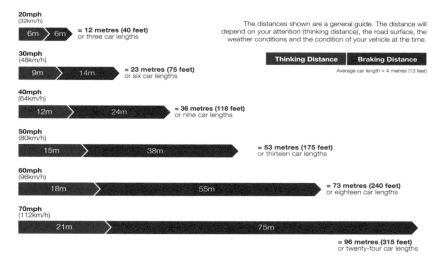

20mph (32km/h)
6m 6m = 12 metres (40 feet) or three car lengths

The distances shown are a general guide. The distance will depend on your attention (thinking distance), the road surface, the weather conditions and the condition of your vehicle at the time.

Thinking Distance	Braking Distance
Average car length = 4 metres (13 feet)	

30mph (48km/h)
9m 14m = 23 metres (75 feet) or six car lengths

40mph (64km/h)
12m 24m = 36 metres (118 feet) or nine car lengths

50mph (80km/h)
15m 38m = 53 metres (175 feet) or thirteen car lengths

60mph (96km/h)
18m 55m = 73 metres (240 feet) or eighteen car lengths

70mph (112km/h)
21m 75m = 96 metres (315 feet) or twenty-four car lengths

Lines and lane markings on the road

Diagrams of all lines are shown in Road markings.

127. A broken white line. This marks the centre of the road. When this line lengthens and the gaps shorten, it means that there is a hazard ahead. Do not cross it unless you can see the road is clear and wish to overtake or turn off.

128. Double white lines where the line nearest to you is broken. This means you may cross the lines to overtake if it is safe, provided you can complete the manoeuvre before reaching a solid white line on your side. White direction arrows on the road indicate that you need to get back onto your side of the road.

129. Double white lines where the line nearest you is solid. This means you **MUST NOT** cross or straddle it unless it is safe and you need to enter adjoining premises or a side road. You may cross the line if necessary, provided the road is clear, to pass a stationary vehicle, or overtake a pedal cycle, horse or road maintenance vehicle, if they are travelling at 10mph (16km/h) or less.

Laws RTA 1988 sect 36 & TSRGD regs 10 & 26

130. Areas of white diagonal stripes or chevrons painted on the road. These are to separate traffic lanes or to protect traffic turning right.

- If the area is bordered by a broken white line, you should not enter the area unless it is necessary and you can see that it is safe to do so.
- If the area is marked with chevrons and bordered by solid white lines you **MUST NOT** enter it except in an emergency.

Laws MT(E&W)R regs 5, 9, 10 & 16, MT(S)R regs 4, 8, 9 & 14, RTA sect 36 & TSRGD 10(1)

131. Lane dividers. These are short, broken white lines which are used on wide carriageways to divide them into lanes. You should keep between them.

132. Reflective road studs may be used with white lines.
- White studs mark the lanes or the middle of the road.
- Red studs mark the left edge of the road.
- Amber studs mark the central reservation of a dual carriageway or motorway.
- Green studs mark the edge of the main carriageway at lay-bys and slip roads.
- Green/yellow studs indicate temporary adjustments to lane layouts, e.g. where road works are taking place.

Reflective road studs mark the lanes and edges of the carriageway

Multi-lane carriageways

Lane discipline

133. If you need to change lane, first use your mirrors and if necessary take a quick sideways glance to make sure you will not force another road user to change course or speed. When it is safe to do so, signal to indicate your intentions to other road users and when clear, move over.

134. You should follow the signs and road markings and get into the lane as directed. In congested road conditions do not change lanes unnecessarily. Merging in turn is recommended but only if safe and appropriate when vehicles are travelling at a very low speed, e.g. when approaching roadworks or a road traffic incident. It is not recommended at high speed.

Single carriageway

135. Where a single carriageway has three lanes and the road markings or signs do not give priority to traffic in either direction
* use the middle lane only for overtaking or turning right. Remember, you have no more right to use the middle lane than a driver coming from the opposite direction
* do not use the right-hand lane.

136. Where a single carriageway has four or more lanes, use only the lanes that signs or markings indicate.

Dual carriageways

A dual carriageway is a road which has a central reservation to separate the carriageways.

137. On a two-lane dual carriageway you should stay in the left-hand lane. Use the right-hand lane for overtaking or turning right. After overtaking, move back to the left-hand lane when it is safe to do so.

138. On a three-lane dual carriageway, you may use the middle lane or the right-hand lane to overtake but return to the middle and then the left-hand lane when it is safe.

139. Climbing and crawler lanes. These are provided on some hills. Use this lane if you are driving a slow-moving vehicle or if there are vehicles behind you wishing to overtake. Be aware of the signs and road markings which indicate the lane is about to end.

140. Cycle lanes. These are shown by road markings and signs. You **MUST NOT** drive or park in a cycle lane marked by a solid white line during its times of operation. Do not drive or park in a cycle lane marked by a broken white line unless it is unavoidable. You **MUST NOT** park in any cycle lane whilst waiting restrictions apply.
Law RTRA sects 5 & 8

141. Bus lanes. These are shown by road markings and signs that indicate which (if any) other vehicles are permitted to use the bus lane. Unless otherwise indicated, you should not drive in a bus lane during its period of operation. You may enter a bus lane to stop, to load or unload where this is not prohibited.

142. High-occupancy vehicle lanes and other designated vehicle lanes. Lanes may be restricted for use by particular types of vehicle; these restrictions may apply some or all of the time. The operating times and vehicle types will be indicated on the accompanying traffic signs. You **MUST NOT** drive in such lanes during their times of operation unless signs indicate that your vehicle is permitted (see Information signs).

Vehicles permitted to use designated lanes may or may not include cycles, buses, taxis, licensed private hire vehicles, motorcycles, heavy goods vehicles (HGVs) and high-occupancy vehicles (HOVs). Where HOV lanes are in operation, they **MUST** ONLY be used by
• vehicles containing at least the minimum number of people indicated on the traffic signs
• any other vehicles, such as buses and motorcycles, as indicated on signs prior to the start of the lane, irrespective of the number of occupants.
Laws RTRA sects 5 & 8, & RTA 1988, sect 36

143. One-way streets. Traffic **MUST** travel in the direction indicated by signs. Buses and/or cycles may have a contraflow lane. Choose the correct lane for your exit as soon as you can. Do not change lanes suddenly. Unless road signs or markings indicate otherwise, you should use
• the left-hand lane when going left
• the right-hand lane when going right
• the most appropriate lane when going straight ahead. Remember – traffic could be passing on both sides.
Laws RTA 1988 sect 36 & RTRA sects 5 & 8

General advice

144. You **MUST NOT**
- drive dangerously
- drive without due care and attention
- drive without reasonable consideration for other road users.

Law RTA 1988 sects 2 & 3 as amended by RTA 1991

145. You **MUST NOT** drive on or over a pavement, footpath or bridleway except to gain lawful access to property, or in the case of an emergency.

Laws HA 1835 sect 72 & RTA 1988 sect 34

146. Adapt your driving to the appropriate type and condition of road you are on. In particular
- do not treat speed limits as a target. It is often not appropriate or safe to drive at the maximum speed limit
- take the road and traffic conditions into account. Be prepared for unexpected or difficult situations, for example, the road being blocked beyond a blind bend. Be prepared to adjust your speed as a precaution
- where there are junctions, be prepared for road users emerging
- in side roads and country lanes look out for unmarked junctions where nobody has priority
- be prepared to stop at traffic control systems, roadworks, pedestrian crossings or traffic lights as necessary
- try to anticipate what pedestrians and cyclists might do. If pedestrians, particularly children, are looking the other way, they may step out into the road without seeing you.

147. Be considerate. Be careful of and considerate towards all types of road users, especially those requiring extra care (see Rule 204). You should
- try to be understanding if other road users cause problems; they may be inexperienced or not know the area well
- be patient; remember that anyone can make a mistake
- not allow yourself to become agitated or involved if someone is behaving badly on the road. This will only make the situation worse. Pull over, calm down and, when you feel relaxed, continue your journey
- slow down and hold back if a road user pulls out into your path at a junction. Allow them to get clear. Do not over-react by driving too close behind to intimidate them
- do not throw anything out of a vehicle, for example, cigarette ends, cans, paper or carrier bags. This can endanger other road users, particularly motorcyclists and cyclists.

148. Safe driving and riding needs concentration. Avoid distractions when driving or riding such as

- loud music (this may mask other sounds)
- trying to read maps
- inserting a cassette or CD or tuning a radio
- arguing with your passengers or other road users
- eating and drinking
- smoking.

You **MUST NOT** smoke in public transport vehicles or in vehicles used for work purposes in certain prescribed circumstances. Separate regulations apply to England, Wales and Scotland.

Laws TSf(EV) regs 2007, TSfP(W) regs 2007 & TPSCP(S) regs 2006

Mobile phones and in-vehicle technology

149. You **MUST** exercise proper control of your vehicle at all times. You **MUST NOT** use a hand-held mobile phone, or similar device, when driving or when supervising a learner driver, except to call 999 or 112 in a genuine emergency when it is unsafe or impractical to stop. Never use a hand-held microphone when driving. Using hands-free equipment is also likely to distract your attention from the road. It is far safer not to use any telephone while you are driving or riding – find a safe place to stop first or use the voicemail facility and listen to messages later.

Laws RTA 1988 sects 2 & 3 & CUR regs 104 & 110

150. There is a danger of driver distraction being caused by in-vehicle systems such as satellite navigation systems, congestion warning systems, PCs, multi-media, etc. You **MUST** exercise proper control of your vehicle at all times. Do not rely on driver assistance systems such as cruise control or lane departure warnings. They are available to assist but you should not reduce your concentration levels. Do not be distracted by maps or screen-based information (such as navigation or vehicle management systems) while driving or riding. If necessary find a safe place to stop.

Laws RTA 1988 sects 2 & 3 & CUR reg 104

151. In slow-moving traffic. You should

- reduce the distance between you and the vehicle ahead to maintain traffic flow
- never get so close to the vehicle in front that you cannot stop safely
- leave enough space to be able to manoeuvre if the vehicle in front breaks down or an emergency vehicle needs to get past
- not change lanes to the left to overtake
- allow access into and from side roads, as blocking these will add to congestion
- be aware of cyclists and motorcyclists who may be passing on either side.

Do not block access to a side road

Driving in built-up areas

152. Residential streets. You should drive slowly and carefully on streets where there are likely to be pedestrians, cyclists and parked cars. In some areas a 20mph (32km/h) maximum speed limit may be in force. Look out for

- vehicles emerging from junctions or driveways
- vehicles moving off
- car doors opening
- pedestrians
- children running out from between parked cars
- cyclists and motorcyclists.

153. Traffic-calming measures. On some roads there are features such as road humps, chicanes and narrowings which are intended to slow you down. When you approach these features reduce your speed. Allow cyclists and motorcyclists room to pass through them. Maintain a reduced speed along the whole of the stretch of road within the calming measures. Give way to oncoming road users if directed to do so by signs. You should not overtake other moving road users while in these areas.

Chicanes may be used to slow traffic down

Country roads

154. Take extra care on country roads and reduce your speed at approaches to bends, which can be sharper than they appear, and at junctions and turnings, which may be partially hidden. Be prepared for pedestrians, horse riders, cyclists, slow-moving farm vehicles or mud on the road surface. Make sure you can stop within the distance you can see to be clear. You should also reduce your speed where country roads enter villages.

155. Single-track roads. These are only wide enough for one vehicle. They may have special passing places. If you see a vehicle coming towards you, or the driver behind wants to overtake, pull into a passing place on your left, or wait opposite a passing place on your right. Give way to vehicles coming uphill whenever you can. If necessary, reverse until you reach a passing place to let the other vehicle pass. Slow down when passing pedestrians, cyclists and horse riders.

156. Do not park in passing places.

Vehicles prohibited from using roads and pavements

157. Certain motorised vehicles do not meet the construction and technical requirements for road vehicles and are generally not intended, not suitable and not legal for road, pavement, footpath, cycle path or bridleway use. These include most types of miniature motorcycles, also called mini motos, and motorised scooters, also called go peds, which are powered by electric or internal combustion engines. These types of vehicle **MUST NOT** be used on roads, pavements, footpaths or bridleways.

Laws RTA 1988 sects 34, 41a, 42, 47, 63 & 66, HA 1835, sect 72, & R(S)A sect 129

158. Certain models of motorcycles, motor tricycles and quadricycles, also called quad bikes, are suitable only for off-road use and do not meet legal standards for use on roads. Vehicles that do not meet these standards **MUST NOT** be used on roads. They **MUST NOT** be used on pavements, footpaths, cycle paths or bridleways either. You **MUST** make sure that any motorcycle, motor tricycle, quadricycle or any other motor vehicle meets legal standards and is properly registered, taxed and insured before using it on the roads. Even when registered, taxed and insured for the road, vehicles **MUST NOT** be used on pavements.

Laws RTA 1988 sects 34, 41a, 42, 47, 63, 66 & 156, HA 1835, sect 72, R(S)A sect 129, & VERA Sects 1, 29, 31A, & 43A

Using the Road

General rules

159. Before moving off you should
- use all mirrors to check the road is clear
- look round to check the blind spots (the areas you are unable to see in the mirrors)
- signal if necessary before moving out
- look round for a final check.

Move off only when it is safe to do so.

Check the blind spot before moving off

160. Once moving you should
- keep to the left, unless road signs or markings indicate otherwise. The exceptions are when you want to overtake, turn right or pass parked vehicles or pedestrians in the road
- keep well to the left on right-hand bends. This will improve your view of the road and help avoid the risk of colliding with traffic approaching from the opposite direction
- drive with both hands on the wheel where possible. This will help you to remain in full control of the vehicle at all times
- be aware of other road users, especially cycles and motorcycles who may be filtering through the traffic. These are more difficult to see than larger vehicles and their riders are particularly vulnerable. Give them plenty of room, especially if you are driving a long vehicle or towing a trailer
- select a lower gear before you reach a long downhill slope. This will help to control your speed
- when towing, remember the extra length will affect overtaking and manoeuvring. The extra weight will also affect the braking and acceleration.

161. Mirrors. All mirrors should be used effectively throughout your journey. You should
- use your mirrors frequently so that you always know what is behind and to each side of you
- use them in good time before you signal or change direction or speed
- be aware that mirrors do not cover all areas and there will be blind spots. You will need to look round and check.

Remember: Mirrors – Signal – Manoeuvre

Overtaking

162. Before overtaking you should make sure
- the road is sufficiently clear ahead
- road users are not beginning to overtake you
- there is a suitable gap in front of the road user you plan to overtake.

163. Overtake only when it is safe and legal to do so. You should
- not get too close to the vehicle you intend to overtake
- use your mirrors, signal when it is safe to do so, take a quick sideways glance if necessary into the blind spot area and then start to move out
- not assume that you can simply follow a vehicle ahead which is overtaking; there may only be enough room for one vehicle
- move quickly past the vehicle you are overtaking, once you have started to overtake. Allow plenty of room. Move back to the left as soon as you can but do not cut in
- take extra care at night and in poor visibility when it is harder to judge speed and distance
- give way to oncoming vehicles before passing parked vehicles or other obstructions on your side of the road
- only overtake on the left if the vehicle in front is signalling to turn right, and there is room to do so
- stay in your lane if traffic is moving slowly in queues. If the queue on your right is moving more slowly than you are, you may pass on the left
- give motorcyclists, cyclists and horse riders at least as much room as you would when overtaking a car (see Rules 211–215).

Remember: Mirrors – Signal – Manoeuvre

Give vulnerable road users at least as much space as you would a car

164. Large vehicles. Overtaking these is more difficult. You should

- drop back. This will increase your ability to see ahead and should allow the driver of the large vehicle to see you in their mirrors. Getting too close to large vehicles, including agricultural vehicles such as a tractor with a trailer or other fixed equipment, will obscure your view of the road ahead and there may be another slow-moving vehicle in front
- make sure that you have enough room to complete your overtaking manoeuvre before committing yourself. It takes longer to pass a large vehicle. If in doubt do not overtake
- not assume you can follow a vehicle ahead which is overtaking a long vehicle. If a problem develops, they may abort overtaking and pull back in.

Do not cut in too quickly

165. You MUST NOT overtake

- if you would have to cross or straddle double white lines with a solid line nearest to you (but see Rule129)
- if you would have to enter an area designed to divide traffic, if it is surrounded by a solid white line
- the nearest vehicle to a pedestrian crossing, especially when it has stopped to let pedestrians cross
- if you would have to enter a lane reserved for buses, trams or cycles during its hours of operation
- after a 'No Overtaking' sign and until you pass a sign cancelling the restriction.

Laws RTA 1988 sect 36, TSRGD regs 10, 22, 23 & 24, ZPPPCRGD reg 24

166. DO NOT overtake if there is any doubt, or where you cannot see far enough ahead to be sure it is safe. For example, when you are approaching

- a corner or bend
- a hump bridge
- the brow of a hill.

167. DO NOT overtake where you might come into conflict with other road users. For example

- approaching or at a road junction on either side of the road
- where the road narrows
- when approaching a school crossing patrol
- between the kerb and a bus or tram when it is at a stop
- where traffic is queuing at junctions or roadworks
- when you would force another road user to swerve or slow down
- at a level crossing
- when a road user is indicating right, even if you believe the signal should have been cancelled. Do not take a risk; wait for the signal to be cancelled
- stay behind if you are following a cyclist approaching a roundabout or junction, and you intend to turn left
- when a tram is standing at a kerbside tram stop and there is no clearly marked passing lane for other traffic.

168. Being overtaken. If a driver is trying to overtake you, maintain a steady course and speed, slowing down if necessary to let the vehicle pass. Never obstruct drivers who wish to pass. Speeding up or driving unpredictably while someone is overtaking you is dangerous. Drop back to maintain a two-second gap if someone overtakes and pulls into the gap in front of you.

169. Do not hold up a long queue of traffic, especially if you are driving a large or slow-moving vehicle. Check your mirrors frequently, and if necessary, pull in where it is safe and let traffic pass.

Road junctions

170. Take extra care at junctions. You should

- watch out for cyclists, motorcyclists, powered wheelchairs/mobility scooters and pedestrians as they are not always easy to see. Be aware that they may not have seen or heard you if you are approaching from behind
- watch out for pedestrians crossing a road into which you are turning. If they have started to cross they have priority, so give way
- watch out for long vehicles which may be turning at a junction ahead; they may have to use the whole width of the road to make the turn (see Rule 221)
- watch out for horse riders who may take a different line on the road from that which you would expect
- not assume, when waiting at a junction, that a vehicle coming from the right and signalling left will actually turn. Wait and make sure
- look all around before emerging. Do not cross or join a road until there is a gap large enough for you to do so safely.

Give way to pedestrians who have started to cross

171. You **MUST** stop behind the line at a junction with a 'Stop' sign and a solid white line across the road. Wait for a safe gap in the traffic before you move off.
Laws RTA 1988 sect 36 & TSRGD regs 10 & 16

172. The approach to a junction may have a 'Give Way' sign or a triangle marked on the road. You **MUST** give way to traffic on the main road when emerging from a junction with broken white lines across the road.
Laws RTA 1988 sect 36 & TSRGD regs 10(1),16(1) & 25

173. Dual carriageways. When crossing or turning right, first assess whether the central reservation is deep enough to protect the full length of your vehicle.
- If it is, then you should treat each half of the carriageway as a separate road. Wait in the central reservation until there is a safe gap in the traffic on the second half of the road.
- If the central reservation is too shallow for the length of your vehicle, wait until you can cross both carriageways in one go.

Assess your vehicle's length and do not obstruct traffic

174. Box junctions. These have criss-cross yellow lines painted on the road (see Road markings). You **MUST NOT** enter the box until your exit road or lane is clear. However, you may enter the box and wait when you want to turn right, and are only stopped from doing so by oncoming traffic, or by other vehicles waiting to turn right. At signalled roundabouts you **MUST NOT** enter the box unless you can cross over it completely without stopping.

Law TSRGD regs 10(1) & 29(2)

Enter a box junction only if your exit road is clear

Junctions controlled by traffic lights

175. You **MUST** stop behind the white 'Stop' line across your side of the road unless the light is green. If the amber light appears you may go on only if you have already crossed the stop line or are so close to it that to stop might cause a collision.

Laws RTA 1988 sect 36 & TSRGD regs 10 & 36

176. You **MUST NOT** move forward over the white line when the red light is showing. Only go forward when the traffic lights are green if there is room for you to clear the junction safely or you are taking up a position to turn right. If the traffic lights are not working, treat the situation as you would an unmarked junction and proceed with great care.

Laws RTA 1988 sect 36 & TSRGD regs 10 & 36

177. Green filter arrow. This indicates a filter lane only. Do not enter that lane unless you want to go in the direction of the arrow. You may proceed in the direction of the green arrow when it, or the full green light shows. Give other traffic, especially cyclists, time and room to move into the correct lane.

178. Advanced stop lines. Some signal-controlled junctions have advanced stop lines to allow cycles to be positioned ahead of other traffic. Motorists, including motorcyclists, **MUST** stop at the first white line reached if the lights are amber or red and should avoid blocking the way or encroaching on the marked area at other times, e.g. if the junction ahead is blocked. If your vehicle has proceeded over the first white line at the time that the signal goes red, you **MUST** stop at the second white line, even if your vehicle is in the marked area. Allow cyclists time and space to move off when the green signal shows.
Laws RTA 1988 sect 36 & TSRGD regs 10, 36(1) & 43(2)

Do not unnecessarily encroach on the cyclists' waiting area

Turning right

179. Well before you turn right you should
- use your mirrors to make sure you know the position and movement of traffic behind you
- give a right-turn signal
- take up a position just left of the middle of the road or in the space marked for traffic turning right
- leave room for other vehicles to pass on the left, if possible.

180. Wait until there is a safe gap between you and any oncoming vehicle. Watch out for cyclists, motorcyclists, pedestrians and other road users. Check your mirrors and blind spot again to make sure you are not being overtaken, then make the turn. Do not cut the corner. Take great care when turning into a main road; you will need to watch for traffic in both directions and wait for a safe gap.
Remember: Mirrors – Signal – Manoeuvre

Position your vehicle correctly to avoid obstructing traffic

181. When turning right at crossroads where an oncoming vehicle is also turning right, there is a choice of two methods

- turn right side to right side; keep the other vehicle on your right and turn behind it. This is generally the safer method as you have a clear view of any approaching traffic when completing your turn
- left side to left side, turning in front of each other. This can block your view of oncoming vehicles, so take extra care. Cyclists and motorcyclists in particular may be hidden from your view. Road layout, markings or how the other vehicle is positioned can determine which course should be taken.

Left – Turning right side to right side.
Right – Turning left side to left side.

Turning left

182. Use your mirrors and give a left-turn signal well before you turn left. Do not overtake just before you turn left and watch out for traffic coming up on your left before you make the turn, especially if driving a large vehicle. Cyclists, motorcyclists and other road users in particular may be hidden from your view.

Do not cut in on cyclists

183. When turning
- keep as close to the left as is safe and practicable
- give way to any vehicles using a bus lane, cycle lane or tramway from either direction.

Roundabouts

184. On approaching a roundabout take notice and act on all the information available to you, including traffic signs, traffic lights and lane markings which direct you into the correct lane. You should
- use **Mirrors – Signal – Manoeuvre** at all stages
- decide as early as possible which exit you need to take
- give an appropriate signal (see Rule 186). Time your signals so as not to confuse other road users
- get into the correct lane
- adjust your speed and position to fit in with traffic conditions
- be aware of the speed and position of all the road users around you.

185. When reaching the roundabout you should
- give priority to traffic approaching from your right, unless directed otherwise by signs, road markings or traffic lights
- check whether road markings allow you to enter the roundabout without giving way. If so, proceed, but still look to the right before joining

- watch out for all other road users already on the roundabout; be aware they may not be signalling correctly or at all
- look forward before moving off to make sure traffic in front has moved off.

Follow the correct procedure at roundabouts

186. Signals and position. When taking the first exit, unless signs or markings indicate otherwise
- signal left and approach in the left-hand lane
- keep to the left on the roundabout and continue signalling left to leave.

When taking an exit to the right or going full circle, unless signs or markings indicate otherwise
- signal right and approach in the right-hand lane
- keep to the right on the roundabout until you need to change lanes to exit the roundabout
- signal left after you have passed the exit before the one you want.

When taking any intermediate exit, unless signs or markings indicate otherwise
- select the appropriate lane on approach to and on the roundabout
- you should not normally need to signal on approach
- stay in this lane until you need to alter course to exit the roundabout
- signal left after you have passed the exit before the one you want.

When there are more than three lanes at the entrance to a roundabout, use the most appropriate lane on approach and through it.

187. In all cases watch out for and give plenty of room to
- pedestrians who may be crossing the approach and exit roads
- traffic crossing in front of you on the roundabout, especially vehicles intending to leave by the next exit
- traffic which may be straddling lanes or positioned incorrectly
- motorcyclists
- cyclists and horse riders who may stay in the left-hand lane and signal right if they intend to continue round the roundabout. Allow them to do so
- long vehicles (including those towing trailers). These might have to take a different course or straddle lanes either approaching or on the roundabout because of their length. Watch out for their signals.

188. Mini-roundabouts. Approach these in the same way as normal roundabouts. All vehicles **MUST** pass round the central markings except large vehicles which are physically incapable of doing so. Remember, there is less space to manoeuvre and less time to signal. Avoid making U-turns at mini-roundabouts. Beware of others doing this.
Laws RTA 1988 sect 36 & TSRGD regs 10(1) & 16(1)

189. At double mini-roundabouts treat each roundabout separately and give way to traffic from the right.

190. Multiple roundabouts. At some complex junctions, there may be a series of mini-roundabouts at each intersection. Treat each mini-roundabout separately and follow the normal rules.

Treat each roundabout separately

Pedestrian crossings

191. You **MUST NOT** park on a crossing or in the area covered by the zig-zag lines. You **MUST NOT** overtake the moving vehicle nearest the crossing or the vehicle nearest the crossing which has stopped to give way to pedestrians.

Laws ZPPPCRGD regs 18, 20 & 24, RTRA sect 25(5) & TSRGD regs 10, 27 & 28

192. In queuing traffic, you should keep the crossing clear.

Keep the crossing clear

193. You should take extra care where the view of either side of the crossing is blocked by queuing traffic or incorrectly parked vehicles. Pedestrians may be crossing between stationary vehicles.

194. Allow pedestrians plenty of time to cross and do not harass them by revving your engine or edging forward.

195. Zebra crossings. As you approach a zebra crossing
- look out for pedestrians waiting to cross and be ready to slow down or stop to let them cross
- you **MUST** give way when a pedestrian has moved onto a crossing
- allow more time for stopping on wet or icy roads
- do not wave or use your horn to invite pedestrians across; this could be dangerous if another vehicle is approaching
- be aware of pedestrians approaching from the side of the crossing.

A zebra crossing with a central island is two separate crossings (see Rule 20).

Law ZPPPCRGD reg 25

Signal-controlled crossings

196. Pelican crossings. These are signal-controlled crossings where flashing amber follows the red 'Stop' light. You **MUST** stop when the red light shows. When the amber light is flashing, you **MUST** give way to any pedestrians on the crossing. If the amber light is flashing and there are no pedestrians on the crossing, you may proceed with caution.
Laws ZPPPCRGD regs 23 & 26 & RTRA sect 25(5)

Allow pedestrians to cross when the amber light is flashing

197. Pelican crossings which go straight across the road are one crossing, even when there is a central island. You **MUST** wait for pedestrians who are crossing from the other side of the island.
Laws ZPPPCRGD reg 26 & RTRA sect 25(5)

198. Give way to anyone still crossing after the signal for vehicles has changed to green. This advice applies to all crossings.

199. Toucan, puffin and equestrian crossings. These are similar to pelican crossings, but there is no flashing amber phase; the light sequence for traffic at these three crossings is the same as at traffic lights. If the signal-controlled crossing is not working, proceed with extreme caution.

Reversing

200. Choose an appropriate place to manoeuvre. If you need to turn your vehicle around, wait until you find a safe place. Try not to reverse or turn round in a busy road; find a quiet side road or drive round a block of side streets.

201. Do not reverse from a side road into a main road. When using a driveway, reverse in and drive out if you can.

202. Look carefully before you start reversing. You should
- use all your mirrors
- check the 'blind spot' behind you (the part of the road you cannot see easily in the mirrors)
- check there are no pedestrians (particularly children), cyclists, other road users or obstructions in the road behind you.

Reverse slowly while
- checking all around
- looking mainly through the rear window
- being aware that the front of your vehicle will swing out as you turn.

Get someone to guide you if you cannot see clearly.

Check all round when reversing

203. You **MUST NOT** reverse your vehicle further than necessary.

Law CUR reg 106

Road users requiring extra care

204. The most vulnerable road users are pedestrians, cyclists, motorcyclists and horse riders. It is particularly important to be aware of children, older and disabled people, and learner and inexperienced drivers and riders.

Pedestrians

205. There is a risk of pedestrians, especially children, stepping unexpectedly into the road. You should drive with the safety of children in mind at a speed suitable for the conditions.

206. Drive carefully and slowly when

- in crowded shopping streets, Home Zones and Quiet Lanes (see Rule 218) or residential areas
- driving past bus and tram stops; pedestrians may emerge suddenly into the road
- passing parked vehicles, especially ice cream vans; children are more interested in ice cream than traffic and may run into the road unexpectedly
- needing to cross a pavement or cycle track; for example, to reach or leave a driveway. Give way to pedestrians and cyclists on the pavement
- reversing into a side road; look all around the vehicle and give way to any pedestrians who may be crossing the road
- turning at road junctions; give way to pedestrians who are already crossing the road into which you are turning
- the pavement is closed due to street repairs and pedestrians are directed to use the road
- approaching pedestrians on narrow rural roads without a footway or footpath. Always slow down and be prepared to stop if necessary, giving them plenty of room as you drive past.

Watch out for children in busy areas

207. Particularly vulnerable pedestrians. These include

- children and older pedestrians who may not be able to judge your speed and could step into the road in front of you. At 40mph (64km/h) your vehicle will probably kill any pedestrians it hits. At 20mph (32km/h) there is only a 1 in 20 chance of the pedestrian being killed. So kill your speed
- older pedestrians who may need more time to cross the road. Be patient and allow them to cross in their own time. Do not hurry them by revving your engine or edging forward
- people with disabilities. People with hearing impairments may not be aware of your vehicle approaching. Those with walking difficulties require more time
- blind or partially sighted people, who may be carrying a white cane or using a guide dog. They may not be able to see you approaching
- deafblind people who may be carrying a white cane with a red band or using a dog with a red and white harness. They may not see or hear instructions or signals.

208. Near schools. Drive slowly and be particularly aware of young cyclists and pedestrians. In some places, there may be a flashing amber signal below the 'School' warning sign which tells you that there may be children crossing the road ahead. Drive very slowly until you are clear of the area.

209. Drive carefully and slowly when passing a stationary bus showing a 'School Bus' sign (see Vehicle markings) as children may be getting on or off.

210. You **MUST** stop when a school crossing patrol shows a 'Stop for children' sign (see pages Signals by authorised persons and Signs giving orders).
Law RTRA sect 28

Motorcyclists and cyclists

211. It is often difficult to see motorcyclists and cyclists, especially when they are coming up from behind, coming out of junctions, at roundabouts, overtaking you or filtering through traffic. Always look out for them before you emerge from a junction; they could be approaching faster than you think. When turning right across a line of slow-moving or stationary traffic, look out for cyclists or motorcyclists on the inside of the traffic you are crossing. Be especially careful when turning, and when changing direction or lane. Be sure to check mirrors and blind spots carefully.

Look out for motorcyclists and cyclists at junctions

212. When passing motorcyclists and cyclists, give them plenty of room (see Rules162–167). If they look over their shoulder it could mean that they intend to pull out, turn right or change direction. Give them time and space to do so.

213. Motorcyclists and cyclists may suddenly need to avoid uneven road surfaces and obstacles such as drain covers or oily, wet or icy patches on the road. Give them plenty of room and pay particular attention to any sudden change of direction they may have to make.

Other road users

214. Animals. When passing animals, drive slowly. Give them plenty of room and be ready to stop. Do not scare animals by sounding your horn, revving your engine or accelerating rapidly once you have passed them. Look out for animals being led, driven or ridden on the road and take extra care. Keep your speed down at bends and on narrow country roads. If a road is blocked by a herd of animals, stop and switch off your engine until they have left the road. Watch out for animals on unfenced roads.

215. Horse riders and horse-drawn vehicles. Be particularly careful of horse riders and horse-drawn vehicles especially when overtaking. Always pass wide and slowly. Horse riders are often children, so take extra care and remember riders may ride in double file when escorting a young or inexperienced horse or rider. Look out for horse riders' and horse drivers' signals and heed a request to slow down or stop. Take great care and treat all horses as a potential hazard; they can be unpredictable, despite the efforts of their rider/driver.

216. Older drivers. Their reactions may be slower than other drivers. Make allowance for this.

217. Learners and inexperienced drivers. They may not be so skilful at anticipating and responding to events. Be particularly patient with learner drivers and young drivers. Drivers who have recently passed their test may display a 'new driver' plate or sticker (see Annexe 8 – Safety code for new drivers).

218. Home Zones and Quiet Lanes. These are places where people could be using the whole of the road for a range of activities such as children playing or for a community event. You should drive slowly and carefully and be prepared to stop to allow people extra time to make space for you to pass them in safety.

Other vehicles

219. Emergency and Incident Support vehicles. You should look and listen for ambulances, fire engines, police, doctors or other emergency vehicles using flashing blue, red or green lights and sirens or flashing headlights, or Highways Agency Traffic Officer and Incident Support vehicles using flashing amber lights. When one approaches do not panic. Consider the route of such a vehicle and take appropriate action to let it pass, while complying with all traffic signs. If necessary, pull to the side of the road and stop, but try to avoid stopping before the brow of a hill, a bend or narrow section of road. Do not endanger yourself, other road users or pedestrians and avoid mounting the kerb. Do not brake harshly on approach to a junction or roundabout, as a following vehicle may not have the same view as you.

220. Powered vehicles used by disabled people. These small vehicles travel at a maximum speed of 8mph (12km/h). On a dual carriageway where the speed limit exceeds 50mph (80km/h) they **MUST** have a flashing amber beacon, but on other roads you may not have that advance warning (see Rules 36–46 inclusive).
Law RVLR reg 17(1) & 26

221. Large vehicles. These may need extra road space to turn or to deal with a hazard that you are not able to see. If you are following a large vehicle, such as a bus or articulated lorry, be aware that the driver may not be able to see you in the mirrors. Be prepared to stop and wait if it needs room or time to turn.

Large vehicles need extra room

222. Large vehicles can block your view. Your ability to see and to plan ahead will be improved if you pull back to increase your separation distance. Be patient, as larger vehicles are subject to lower speed limits than cars and motorcycles. Many large vehicles may be fitted with speed limiting devices which will restrict speed to 56mph (90km/h) even on a motorway.

223. Buses, coaches and trams. Give priority to these vehicles when you can do so safely, especially when they signal to pull away from stops. Look out for people getting off a bus or tram and crossing the road.

224. Electric vehicles. Be careful of electric vehicles such as milk floats and trams. Trams move quickly but silently and cannot steer to avoid you.

225. Vehicles with flashing amber beacons. These warn of a slow-moving or stationary vehicle (such as a Traffic Officer vehicle, salt spreader, snow plough or recovery vehicle) or abnormal loads, so approach with caution. On unrestricted dual carriageways, motor vehicles first used on or after 1 January 1947 with a maximum speed of 25mph (40km/h) or less (such as tractors) **MUST** use a flashing amber beacon (also see Rule 220).
Law RVLR 1989, reg 17

Driving in adverse weather conditions

226. You **MUST** use headlights when visibility is seriously reduced, generally when you cannot see for more than 100 metres (328 feet). You may also use front or rear fog lights but you **MUST** switch them off when visibility improves (see Rule 236).
Law RVLR regs 25 & 27

227. Wet weather. In wet weather, stopping distances will be at least double those required for stopping on dry roads (see Rule 126). This is because your tyres have less grip on the road. In wet weather
- you should keep well back from the vehicle in front. This will increase your ability to see and plan ahead
- if the steering becomes unresponsive, it probably means that water is preventing the tyres from gripping the road. Ease off the accelerator and slow down gradually
- the rain and spray from vehicles may make it difficult to see and be seen
- be aware of the dangers of spilt diesel that will make the surface very slippery (see Annexe 6)
- take extra care around pedestrians, cyclists, motorcyclists and horse riders.

Icy and snowy weather

228. In winter check the local weather forecast for warnings of icy or snowy weather. **DO NOT** drive in these conditions unless your journey is essential. If it is, take great care and allow more time for your journey. Take an emergency kit of de-icer and ice scraper, torch, warm clothing and boots, first aid kit, jump leads and a shovel, together with a warm drink and emergency food in case you get stuck or your vehicle breaks down.

229. Before you set off
- you **MUST** be able to see, so clear all snow and ice from all your windows
- you **MUST** ensure that lights are clean and number plates are clearly visible and legible
- make sure the mirrors are clear and the windows are demisted thoroughly
- remove all snow that might fall off into the path of other road users
- check your planned route is clear of delays and that no further snowfalls or severe weather are predicted.
Laws CUR reg 30, RVLR reg 23, VERA sect 43 & RV(DRM)R reg 11

Make sure your windscreen is completely clear

230. When driving in icy or snowy weather
- drive with care, even if the roads have been treated
- keep well back from the road user in front as stopping distances can be ten times greater than on dry roads
- take care when overtaking vehicles spreading salt or other de-icer, particularly if you are riding a motorcycle or cycle
- watch out for snowploughs which may throw out snow on either side. Do not overtake them unless the lane you intend to use has been cleared
- be prepared for the road conditions to change over relatively short distances
- listen to travel bulletins and take note of variable message signs that may provide information about weather, road and traffic conditions ahead.

231. Drive extremely carefully when the roads are icy. Avoid sudden actions as these could cause loss of control. You should
- drive at a slow speed in as high a gear as possible; accelerate and brake very gently
- drive particularly slowly on bends where loss of control is more likely. Brake progressively on the straight before you reach a bend. Having slowed down, steer smoothly round the bend, avoiding sudden actions
- check your grip on the road surface when there is snow or ice by choosing a safe place to brake gently. If the steering feels unresponsive this may indicate ice and your vehicle losing its grip on the road. When travelling on ice, tyres make virtually no noise.

Windy weather

232. High-sided vehicles are most affected by windy weather, but strong gusts can also blow a car, cyclist, motorcyclist or horse rider off course. This can happen on open stretches of road exposed to strong crosswinds, or when passing bridges or gaps in hedges.

233. In very windy weather your vehicle may be affected by turbulence created by large vehicles. Motorcyclists are particularly affected, so keep well back from them when they are overtaking a high-sided vehicle.

Fog

234. Before entering fog check your mirrors then slow down. If the word 'Fog' is shown on a roadside signal but the road is clear, be prepared for a bank of fog or drifting patchy fog ahead. Even if it seems to be clearing, you can suddenly find yourself in thick fog.

235. When driving in fog you should
- use your lights as required (see Rule 226)
- keep a safe distance behind the vehicle in front. Rear lights can give a false sense of security
- be able to pull up well within the distance you can see clearly. This is particularly important on motorways and dual carriageways, as vehicles are travelling faster
- use your windscreen wipers and demisters
- beware of other drivers not using headlights
- not accelerate to get away from a vehicle which is too close behind you
- check your mirrors before you slow down. Then use your brakes so that your brake lights warn drivers behind you that you are slowing down
- stop in the correct position at a junction with limited visibility and listen for traffic. When you are sure it is safe to emerge, do so positively and do not hesitate in a position that puts you directly in the path of approaching vehicles.

236. You **MUST NOT** use front or rear fog lights unless visibility is seriously reduced (see Rule 226) as they dazzle other road users and can obscure your brake lights. You **MUST** switch them off when visibility improves.
Law RVLR regs 25 & 27

Hot weather

237. Keep your vehicle well ventilated to avoid drowsiness. Be aware that the road surface may become soft or if it rains after a dry spell it may become slippery. These conditions could affect your steering and braking. If you are dazzled by bright sunlight, slow down and if necessary, stop.

Waiting and parking

238. You **MUST NOT** wait or park on yellow lines during the times of operation shown on nearby time plates (or zone entry signs if in a Controlled Parking Zone) – see Information signs and Road markings. Double yellow lines indicate a prohibition of waiting at any time even if there are no upright signs. You **MUST NOT** wait or park, or stop to set down and pick up passengers, on school entrance markings (see Road markings) when upright signs indicate a prohibition of stopping.
Law RTRA sects 5 & 8

Parking

239. Use off-street parking areas, or bays marked out with white lines on the road as parking places, wherever possible. If you have to stop on the roadside
- do not park facing against the traffic flow
- stop as close as you can to the side
- do not stop too close to a vehicle displaying a Blue Badge: remember, the occupant may need more room to get in or out
- you **MUST** switch off the engine, headlights and fog lights
- you **MUST** apply the handbrake before leaving the vehicle
- you **MUST** ensure you do not hit anyone when you open your door. Check for cyclists or other traffic
- it is safer for your passengers (especially children) to get out of the vehicle on the side next to the kerb
- put all valuables out of sight and make sure your vehicle is secure
- lock your vehicle.

Laws CUR reg 98, 105 & 107, RVLR reg 27 & RTA 1988 sect 42

Check before opening your door

240. You **MUST NOT** stop or park on

- the carriageway or the hard shoulder of a motorway except in an emergency (see Rule 270)
- a pedestrian crossing, including the area marked by the zig-zag lines (see Rule 191)
- a clearway (see Traffic signs)
- taxi bays as indicated by upright signs and markings
- an Urban Clearway within its hours of operation, except to pick up or set down passengers (see Traffic signs)
- a road marked with double white lines, even when a broken white line is on your side of the road, except to pick up or set down passengers, or to load or unload goods
- a tram or cycle lane during its period of operation
- a cycle track
- red lines, in the case of specially designated 'red routes', unless otherwise indicated by signs.

Any vehicle may enter a bus lane to stop, load or unload where this is not prohibited (see Rule 141).

Laws MT(E&W)R regs 7 & 9, MT(S)R regs 6 & 8, ZPPPCRGD regs 18 & 20, RTRA sects 5, 6 & 8, TSRGD regs 10, 26 & 27, RTA 1988 sects 21(1) & 36

241. You **MUST NOT** park in parking spaces reserved for specific users, such as Blue Badge holders, residents or motorcycles, unless entitled to do so.

Laws CSDPA sect 21 & RTRA sects 5 & 8

242. You **MUST NOT** leave your vehicle or trailer in a dangerous position or where it causes any unnecessary obstruction of the road.

Laws RTA 1988, sect 22 & CUR reg 103

243. DO NOT stop or park

- near a school entrance
- anywhere you would prevent access for Emergency Services
- at or near a bus or tram stop or taxi rank
- on the approach to a level crossing/tramway crossing
- opposite or within 10 metres (32 feet) of a junction, except in an authorised parking space
- near the brow of a hill or hump bridge
- opposite a traffic island or (if this would cause an obstruction) another parked vehicle
- where you would force other traffic to enter a tram lane
- where the kerb has been lowered to help wheelchair users and powered mobility vehicles

- in front of an entrance to a property
- on a bend
- where you would obstruct cyclists' use of cycle facilities

except when forced to do so by stationary traffic.

244. You **MUST NOT** park partially or wholly on the pavement in London, and should not do so elsewhere unless signs permit it. Parking on the pavement can obstruct and seriously inconvenience pedestrians, people in wheelchairs or with visual impairments and people with prams or pushchairs.

Law GL(GP)A sect 15

245. Controlled Parking Zones. The zone entry signs indicate the times when the waiting restrictions within the zone are in force. Parking may be allowed in some places at other times. Otherwise parking will be within separately signed and marked bays.

246. Goods vehicles. Vehicles with a maximum laden weight of over 7.5 tonnes (including any trailer) **MUST NOT** be parked on a verge, pavement or any land situated between carriageways, without police permission. The only exception is when parking is essential for loading and unloading, in which case the vehicle **MUST NOT** be left unattended.

Law RTA 1988 sect 19

247. Loading and unloading. Do not load or unload where there are yellow markings on the kerb and upright signs advise restrictions are in place (see Road markings). This may be permitted where parking is otherwise restricted. On red routes, specially marked and signed bays indicate where and when loading and unloading is permitted.

Law RTRA sects 5 & 8

Parking at night

248. You **MUST NOT** park on a road at night facing against the direction of the traffic flow unless in a recognised parking space.

Laws CUR reg 101 & RVLR reg 24

249. All vehicles **MUST** display parking lights when parked on a road or a lay-by on a road with a speed limit greater than 30mph (48km/h).

Law RVLR reg 24

250. Cars, goods vehicles not exceeding 1525kg unladen weight, invalid carriages, motorcycles and pedal cycles may be parked without lights on a road (or lay-by) with a speed limit of 30mph (48km/h) or less if they are

- at least 10 metres (32 feet) away from any junction, close to the kerb and facing in the direction of the traffic flow
- in a recognised parking place or lay-by.

Other vehicles and trailers, and all vehicles with projecting loads, **MUST NOT** be left on a road at night without lights.

Laws RVLR reg 24 & CUR reg 82(7)

251. Parking in fog. It is especially dangerous to park on the road in fog. If it is unavoidable, leave your parking lights or sidelights on.

252. Parking on hills. If you park on a hill you should

- park close to the kerb and apply the handbrake firmly
- select a forward gear and turn your steering wheel away from the kerb when facing uphill
- select reverse gear and turn your steering wheel towards the kerb when facing downhill
- use 'park' if your car has an automatic gearbox.

Turn your wheels away from the kerb when parking facing uphill.

Turn your wheels towards the kerb when parking facing downhill.

Decriminalised Parking Enforcement (DPE)

DPE is becoming increasingly common as more authorities take on this role. The local traffic authority assumes responsibility for enforcing many parking contraventions in place of the police. Further details on DPE may be found at the following websites:

www.parking-appeals.gov.uk (outside London)

www.parkingandtrafficappeals.gov.uk (inside London)

Motorways

Many other Rules apply to motorway driving, either wholly or in part: Rules 46, 57, 83–126, 130–134, 139, 144, 146–151, 160, 161, 219, 221–222, 225, 226–237, 274–278, 280, and 281–290.

General

253. Prohibited vehicles. Motorways **MUST NOT** be used by pedestrians, holders of provisional motorcycle or car licences, riders of motorcycles under 50cc, cyclists, horse riders, certain slow-moving vehicles and those carrying oversized loads (except by special permission), agricultural vehicles and powered wheelchairs/powered mobility scooters (see Rules 36–46 incl)

Laws HA 1980 sects 16, 17 & sch 4, MT(E&W)R regs 3(d), 4 & 11, MT(E&W)(A)R, R(S)A sects 7, 8 & sch 3, RTRA sects 17(2) & (3), & MT(S)R reg 10

254. Traffic on motorways usually travels faster than on other roads, so you have less time to react. It is especially important to use your mirrors earlier and look much further ahead than you would on other roads.

Motorway signals

255. Motorway signals (see Motorway signals) are used to warn you of a danger ahead. For example, there may be an incident, fog, a spillage or road workers on the carriageway which you may not immediately be able to see.

256. Signals situated on the central reservation apply to all lanes. On very busy stretches, signals may be overhead with a separate signal for each lane.

257. Amber flashing lights. These warn of a hazard ahead. The signal may show a temporary maximum speed limit, lanes that are closed or a message such as 'Fog'. Adjust your speed and look out for the danger until you pass a signal which is not flashing or one that gives the 'All clear' sign and you are sure it is safe to increase your speed.

258. Red flashing lights. If red lights on the overhead signals flash above your lane and a red 'X' is showing, you **MUST NOT** go beyond the signal in that lane. If red lights flash on a signal in the central reservation or at the side of the road, you **MUST NOT** go beyond the signal in any lane.

Laws RTA 1988 sect 36 & TSRGD regs 10 & 38

Driving on the motorway

Joining the motorway.

259. When you join the motorway you will normally approach it from a road on the left (a slip road) or from an adjoining motorway. You should

- give priority to traffic already on the motorway
- check the traffic on the motorway and match your speed to fit safely into the traffic flow in the left-hand lane
- not cross solid white lines that separate lanes or use the hard shoulder
- stay on the slip road if it continues as an extra lane on the motorway
- remain in the left-hand lane long enough to adjust to the speed of traffic before considering overtaking.

On the motorway

260. When you can see well ahead and the road conditions are good, you should

- drive at a steady cruising speed which you and your vehicle can handle safely and is within the speed limit (see Rule 124)
- keep a safe distance from the vehicle in front and increase the gap on wet or icy roads, or in fog (see Rules 126 and 235).

261. You **MUST NOT** exceed 70mph (112km/h), or the maximum speed limit permitted for your vehicle (see Rule 124). If a lower speed limit is in force, either permanently or temporarily, at roadworks for example, you **MUST NOT** exceed the lower limit. On some motorways, mandatory motorway signals (which display the speed within a red ring) are used to vary the maximum speed limit to improve traffic flow. You **MUST NOT** exceed this speed limit.
Law RTRA sects 17, 86, 89 & sch 6

262. The monotony of driving on a motorway can make you feel sleepy. To minimise the risk, follow the advice in Rule 91.

263. You **MUST NOT** reverse, cross the central reservation, or drive against the traffic flow. If you have missed your exit, or have taken the wrong route, carry on to the next exit.
Laws MT(E&W)R regs 6, 8 & 10 & MT(S)R regs 4, 5, 7 & 9

Lane discipline

264. You should always drive in the left-hand lane when the road ahead is clear. If you are overtaking a number of slower-moving vehicles, you should return to the left-hand lane as soon as you are safely past. Slow-moving or speed-restricted vehicles should always remain in the left-hand lane of the carriageway unless overtaking. You **MUST NOT** drive on the hard shoulder except in an emergency or if directed to do so by the police, HA traffic officers in uniform or by signs.

Laws MT(E&W)R regs 5, 9 & 16(1)(a), MT(S)R regs 4, 8 & 14(1)(a), and RTA 1988, sects 35 & 186, as amended by TMA 2004 sect 6

265. The right-hand lane of a motorway with three or more lanes **MUST NOT** be used (except in prescribed circumstances) if you are driving

- any vehicle drawing a trailer
- a goods vehicle with a maximum laden weight exceeding 3.5 tonnes but not exceeding 7.5 tonnes, which is required to be fitted with a speed limiter
- a goods vehicle with a maximum laden weight exceeding 7.5 tonnes
- a passenger vehicle with a maximum laden weight exceeding 7.5 tonnes constructed or adapted to carry more than eight seated passengers in addition to the driver
- a passenger vehicle with a maximum laden weight not exceeding 7.5 tonnes which is constructed or adapted to carry more than eight seated passengers in addition to the driver, which is required to be fitted with a speed limiter.

Laws MT(E&W)R reg 12, MT(E&W)AR (2004), MT(S)R reg 11 & MT(S)AR (2004)

266. Approaching a junction. Look well ahead for signals or signs. Direction signs may be placed over the road. If you need to change lanes, do so in good time. At some junctions a lane may lead directly off the motorway. Only get in that lane if you wish to go in the direction indicated on the overhead signs.

Overtaking

267. Do not overtake unless you are sure it is safe and legal to do so. Overtake only on the right. You should

- check your mirrors
- take time to judge the speeds correctly
- make sure that the lane you will be joining is sufficiently clear ahead and behind
- take a quick sideways glance into the blind spot area to verify the position of a vehicle that may have disappeared from your view in the mirror
- remember that traffic may be coming up behind you very quickly. Check all your mirrors carefully. Look out for motorcyclists. When it is safe to do so, signal in plenty of time, then move out
- ensure you do not cut in on the vehicle you have overtaken
- be especially careful at night and in poor visibility when it is harder to judge speed and distance.

268. Do not overtake on the left or move to a lane on your left to overtake. In congested conditions, where adjacent lanes of traffic are moving at similar speeds, traffic in left-hand lanes may sometimes be moving faster than traffic to the right. In these conditions you may keep up with the traffic in your lane even if this means passing traffic in the lane to your right. Do not weave in and out of lanes to overtake.

269. Hard shoulder. You **MUST NOT** use the hard shoulder for overtaking. In areas where an Active Traffic Management (ATM) Scheme is in force, the hard shoulder may be used as a running lane. You will know when you can use this because a speed limit sign will be shown above all open lanes, including the hard shoulder. A red cross or blank sign above the hard shoulder means that you **MUST NOT** drive on the hard shoulder except in an emergency or breakdown. Emergency refuge areas have also been built into these areas for use in cases of emergency or breakdown.

Laws MT(E&W)R regs 5, 5A & 9, MT(S)R regs 4 & 8

Overhead gantry showing red cross over hard shoulder

Stopping

270. You **MUST NOT** stop on the carriageway, hard shoulder, slip road, central reservation or verge except in an emergency, or when told to do so by the police, HA traffic officers in uniform, an emergency sign or by flashing red light signals. Do not stop on the hard shoulder to either make or receive mobile phone calls.

Laws MT(E&W)R regs 5A, 7, 9, 10 & 16, MT(S)R regs 6(1), 8, 9 & 14, PRA 2002 sect 41 & sched 5(8), & RTA 1988 sects 35 & 163 as amended by TMA 2004, sect 6

271. You **MUST NOT** pick up or set down anyone, or walk on a motorway, except in an emergency.

Laws RTRA sect 17 & MT(E&W)R reg 15

Leaving the motorway

272. Unless signs indicate that a lane leads directly off the motorway, you will normally leave the motorway by a slip road on your left. You should

- watch for the signs letting you know you are getting near your exit
- move into the left-hand lane well before reaching your exit
- signal left in good time and reduce your speed on the slip road as necessary.

273. On leaving the motorway or using a link road between motorways, your speed may be higher than you realise – 50mph (80km/h) may feel like 30mph (48km/h). Check your speedometer and adjust your speed accordingly. Some slip-roads and link roads have sharp bends, so you will need to slow down.

Breakdowns and incidents

Breakdowns

274. If your vehicle breaks down, think first of all other road users and

- get your vehicle off the road if possible
- warn other traffic by using your hazard warning lights if your vehicle is causing an obstruction
- help other road users see you by wearing light-coloured or fluorescent clothing in daylight and reflective clothing at night or in poor visibility
- put a warning triangle on the road at least 45 metres (147 feet) behind your broken-down vehicle on the same side of the road, or use other permitted warning devices if you have them. Always take great care when placing or retrieving them, but never use them on motorways
- if possible, keep your sidelights on if it is dark or visibility is poor
- do not stand (or let anybody else stand) between your vehicle and oncoming traffic
- at night or in poor visibility do not stand where you will prevent other road users seeing your lights.

Additional rules for the motorway

275. If your vehicle develops a problem, leave the motorway at the next exit or pull into a service area. If you cannot do so, you should

- pull on to the hard shoulder and stop as far to the left as possible, with your wheels turned to the left
- try to stop near an emergency telephone (situated at approximately one-mile (1.6km) intervals along the hard shoulder)
- leave the vehicle by the left-hand door and ensure your passengers do the same. You **MUST** leave any animals in the vehicle or, in an emergency, keep them under proper control on the verge. Never attempt to place a warning triangle on a motorway
- do not put yourself in danger by attempting even simple repairs
- ensure that passengers keep away from the carriageway and hard shoulder, and that children are kept under control
- walk to an emergency telephone on your side of the carriageway (follow the arrows on the posts at the back of the hard shoulder) – the telephone is free of charge and connects directly to the Highways Agency or the police. Use these in preference to a mobile phone (see Rule 283). Always face the traffic when you speak on the phone
- give full details to the Highways Agency or the police; also inform them if you are a vulnerable motorist such as disabled, older or travelling alone
- return and wait near your vehicle (well away from the carriageway and hard shoulder)
- if you feel at risk from another person, return to your vehicle by a left-hand door and lock all doors. Leave your vehicle again as soon as you feel this danger has passed.

Laws MT(E&W)R reg 14 & MT(S)R reg 12

Keep well back from the hard shoulder

276. Before you rejoin the carriageway after a breakdown, build up speed on the hard shoulder and watch for a safe gap in the traffic. Be aware that other vehicles may be stationary on the hard shoulder.

277. If you cannot get your vehicle onto the hard shoulder
- do not attempt to place any warning device on the carriageway
- switch on your hazard warning lights
- leave your vehicle only when you can safely get clear of the carriageway.

Disabled drivers
278. If you have a disability which prevents you from following the above advice you should
- stay in your vehicle
- switch on your hazard warning lights
- display a 'Help' pennant or, if you have a car or mobile telephone, contact the emergency services and be prepared to advise them of your location.

Obstructions
279. If anything falls from your vehicle (or any other vehicle) on to the road, stop and retrieve it only if it is safe to do so.

280. Motorways. On a motorway do not try to remove the obstruction yourself. Stop at the next emergency telephone and call the Highways Agency or the police.

Incidents
281. Warning signs or flashing lights. If you see or hear emergency or incident support vehicles in the distance, be aware there may be an incident ahead (see Rule 219). Police Officers and Highways Agency Traffic Officers may be required to work in the carriageway, for example dealing with debris, collisions or conducting rolling road blocks. Police officers will use rear-facing flashing red and blue lights and HA Traffic Officers will use rear-facing flashing red and amber lights in these situations. Watch out for such signals, slow down and be prepared to stop. You **MUST** follow any directions given by Police officers or Traffic officers as to whether you can safely pass the incident or blockage.
Laws RTA1988, sects 35 & 163, and as amended by TMA 2004, sect 6

282. When passing the scene of an incident or crash do not be distracted or slow down unnecessarily (for example if an incident is on the other side of a dual carriageway). This may cause a collision or traffic congestion, but see Rule 283.

283. If you are involved in a crash or stop to give assistance
- use your hazard warning lights to warn other traffic
- ask drivers to switch off their engines and stop smoking
- arrange for the emergency services to be called immediately with full details of the incident location and any casualties (on a motorway, use the emergency telephone which allows easy location by the emergency services. If you use a mobile phone, first make sure you have identified your location from the marker posts on the side of the hard shoulder)
- move uninjured people away from the vehicles to safety; on a motorway this should, if possible, be well away from the traffic, the hard shoulder and the central reservation
- do not move injured people from their vehicles unless they are in immediate danger from fire or explosion
- do not remove a motorcyclist's helmet unless it is essential to do so
- be prepared to give first aid as shown in Annexe 7, First aid on the road
- stay at the scene until emergency services arrive.

If you are involved in any other medical emergency on the motorway you should contact the emergency services in the same way.

Incidents involving dangerous goods
284. Vehicles carrying dangerous goods in packages will be marked with plain orange reflective plates. Road tankers and vehicles carrying tank containers of dangerous goods will have hazard warning plates (see Vehicle markings).

285. If an incident involves a vehicle containing dangerous goods, follow the advice in Rule 283 and, in particular
- switch off engines and **DO NOT SMOKE**
- keep well away from the vehicle and do not be tempted to try to rescue casualties as you yourself could become one
- call the emergency services and give as much information as possible about the labels and markings on the vehicle. **DO NOT** use a mobile phone close to a vehicle carrying flammable loads.

Documentation
286. If you are involved in a collision which causes damage or injury to any other person, vehicle, animal or property, you **MUST**
- stop
- give your own and the vehicle owner's name and address, and the registration number of the vehicle, to anyone having reasonable grounds for requiring them
- if you do not give your name and address at the time of the collision, report it to the police as soon as reasonably practicable, and in any case within 24 hours.

Law RTA 1988 sect 170

287. If another person is injured and you do not produce your insurance certificate at the time of the crash to a police officer or to anyone having reasonable grounds to request it, you **MUST**
- report it to the police as soon as possible and in any case within 24 hours
- produce your insurance certificate for the police within seven days.

Law RTA 1988 sect 170

Roadworks

288. When the 'Road Works Ahead' sign is displayed, you will need to be more watchful and look for additional signs providing more specific instructions. Observe all signs – they are there for your safety and the safety of road workers.
- You **MUST NOT** exceed any temporary maximum speed limit.
- Use your mirrors and get into the correct lane for your vehicle in good time and as signs direct.
- Do not switch lanes to overtake queuing traffic.
- Take extra care near cyclists and motorcyclists as they are vulnerable to skidding on grit, mud or other debris at roadworks.
- Where lanes are restricted due to roadworks, merge in turn (see Rule 134).
- Do not drive through an area marked off by traffic cones.
- Watch out for traffic entering or leaving the works area, but do not be distracted by what is going on there. Concentrate on the road ahead, not the roadworks.
- Bear in mind that the road ahead may be obstructed by the works or by slow moving or stationary traffic.
- Keep a safe distance – there could be queues in front.

To obtain further information about roadworks see Other information.

Law RTRA sect 16

Additional rules for high-speed roads
289. Take special care on motorways and other high-speed dual carriageways.
- One or more lanes may be closed to traffic and a lower speed limit may apply.
- Works vehicles that are slow moving or stationary with a large 'Keep Left' or 'Keep Right' sign on the back are sometimes used to close lanes for repairs, and a flashing light arrow may also be used to make the works vehicle more conspicuous from a distance and give earlier warning to drivers that they need to move over to the next lane.
- Check mirrors, slow down and change lanes if necessary.
- Keep a safe distance from the vehicle in front (see Rule 126).

290. Contraflow systems mean that you may be travelling in a narrower lane than normal and with no permanent barrier between you and oncoming traffic. The hard shoulder may be used for traffic, but be aware that there may be broken-down vehicles ahead of you. Keep a good distance from the vehicle ahead and observe any temporary speed limits.

Level crossings

291. A level crossing is where a road crosses a railway or tramway line. Approach and cross it with care. Never drive onto a crossing until the road is clear on the other side and do not get too close to the car in front. Never stop or park on, or near a crossing.

292. Overhead electric lines. It is dangerous to touch overhead electric lines. You **MUST** obey the safe height warning road signs and you should not continue forward onto the railway if your vehicle touches any height barrier or bells. The clearance available is usually 5 metres (16 feet 6 inches) but may be lower.

Laws RTA 1988 sect 36, TSRGD 2002 reg 17(5)

293. Controlled Crossings. Most crossings have traffic light signals with a steady amber light, twin flashing red stop lights (see Light signals controlling traffic and Warning signs) and an audible alarm for pedestrians. They may have full, half or no barriers.
- You **MUST** always obey the flashing red stop lights.
- You **MUST** stop behind the white line across the road.
- Keep going if you have already crossed the white line when the amber light comes on.
- Do not reverse onto or over a controlled crossing.
- You **MUST** wait if a train goes by and the red lights continue to flash. This means another train will be passing soon.
- Only cross when the lights go off and barriers open.
- Never zig-zag around half-barriers, they lower automatically because a train is approaching.
- At crossings where there are no barriers, a train is approaching when the lights show.

Laws RTA 1988 sect 36 & TSRGD regs 10 & 40

Stop when the traffic lights show

294. Railway telephones. If you are driving a large or slow-moving vehicle, a long, low vehicle with a risk of grounding, or herding animals, a train could arrive before you are clear of the crossing. You **MUST** obey any sign instructing you to use the railway telephone to obtain permission to cross. You **MUST** also telephone when clear of the crossing if requested to do so.

Laws RTA 1988 sect 36 & TSRGD regs 10 & 16(1)

295. Crossings without traffic lights. Vehicles should stop and wait at the barrier or gate when it begins to close and not cross until the barrier or gate opens.

296. User-operated gates or barriers. Some crossings have 'Stop' signs and small red and green lights. You **MUST NOT** cross when the red light is showing, only cross if the green light is on. If crossing with a vehicle, you should

- open the gates or barriers on both sides of the crossing
- check that the green light is still on and cross quickly
- close the gates or barriers when you are clear of the crossing.

Laws RTA 1988 sect 36 & TSRGD regs 10 & 52(2)

297. If there are no lights, follow the procedure in Rule 295. Stop, look both ways and listen before you cross. If there is a railway telephone, always use it to contact the signal operator to make sure it is safe to cross. Inform the signal operator again when you are clear of the crossing.

298. Open crossings. These have no gates, barriers, attendant or traffic lights but will have a 'Give Way' sign. You should look both ways, listen and make sure there is no train coming before you cross.

299. Incidents and breakdowns. If your vehicle breaks down, or if you have an incident on a crossing you should

- get everyone out of the vehicle and clear of the crossing immediately
- use a railway telephone if available to tell the signal operator. Follow the instructions you are given
- move the vehicle clear of the crossing if there is time before a train arrives. If the alarm sounds, or the amber light comes on, leave the vehicle and get clear of the crossing immediately.

Tramways

300. You **MUST NOT** enter a road, lane or other route reserved for trams. Take extra care where trams run along the road. You should avoid driving directly on top of the rails and should take care where trams leave the main carriageway to enter the reserved route, to ensure you do not follow them. The width taken up by trams is often shown by tram lanes marked by white lines, yellow dots or by a different type of road surface. Diamond-shaped signs and white light signals give instructions to tram drivers only.
Law RTRA sects 5 & 8

301. Take extra care where the track crosses from one side of the road to the other and where the road narrows and the tracks come close to the kerb. Tram drivers usually have their own traffic signals and may be permitted to move when you are not. Always give way to trams. Do not try to race or overtake them or pass them on the inside, unless they are at tram stops or stopped by tram signals and there is a designated tram lane for you to pass.

302. You **MUST NOT** park your vehicle where it would get in the way of trams or where it would force other drivers to do so. Do not stop on any part of a tram track, except in a designated bay where this has been provided alongside and clear of the track. When doing so, ensure that all parts of your vehicle are outside the delineated tram path. Remember that a tram cannot steer round an obstruction.
Law RTRA sects 5 & 8

303. Tram stops. Where the tram stops at a platform, either in the middle or at the side of the road, you **MUST** follow the route shown by the road signs and markings. At stops without platforms you **MUST NOT** drive between a tram and the left-hand kerb when a tram has stopped to pick up passengers. If there is no alternative route signed, do not overtake the tram – wait until it moves off.
Law RTRA sects 5 & 8

304. Look out for pedestrians, especially children, running to catch a tram approaching a stop.

305. Always give priority to trams, especially when they signal to pull away from stops, unless it would be unsafe to do so. Remember that they may be carrying large numbers of standing passengers who could be injured if the tram had to make an emergency stop. Look out for people getting off a bus or tram and crossing the road.

306. All road users, but particularly cyclists and motorcyclists, should take extra care when driving or riding close to or crossing the tracks, especially if the rails are wet. You should take particular care when crossing the rails at shallow angles, on bends and at junctions. It is safest to cross the tracks directly at right angles. Other road users should be aware that cyclists and motorcyclists may need more space to cross the tracks safely.

307. Overhead electric lines. Tramway overhead wires are normally 5.8 metres above any carriageway, but can be lower. You should ensure that you have sufficient clearance between the wire and your vehicle (including any load you are carrying) before driving under an overhead wire. Drivers of vehicles with extending cranes, booms, tipping apparatus or other types of variable height equipment should ensure that the equipment is fully lowered. Where overhead wires are set lower than 5.8 metres (19 feet), these will be indicated by height clearance markings – similar to 'low bridge' signs. The height clearances on these plates should be carefully noted and observed. If you are in any doubt as to whether your vehicle will pass safely under the wires, you should always contact the local police or the tramway operator. Never take a chance as this can be extremely hazardous.

Light signals controlling traffic

Traffic Light Signals

RED means 'Stop'. Wait behind the stop line on the carriageway	RED AND AMBER also means 'Stop'. Do not pass through or start until GREEN shows	GREEN means you may go on if the way is clear. Take special care if you intend to turn left or right and give way to pedestrians who are crossing	AMBER means 'Stop' at the stop line. You may go on only if the AMBER appears after you have crossed the stop line or are so close to it that to pull up might cause an accident	A GREEN ARROW may be provided in addition to the full green signal if movement in a certain direction is allowed before or after the full green phase. If the way is clear you may go but only in the direction shown by the arrow. You may do this whatever other lights may be showing. White light signals may be provided for trams

Flashing red lights

Alternately flashing red lights mean YOU MUST STOP

At level crossings, lifting bridges, airfields, fire stations, etc.

Motorway signals

You **MUST NOT** proceed further in this lane

Change lane

Reduced visibility ahead

Lane ahead closed

Temporary maximum speed advised and information message

Leave motorway at next exit

Temporary maximum speed advised

End of restriction

Lane control signals

Green arrow – lane available to traffic facing the sign

Red crosses – lane closed to traffic facing the sign

White diagonal arrow – change lanes in direction shown

Signals to other road users

Direction indicator signals

I intend to move out to the
right or turn right

I intend to move in to the left
or turn left or stop on the left

Brake light signals

I am applying the brakes

Reversing light signals

I intend to reverse

These signals should not be used except for the purposes described.

Arm signals

For use when direction indicator signals are not used, or when necessary to reinforce direction
indicator signals and stop lights. ***Also for use by pedal cyclists and those in charge of horses.***

I intend to move in to
the left or turn left

I intend to move out to
the right or turn right

I intend to slow
down or stop

Signals by authorised persons

Police officers

Stop

Traffic approaching from the front	Traffic approaching from both front and behind	Traffic approaching from behind

To beckon traffic on

From the side	From the front	From behind*

Arm signals to persons controlling traffic

I want to go straight on	I want to turn left; use either hand	I want to turn right

* In Wales, bilingual signs appear on emergency services vehicles and clothing

Vehicle and Operator Services Agency and Highways Agency Traffic Officers

Highways Agency Traffic Officer

VOSA Traffic Officer

These officers now have new powers to stop/direct vehicles and will be using hand signals and light signals similar to those used by police. You **MUST** obey any signals given (see Rules 107 and 108).

School Crossing Patrols

Not ready to cross pedestrians

Barrier to stop pedestrians crossing

Ready to cross pedestrians, vehicles must be prepared to stop

All vehicles must stop

Traffic signs

Signs giving orders

Signs with red circles are mostly prohibitive.
Plates below signs qualify their message.

Entry to
20mph zone

End of
20mph zone

Maximum
speed

National speed
limit applies

School crossing
patrol

Stop and
give way

Give way to
traffic on
major road

Manually operated temporary
STOP and GO signs

No entry for
vehicular traffic

No vehicles
except bicycles
being pushed

No cycling

No motor
vehicles

No buses
(over 8
passenger
seats)

No
overtaking

No
towed
caravans

No vehicles
carrying
explosives

No vehicle or
combination of
vehicles over
length shown

No vehicles
over
height shown

No vehicles
over
width shown

Give priority to
vehicles from
opposite
direction

No right turn

No left turn

No
U-turns

No goods vehicles
over maximum
gross weight
shown (in tonnes)
except for loading
and unloading

Note: Although *The Highway Code* shows many of the signs commonly in use, a comprehensive explanation of our signing system is given in the Department's booklet *Know Your Traffic Signs*, which is on sale at booksellers. The booklet also illustrates and explains the vast majority of signs the road user is likely to encounter. The signs illustrated in *The Highway Code* are not all drawn to the same scale. In Wales, bilingual versions of some signs are used including Welsh and English versions of place names. Some older designs of signs may still be seen on the roads.

WEAK BRIDGE

18T m g w

No vehicles over maximum gross weight shown (in tonnes)

P Permit holders only

Parking restricted to permit holders

RED ROUTE
No stopping at any time except buses

No stopping during period indicated except for buses

URBAN CLEARWAY
Monday to Friday

am	pm
8.00 - 9.30	4.30 - 6.30

No stopping during times shown except for as long as necessary to set down or pick up passengers

No waiting

No stopping (Clearway)

Signs with blue circles but no red border mostly give positive instruction.

Ahead only

Turn left ahead (right if symbol reversed)

Turn left (right if symbol reversed)

Keep left (right if symbol reversed)

Vehicles may pass either side to reach same destination

Mini-roundabout (roundabout circulation – give way to vehicles from the immediate right)

Route to be used by pedal cycles only

Segregated pedal cycle and pedestrian route

Minimum speed

End of minimum speed

Buses and cycles only

Trams only

TRAMWAY
LOOK BOTH WAYS

Pedestrian crossing point over tramway

One-way traffic (note: compare circular 'Ahead only' sign)

With-flow bus and cycle lane

Contraflow bus lane

With-flow pedal cycle lane

Warning signs

Mostly triangular

STOP
100 yds

Distance to
'STOP' line
ahead

Dual
carriageway
ends

Road narrows on
right (left if
symbol reversed)

Road
narrows on
both sides

GIVE WAY
50 yds

Distance to
'Give Way'
line ahead

Crossroads

Junction on
bend ahead

T-junction with
priority over
vehicles from
the right

Staggered
junction

Traffic merging
from left ahead

The priority through route is indicated by the broader line.

Double bend first
to left (symbol
may be reversed)

Bend to right
(or left if symbol
reversed)

Roundabout

Uneven road

REDUCE
SPEED
NOW

Plate below
some signs

Two-way
traffic crosses
one-way road

Two-way traffic
straight ahead

Opening or
swing bridge
ahead

Low-flying aircraft
or sudden
aircraft noise

Falling or
fallen rocks

Traffic signals
not in use

Traffic signals

Slippery road

Steep hill
downwards

Steep hill
upwards

Gradients may be shown as a ratio i.e. 20% = 1:5

Tunnel ahead

Trams
crossing
ahead

Level crossing
with barrier or
gate ahead

Level crossing
without barrier
or gate ahead

Level crossing
without barrier

Warning signs – continued

Patrol

School crossing patrol ahead (some signs have amber lights which flash when crossings are in use)

Frail (or blind or disabled if shown) pedestrians likely to cross road ahead

No footway for 400 yds

Pedestrians in road ahead

Zebra crossing

Safe height 16'-6"

Overhead electric cable; plate indicates maximum height of vehicles which can pass safely

Available width of headroom indicated

Sharp deviation of route to left (or right if chevrons reversed)

STOP when lights show

Light signals ahead at level crossing, airfield or bridge

| Red | STOP |
| Green | Clear |

IF NO LIGHT - PHONE CROSSING OPERATOR

Miniature warning lights at level crossings

Cattle

Wild animals

Wild horses or ponies

Accompanied horses or ponies

Cycle route ahead

Ice

Risk of ice

Queues likely

Traffic queues likely ahead

Humps for ½ mile

Distance over which road humps extend

Hidden dip

Other danger; plate indicates nature of danger

Soft verges for 2 miles

Soft verges

Side winds

Hump bridge

Ford

Worded warning sign

Quayside or river bank

Risk of grounding

Direction signs

Mostly rectangular

Signs on motorways – blue backgrounds

At a junction leading directly
into a motorway (junction
number may be shown
on a black background)

On approaches to
junctions (junction number
on black background)

Route confirmatory
sign after junction

Downward pointing arrows mean 'Get in lane'
The left-hand lane leads to a different destination from the other lanes.

The panel with the inclined arrow indicates the destinations which can be reached
by leaving the motorway at the next junction

Signs on primary routes - green backgrounds

On approaches to junctions

At the junction

Route confirmatory
sign after junction

On approaches
to junctions

On approach to a junction
in Wales (bilingual)

Blue panels indicate that the motorway starts at the junction ahead.
Motorways shown in brackets can also be reached along the route indicated.
White panels indicate local or non-primary routes leading from the junction ahead.
Brown panels show the route to tourist attractions.
The name of the junction may be shown at the top of the sign.
The aircraft symbol indicates the route to an airport.
A symbol may be included to warn of a hazard or restriction along that route.

Green background signs – continued

Primary route forming part of a ring road

Signs on non-primary and local routes - black borders

On approaches to junctions

Market Walborough 7
B 486

At the junction

Direction to toilets with access for the disabled

Green panels indicate that the primary route starts at the junction ahead.
Route numbers on a blue background show the direction to a motorway.
Route numbers on a green background show the direction to a primary route.

Other direction signs

Picnic site

Ancient monument in the care of English Heritage

Saturday only

Direction to a car park

Tourist attraction

Direction to camping and caravan site

Advisory route for lorries

Route for pedal cycles forming part of a network

Recommended route for pedal cycles to place shown

Route for pedestrians

Northtown

Symbols showing emergency diversion route for motorway and other main road traffic

Diversion route

Information signs

All rectangular

Entrance to controlled parking zone

Entrance to congestion charging zone

End of controlled parking zone

Advance warning of restriction or prohibition ahead

Parking place for solo motorcycles

With-flow bus lane ahead which pedal cycles and taxis may also use

Lane designated for use by high occupancy vehicles (HOV) - see rule 142

Vehicles permitted to use an HOV lane ahead

End of motorway

Start of motorway and point from which motorway regulations apply

Appropriate traffic lanes at junction ahead

Traffic on the main carriageway coming from right has priority over joining traffic

Additional traffic joining from left ahead. Traffic on main carriageway has priority over joining traffic from right hand lane of slip road

Traffic in right hand lane of slip road joining the main carriageway has prority over left hand lane

'Countdown' markers at exit from motorway (each bar represents 100 yards to the exit). Green-backed markers may be used on primary routes and white-backed markers with black bars on other routes. At approaches to concealed level crossings white-backed markers with red bars may be used. Although these will be erected at equal distances the bars do not represent 100 yard intervals.

Motorway service area sign showing the operator's name

Information signs – continued

Traffic has priority over oncoming vehicles

Hospital ahead with Accident and Emergency facilities

Tourist information point

No through road for vehicles

Recommended route for pedal cycles

Home Zone Entry

Area in which cameras are used to enforce traffic regulations

Bus lane on road at junction ahead

Roadworks signs

Road works

Loose chippings

Temporary hazard at roadworks

Temporary lane closure (the number and position of arrows and red bars may be varied according to lanes open and closed)

Slow-moving or stationary works vehicle blocking a traffic lane. Pass in the direction shown by the arrow.

Mandatory speed limit ahead

Roadworks 1 mile ahead

End of roadworks and any temporary restrictions including speed limits

Signs used on the back of slow-moving or stationary vehicles warning of a lane closed ahead by a works vehicle. There are no cones on the road.

Lane restrictions at roadworks ahead

One lane crossover at contraflow roadworks

Road markings

Across the carriageway

Stop line at signals or police control

Stop line at 'Stop' sign

Stop line for pedestrians at a level crossing

Give way to traffic on major road (can also be used at mini roundabouts)

Give way to traffic from the right at a roundabout

Give way to traffic from the right at a mini-roundabout

Along the carriageway

Edge line

Centre line
See Rule 127

Hazard warning line
See Rule 127

Double white lines
See Rules 128 and 129

See Rule 130

Lane line See
Rule 131

Along the edge of the carriageway

Waiting restrictions

Waiting restrictions indicated by yellow lines apply to the carriageway, pavement and verge. You may stop to load or unload (unless there are also loading restrictions as described below) or while passengers board or alight. Double yellow lines mean no waiting at any time, unless there are signs that specifically indicate seasonal restrictions. The times at which the restrictions apply for other road markings are shown on nearby plates or on entry signs to controlled parking zones. If no days are shown on the signs, the restrictions are in force every day including Sundays and Bank Holidays. White bay markings and upright signs (see below) indicate where parking is allowed.

No waiting at any time	No waiting during times shown on sign	Waiting is limited to the duration specified during the days and times shown

Red Route stopping controls

Red lines are used on some roads instead of yellow lines. In London the double and single red lines used on Red Routes indicate that stopping to park, load/unload or to board and alight from a vehicle (except for a licensed taxi or if you hold a Blue Badge) is prohibited. The red lines apply to the carriageway, pavement and verge. The times that the red line prohibitions apply are shown on nearby signs, but the double red line ALWAYS means no stopping at any time. On Red Routes you may stop to park, load/unload in specially marked boxes and adjacent signs specify the times and purposes and duration allowed. A box MARKED IN RED indicates that it may only be available for the purpose specified for part of the day (e.g. between busy peak periods). A box MARKED IN WHITE means that it is available throughout the day.

RED AND SINGLE YELLOW LINES CAN ONLY GIVE A GUIDE TO THE RESTRICTIONS AND CONTROLS IN FORCE AND SIGNS, NEARBY OR AT A ZONE ENTRY, MUST BE CONSULTED.

No stopping at any time	No stopping during times shown on sign	Parking is limited to the duration specified during the days and times shown	Only loading may take place at the times shown for up to a maximum duration of 20 mins

On the kerb or at the edge of the carriageway

Loading restrictions on roads other than Red Routes

Yellow marks on the kerb or at the edge of the carriageway indicate that loading or unloading is prohibited at the times shown on the nearby black and white plates. You may stop while passengers board or alight. If no days are indicated on the signs the restrictions are in force every day including Sundays and Bank Holidays.

ALWAYS CHECK THE TIMES SHOWN ON THE PLATES.

Lengths of road reserved for vehicles loading and unloading are indicated by a white 'bay' marking with the words 'Loading Only' and a sign with the white on blue 'trolley' symbol. This sign also shows whether loading and unloading is restricted to goods vehicles and the times at which the bay can be used. If no times or days are shown it may be used at any time. Vehicles may not park here if they are not loading or unloading.

No loading or unloading
at any time

No loading or unloading
at the times shown

Loading bay

Other road markings

Keep entrance clear of stationary vehicles, even if picking up or setting down children

Warning of 'Give Way'
just ahead

Parking space reserved
for vehicles named

See Rule 243

See Rule 141

Box junction - See Rule 174

Do not block that part of
the carriageway indicated

Indication of traffic lanes

Vehicle markings

Large goods vehicle rear markings

Motor vehicles over 7500 kilograms maximum gross weight and trailers over 3500 kilograms maximum gross weight

Left   Right

LONG VEHICLE

LONG VEHICLE

LONG VEHICLE

Central

The vertical markings are also required to be fitted to builders' skips placed in the road, commercial vehicles or combinations longer than 13 metres (optional on combinations between 11 and 13 metres)

Hazard warning plates

Certain tank vehicles carrying dangerous goods must display hazard information panels

2YE
1089
FLAMMABLE LIQUID
3
Newtown-on-Moors
(0123) 45678

The panel illustrated is for flammable liquid. Diamond symbols indicating other risks include:

The above panel will be displayed by vehicles carrying certain dangerous goods in packages

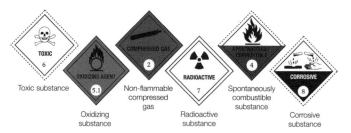

TOXIC
6

Toxic substance

OXIDIZING AGENT
5.1

Oxidizing substance

COMPRESSED GAS
2

Non-flammable compressed gas

RADIOACTIVE
7

Radioactive substance

SPONTANEOUSLY COMBUSTIBLE
4

Spontaneously combustible substance

CORROSIVE
8

Corrosive substance

Projection markers

Side marker   End marker

Both required when load or equipment (eg crane jib) overhangs front or rear by more than two metres

Other

School bus (displayed in front or rear window of bus or coach)

Annexes

1. You and your bicycle

Make sure that you feel confident of your ability to ride safely on the road. Be sure that
- you choose the right size and type of cycle for comfort and safety
- lights and reflectors are kept clean and in good working order
- tyres are in good condition and inflated to the pressure shown on the tyre
- gears are working correctly
- the chain is properly adjusted and oiled
- the saddle and handlebars are adjusted to the correct height.

It is recommended that you fit a bell to your cycle.

You **MUST**
- ensure your brakes are efficient
- at night, use lit front and rear lights and have a red rear reflector.

Laws PCUR regs 6 & 10 & RVLR reg 18

Cycle training can help both children and adults, especially those adults returning to cycling to develop the skills needed to cycle safely on today's roads. A new national cycle training standard has been developed which the Government is promoting and making funding available for delivery in schools.

All cyclists should consider the benefits of undertaking cycle training. For information, contact your local authority.

2. Motorcycle licence requirements

If you have a provisional motorcycle licence, you **MUST** satisfactorily complete a Compulsory Basic Training (CBT) course. You can then ride on the public road, with L plates (in Wales either D plates, L plates or both can be used), for up to two years. To obtain your full motorcycle licence you **MUST** pass a motorcycle theory test and then a practical test.

Law MV(DL)R regs 16 & 68

If you have a full car licence you may ride motorcycles up to 125cc and 11kW power output, with L plates (and/or D plates in Wales), on public roads, but you **MUST** first satisfactorily complete a CBT course if you have not already done so.

Law MV(DL)R reg 43

If you have a full moped licence and wish to obtain full motorcycle entitlement, you will be required to take a motorcycle theory test if you did not take a separate theory test when you obtained your moped licence. You **MUST** then pass a practical motorcycle test. Note that if CBT was completed for the full moped licence there is no need to repeat it, but if the moped test was taken before 1/12/90 CBT will need to be completed before riding a motorcycle as a learner.
Law MV(DL)R regs 42(1) & 69(1)

Light motorcycle licence (A1): you take a test on a motorcycle of between 75 and 125cc. If you pass you may ride a motorcycle up to 125cc with power output up to 11kW.

Standard motorcycle licence (A): if your test vehicle is between 120 and 125cc and capable of more than 100km/h you will be given a standard (A) licence. You will then be restricted to motorcycles of up to 25kW for two years. After two years you may ride any size machine.

Direct or Accelerated Access enables riders over the age of 21, or those who reach 21 before their two-year restriction ends, to ride larger motorcycles sooner. To obtain a licence to do so they are required to
• have successfully completed a CBT course
• pass a theory test, if they are required to do so
• pass a practical test on a machine with power output of at least 35kW.
To practise, they can ride larger motorcycles, with L plates (and/or D plates in Wales), on public roads, but only when accompanied by an approved instructor on another motorcycle in radio contact.

You **MUST NOT** carry a pillion passenger or pull a trailer until you have passed your test.
Law MV(DL)R reg 16

Moped licence requirements

A moped **MUST** have an engine capacity not exceeding 50cc, not weigh more than 250kg and be designed to have a maximum speed not exceeding 31mph (50km/h). From June 2003 all EC Type Approved mopeds have been restricted to 28mph (45km/h).

Law RTA 1988 (as amended) sect 108

To ride a moped, learners **MUST**

- be 16 or over
- have a provisional moped licence
- complete CBT training.

You **MUST** first pass the theory test for motorcycles and then the moped practical test to obtain your full moped licence. If you passed your driving test before 1 February 2001 you are qualified to ride a moped without L plates (and/or D plates in Wales), although it is recommended that you complete CBT before riding on the road. If you passed your driving test after this date you **MUST** complete CBT before riding a moped on the road.

Laws RTA 1988 sects 97(e) & 101 & MV(DL)R regs 38(4) & 43

Note. For motorcycle and moped riders wishing to upgrade, the following give exemption from taking the motorcycle theory test
- full A1 motorcycle licence
- full moped licence, if gained after 1 July 1996.

Law MV(DL)R reg 42

3. Motor vehicle documentation and learner driver requirements

Documents

Driving licence. You **MUST** have a valid driving licence for the category of motor vehicle you are driving. You **MUST** inform the Driver and Vehicle Licensing Agency (DVLA) if you change your name and/or address.

Law RTA 1988 sects 87 & 99(4)

Holders of non-European Community licences who are now resident in the UK may only drive on that licence for a maximum of 12 months from the date they become resident in this country. To ensure continuous driving entitlement
- a British provisional licence should be obtained and a driving test(s) passed before the 12-month period elapses, or
- in the case of a driver who holds a licence from a country which has been designated in law for licence exchange purposes, the driver should exchange the licence for a British one.

MOT. Cars and motorcycles **MUST** normally pass an MOT test three years from the date of the first registration and every year after that. You **MUST NOT** drive a motor vehicle without an MOT certificate when it should have one. Exceptionally, you may drive to a pre-arranged test appointment or to a garage for repairs required for the test. Driving an unroadworthy motor vehicle may invalidate your insurance.
Law RTA 1988 sects 45, 47, 49 & 53

Insurance. To use a motor vehicle on the road, you **MUST** have a valid insurance policy. This **MUST** at least cover you for injury or damage to a third party while using that motor vehicle. Before driving any motor vehicle, make sure that it has this cover for your use or that your own insurance provides adequate cover. You **MUST NOT** drive a motor vehicle without insurance. Also, be aware that even if a road traffic incident is not your fault, you may still be held liable by insurance companies.
Law RTA 1988 sect 143

Uninsured drivers can now be automatically detected by roadside cameras. Further to the penalties for uninsured driving listed in Annexe 5, Penalties, an offender's vehicle can now be seized by the Police, taken away and crushed.
Law RTA 1988, sects 165a & 165b

The types of cover available are indicated below:

Third-Party insurance – this is often the cheapest form of insurance, and is the minimum cover required by law. It covers anyone you might injure or whose property you might damage. It does not cover damage to your own motor vehicle or injury to yourself.

Third-Party, Fire and Theft insurance – similar to third-party, but also covers you against your motor vehicle being stolen, or damaged by fire.

Comprehensive insurance – this is the most expensive but the best insurance. Apart from covering other persons and property against injury or damage, it also covers damage to your own motor vehicle, up to the market value of that vehicle, and personal injury to yourself.

Registration certificate. Registration certificates (also called harmonised registration certificates) are issued for all motor vehicles used on the road, describing them (make, model, etc) and giving details of the registered keeper. You **MUST** notify the Driver and Vehicle Licensing Agency in Swansea as soon as possible when you buy or sell a motor vehicle, or if you change your name or address.

For registration certificates issued after 27 March 1997, the buyer and seller are responsible for completing the registration certificates. The seller is responsible for forwarding them to DVLA. The procedures are explained on the back of the registration certificates.

Law RV(R&L)R regs 21, 22, 23 & 24

Vehicle Excise Duty (VED). All motor vehicles used or kept on public roads **MUST** display a valid Vehicle Excise Duty disc (tax disc) displayed at all times. Even motor vehicles exempt from duty **MUST** display a tax disc at all times.

Law VERA sects 29 and 33

Statutory Off-Road Notification (SORN). This is a notification to the DVLA that a motor vehicle is not being used on the road. If you are the vehicle keeper and want to keep a motor vehicle untaxed and off the public road you **MUST** declare SORN – it is an offence not to do so. You then won't have to pay any road tax for that vehicle for a period of 12 months. You need to send a further declaration after that period if the vehicle is still off the public road. The SORN will end if you sell the vehicle and the new owner will become immediately responsible.

Law RV(RL)R 2002, reg 26 sched 4

Production of documents. You **MUST** be able to produce your driving licence and counterpart, a valid insurance certificate and (if appropriate) a valid MOT certificate, when requested by a police officer. If you cannot do this you may be asked to take them to a police station within seven days.

Law RTA 1988 sects 164 & 165

Learner drivers

Learners driving a car **MUST** hold a valid provisional licence. They **MUST** be supervised by someone at least 21 years old who holds a full EC/EEA licence for that type of car (automatic or manual) and has held one for at least three years.

Laws MV(DL)R reg 16 & RTA 1988 sect 87

Vehicles. Any vehicle driven by a learner **MUST** display red L plates. In Wales, either red D plates, red L plates, or both, can be used. Plates **MUST** conform to legal specifications and **MUST** be clearly visible to others from in front of the vehicle and from behind. Plates should be removed or covered when not being driven by a learner (except on driving school vehicles).

Law MV(DL)R reg 16 & sched 4

You **MUST** pass the theory test (if one is required) and then a practical driving test for the category of vehicle you wish to drive before driving unaccompanied.

Law MV(DL)R reg 40

4. The road user and the law
Road traffic law
The following list can be found abbreviated throughout The Code. It is not intended to be a comprehensive guide, but a guide to some of the important points of law. For the precise wording of the law, please refer to the various Acts and Regulations (as amended) indicated in The Code. Abbreviations are listed on the following page.

Most of the provisions apply on all roads throughout Great Britain, although there are some exceptions. The definition of a road in England and Wales is 'any highway and any other road to which the public has access and includes bridges over which a road passes' (RTA 1988 sect 192(1)). In Scotland, there is a similar definition which is extended to include any way over which the public have a right of passage (R(S)A 1984 sect 151(1)).

It is important to note that references to 'road' therefore generally include footpaths, bridleways and cycle tracks, and many roadways and driveways on private land (including many car parks). In most cases, the law will apply to them and there may be additional rules for particular paths or ways. Some serious driving offences, including drink-driving offences, also apply to all public places, for example public car parks.

Chronically Sick & Disabled Persons Act 1970	CSDPA
Functions of Traffic Wardens Order 1970	FTWO
Greater London (General Powers) Act 1974	GL(GP)A
Highway Act 1835 or 1980 (as indicated)	HA
Horses (Protective Headgear for Young Riders) Act 1990	H(PHYR)A
Horses (Protective Headgear for Young Riders) Regulations 1992	H(PHYR)R
Motor Cycles (Eye Protectors) Regulations 1999	MC(EP)R
Motor Cycles (Protective Helmets) Regulations 1980	MC(PH)R
Motorways Traffic (England & Wales) Regulations 1982	MT(E&W)R
Motorways Traffic (England & Wales) Amended Regulations	MT(E&W)(A)R
Motorways Traffic (Scotland) Regulations 1995	MT(S)R
Motor Vehicles (Driving Licences) Regulations 1999	MV(DL)R
Motor Vehicles (Wearing of Seat Belts) Regulations 1993	MV(WSB)R
Motor Vehicles (Wearing of Seat Belts) (Amendment) Regulations 2006	MV(WSB)(A)R
Motor Vehicles (Wearing of Seat Belts by Children in Front Seats) Regulations 1993	MV(WSBCFS)R
New Roads and Streetworks Act 1991	NRSWA
Pedal Cycles (Construction & Use) Regulations 1983	PCUR
Powers of Criminal Courts (Sentencing) Act 2000	PCC(S)A
Police Reform Act 2002	PRA
Prohibition of Smoking in Certain Premises (Scotland) Regulations 2006 (SI no 90)	PSCP(S)R*
Public Passenger Vehicles Act 1981	PPVA
Road Safety Act 2006	RSA
Road Traffic Act 1984, 1988 or 1991 (as indicated)	RTA
Road Traffic (New Drivers) Act 1995	RT(ND)A
Road Traffic Offenders Act 1988	RTOA
Road Traffic Regulation Act 1984	RTRA
Road Vehicles (Construction & Use) Regulations 1986	CUR
Road Vehicles (Display of Registration Marks) Regulations 2001	RV(DRM)R
Road Vehicles Lighting Regulations 1989	RVLR
Road Vehicles (Registration & Licensing) Regulations 2002	RV(R&L)R
Roads (Scotland) Act 1984	R(S)A
Traffic Management Act 2004	TMA
Traffic Signs Regulations & General Directions 2002	TSRGD
Use of Invalid Carriages on Highways Regulations 1988	UICHR
Vehicle Excise and Registration Act 1994	VERA
Zebra, Pelican and Puffin Pedestrian Crossings Regulations and General Directions 1997	ZPPPCRGD

Acts and regulations from 1988 can be viewed on the Office of Public Sector Information website (www.opsi.gov.uk). Acts and regulations prior to 1988 are only available in their original print format which may be obtained from The Stationery Office as detailed inside the back cover.

*Specific legislation applies to smoking in vehicles which constitute workplaces. For information, visit
www.smokefreeengland.co.uk
www.clearingtheairscotland.com
www.smokingbanwales.co.uk

5. Penalties

Parliament sets the maximum penalties for road traffic offences. The seriousness of the offence is reflected in the maximum penalty. It is for the courts to decide what sentence to impose according to circumstances.

The penalty table on the next page indicates some of the main offences, and the associated penalties. There is a wide range of other more specific offences which, for the sake of simplicity, are not shown here. The penalty points and disqualification system is described below.

Penalty points and disqualification

The penalty point system is intended to deter drivers and motorcyclists from following unsafe motoring practices. Certain non-motoring offences, e.g. failure to rectify vehicle defects, can also attract penalty points. The court **MUST** order points to be endorsed on the licence according to the fixed number or the range set by Parliament. The accumulation of penalty points acts as a warning to drivers and motorcyclists that they risk disqualification if further offences are committed.
Law RTOA sects 44 & 45

A driver or motorcyclist who accumulates 12 or more penalty points within a three-year period **MUST** be disqualified. This will be for a minimum period of six months, or longer if the driver or motorcyclist has previously been disqualified.
Law RTOA sect 35

For every offence which carries penalty points the court has a discretionary power to order the licence holder to be disqualified. This may be for any period the court thinks fit, but will usually be between a week and a few months.

In the case of serious offences, such as dangerous driving and drink-driving, the court **MUST** order disqualification. The minimum period is 12 months, but for repeat offenders or where the alcohol level is high, it may be longer. For example, a second drink-drive offence in the space of 10 years will result in a minimum of three years' disqualification.
Law RTOA sect 34

Penalty Table

Offence	Maximum Penalties			
	Imprisonment	Fine	Disqualification	Penalty Points
*Causing death by dangerous driving	14 years	Unlimited	Obligatory – 2 years minimum	3–11 (if exceptionally not disqualified)
*Dangerous driving	2 years	Unlimited	Obligatory	3–11 (if exceptionally not disqualified)
*Causing death by careless driving under the influence of drink or drugs	14 years	Unlimited	Obligatory - 2 years minimum	3–11 (if exceptionally not disqualified)
Careless and inconsiderate driving	-	£5,000	Discretionary	3–9
Driving while unfit through drink or drugs or with excess alcohol; or failing to provide a specimen for analysis	6 months	£5,000	Obligatory	3–11 (if exceptionally not disqualified)
Failing to stop after an accident or failing to report an accident	6 months	£5,000	Discretionary	5–10
Driving when disqualified	6 months (12 months in Scotland)	£5,000	Discretionary	6
Driving after refusal or revocation of licence on medical grounds	6 months	£5,000	Discretionary	3–6
Driving without insurance	-	£5,000	Discretionary	6–8
Using a vehicle in a dangerous condition	-	LGV £5,000 PCV £5,000 Other £2,500	Obligatory for 2 offences in 3 yrs – 6 mths min. Otherwise Discretionary in each case	3 in each case
Driving otherwise than in accordance with a licence	-	£1,000	Discretionary	3–6
Speeding	-	£1,000 (£2,500 for motorway offences)	Discretionary	3–6 or 3 (fixed penalty)
Traffic light offences	-	£1,000	Discretionary	3
No MOT certificate	-	£1,000	-	-
Seat belt offences	-	£500	-	-
Dangerous cycling	-	£2,500	-	-
Careless cycling	-	£1,000	-	-
Cycling on pavement	-	£500	-	-
Failing to identify driver of a vehicle	-	£1,000	Discretionary	6

*Where a court disqualifies a person on conviction for one of these offences, it must order an extended retest. The courts also have discretion to order a retest for any other offence which carries penalty points, an extended retest where disqualification is obligatory, and an ordinary test where disqualification is not obligatory.

Furthermore, in some serious cases, the court **MUST** (in addition to imposing a fixed period of disqualification) order the offender to be disqualified until they pass a driving test. In other cases the court has a discretionary power to order such disqualification. The test may be an ordinary length test or an extended test according to the nature of the offence.
Law RTOA sect 36

New drivers. Special rules as set out below apply for a period of two years from the date of passing their first driving test, to drivers and motorcyclists from
*   the UK, EU/EEA, the Isle of Man, the Channel Islands or Gibraltar who passed their first driving test in any of those countries
*   other foreign countries who have to pass a UK driving test to gain a UK licence, in which case the UK driving test is treated as their first driving test; and
*   other foreign countries who (without needing a test) exchanged their licence for a UK licence and subsequently passed a UK driving test to drive another type of vehicle, in which case the UK driving test is treated as their first driving test. For example a driver who exchanges a foreign licence (car) for a UK licence (car) and who later passes a test to drive another type of vehicle (e.g. an HGV) will be subject to the special rules.

Where a person subject to the special rules accumulates six or more penalty points before the end of the two-year period (including any points acquired before passing the test) their licence will be revoked automatically. To regain the licence they **MUST** reapply for a provisional licence and may drive only as a learner until they pass a further driving test (also see Annexe 8 – Safety code for new drivers.)
Law RT(ND)A

Note. This applies even if they pay for offences by fixed penalty. Drivers in the first group (UK, EU/EEA etc.) who already have a full licence for one type of vehicle are not affected by the special rules if they later pass a test to drive another type of vehicle.

Other consequences of offending
Where an offence is punishable by imprisonment then the vehicle used to commit the offence may be confiscated.
Law PCC(S)A, sect 143

In addition to the penalties a court may decide to impose, the cost of insurance is likely to rise considerably following conviction for a serious driving offence. This is because insurance companies consider such drivers are more likely to be involved in a collision.

Drivers disqualified for drinking and driving twice within 10 years, or once if they are over two and a half times the legal limit, or those who refused to give a specimen, also have to satisfy the Driver and Vehicle Licensing Agency's Medical Branch that they do not have an alcohol problem and are otherwise fit to drive before their licence is returned at the end of their period of disqualification. Persistent misuse of drugs or alcohol may lead to the withdrawal of a driving licence.

6. Vehicle maintenance, safety and security

Vehicle maintenance

Take special care that lights, brakes, steering, exhaust system, seat belts, demisters, wipers and washers are all working. Also

- lights, indicators, reflectors, and number plates **MUST** be kept clean and clear
- windscreens and windows **MUST** be kept clean and free from obstructions to vision
- lights **MUST** be properly adjusted to prevent dazzling other road users. Extra attention needs to be paid to this if the vehicle is heavily loaded
- exhaust emissions **MUST NOT** exceed prescribed levels
- ensure your seat, seat belt, head restraint and mirrors are adjusted correctly before you drive
- ensure that items of luggage are securely stowed.

Laws RVLR 1989 regs 23 & 27 & CUR 1986, regs 30 & 61

Warning displays

Make sure that you understand the meaning of all warning displays on the vehicle instrument panel. Do not ignore warning signs, they could indicate a dangerous fault developing.

- When you turn the ignition key, warning lights will be illuminated but will go out when the engine starts (except the handbrake warning light). If they do not, or if they come on while you are driving, stop and investigate the problem, as you could have a serious fault.
- If the charge warning light comes on while you are driving, it may mean that the battery isn't charging. This should also be checked as soon as possible to avoid loss of power to lights and other electrical systems.

Window tints

You **MUST NOT** use a vehicle with excessively dark tinting applied to the windscreen, or to the glass in any front window to either side of the driver. Window tinting applied during manufacture complies with the Visual Light Transmittance (VLT) standards. There are no VLT limits for rear windscreens or rear passenger windows.

Laws RTA 1988 sect 42 & CUR reg 32

Tyres

Tyres **MUST** be correctly inflated to the vehicle manufacturer's specification for the load being carried. Always refer to the vehicle's handbook or data. Tyres should also be free from certain cuts and other defects.

Cars, light vans and light trailers **MUST** have a tread depth of at least 1.6 mm across the central three-quarters of the breadth of the tread and around the entire circumference.

Motorcycles, large vehicles and passenger-carrying vehicles **MUST** have a tread depth of at least 1 mm across three-quarters of the breadth of the tread and in a continuous band around the entire circumference.

Mopeds should have visible tread.

Be aware that some vehicle defects can attract penalty points.

Law CUR reg 27

If a tyre bursts while you are driving, try to keep control of your vehicle. Grip the steering wheel firmly and allow the vehicle to roll to a stop at the side of the road.

If you have a flat tyre, stop as soon as it is safe to do so. Only change the tyre if you can do so without putting yourself or others at risk – otherwise call a breakdown service.

Tyre pressures

Check weekly. Do this before your journey, when tyres are cold. Warm or hot tyres may give a misleading reading.

Your brakes and steering will be adversely affected by under-inflated or over-inflated tyres. Excessive or uneven tyre wear may be caused by faults in the braking or suspension systems, or wheels which are out of alignment. Have these faults corrected as soon as possible.

Fluid levels

Check the fluid levels in your vehicle at least weekly. Low brake fluid may result in brake failure and a crash. Make sure you recognise the low fluid warning lights if your vehicle has them fitted.

Before winter

Ensure that the battery is well maintained and that there are appropriate anti-freeze agents in your radiator and windscreen bottle.

Other problems

If your vehicle

- pulls to one side when braking, it is most likely to be a brake fault or incorrectly inflated tyres. Consult a garage or mechanic immediately

- continues to bounce after pushing down on the front or rear, its shock absorbers are worn. Worn shock absorbers can seriously affect the operation of a vehicle and should be replaced
- smells of anything unusual such as burning rubber, petrol or an electrical fault; investigate immediately. Do not risk a fire.

Overheated engines or fire

Most engines are water-cooled. If your engine overheats you should wait until it has cooled naturally. Only then remove the coolant filler cap and add water or other coolant.

If your vehicle catches fire, get the occupants out of the vehicle quickly and to a safe place. Do not attempt to extinguish a fire in the engine compartment, as opening the bonnet will make the fire flare. Call the fire brigade.

Petrol stations/fuel tank/fuel leaks

Ensure that, when filling up your vehicle's tank or any fuel cans you are carrying, you do not spill fuel on the forecourt. Any spilled fuel should be immediately reported to the petrol station attendant. Diesel spillage is dangerous to other road users, particularly motorcyclists, as it will significantly reduce the level of grip between the tyres and road surface. Double-check for fuel leaks and make sure that

- you do not overfill your fuel tank
- the fuel cap is fastened securely
- the seal in the cap is not torn, perished or missing
- there is no visual damage to the cap or the fuel tank

Emergency fuel caps, if fitted, should form a good seal.

Never smoke, or use a mobile phone, on the forecourt of petrol stations as these are major fire risks and could cause an explosion.

Vehicle security

When you leave your vehicle you should

- remove the ignition key and engage the steering lock
- lock the car, even if you only leave it for a few minutes
- close the windows completely
- never leave children or pets in an unventilated car
- take all contents with you, or lock them in the boot. Remember, for all a thief knows a carrier bag may contain valuables
- never leave vehicle documents in the car.

For extra security fit an anti-theft device such as an alarm or immobiliser. If you are buying a new car it is a good idea to check the level of built-in security features. Consider having your registration number etched on all your car windows. This is a cheap and effective deterrent to professional thieves.

7. First Aid on the road

In the event of an incident, you can do a number of things to help, even if you have had no training.

1. Deal with danger

Further collisions and fire are the main dangers following a crash. Approach any vehicle involved with care. Switch off all engines and, if possible, warn other traffic. Stop anyone from smoking.

2. Get help

Try to get the assistance of bystanders. Get someone to call the appropriate emergency services as soon as possible. They will need to know the exact location of the incident and the number of vehicles involved.

3. Help those involved

DO NOT move casualties still in vehicles unless further danger is threatened. **DO NOT** remove a motorcyclist's helmet unless it is essential. Remember the casualty may be suffering from shock. **DO NOT** give them anything to eat or drink. **DO** try to make them warm and as comfortable as you can, but avoid unnecessary movement. **DO** give reassurance confidently and try not to leave them alone or let them wander into the path of other traffic.

4. Provide emergency care

Remember the letters **D R A B C:**

D – Danger – check that you are not in danger.

R – Response – try to get a response by asking questions and gently shaking their shoulders.

A – Airway – the airway should be clear and kept open. Place one hand on the forehead, two fingers under the chin and gently tilt the head back.

B – Breathing – normal breathing should be established. Once the airway is open check breathing for up to 10 seconds.

C – Compressions – if they are not breathing normally compressions should be administered to maintain circulation; place two hands in the centre of the chest and press down 4–5cms at a rate of 100/minute. You may only need one hand for a child. Give 30 chest compressions. Then tilt the head back gently, pinch the casualty's nostrils together and place your mouth over theirs. Give two breaths, each lasting one second (use gentle breaths for a small child).

If the casualty is unconscious and breathing, place them in the recovery position until medical help arrives

Bleeding. First check for anything that may be in the wound, such as glass. If there is nothing embedded apply firm pressure over the wound. Take care not to press on the object – build up padding on either side of it. Fasten a pad to the wound with a bandage or length of cloth. Use the cleanest material available. If a limb is bleeding, but not broken, raise it above the level of the heart to reduce the flow of blood. Any restriction of blood circulation for more than a short time could cause long-term injuries.

Burns. Try to cool the burn by dousing it with clean, cold water or similar non-toxic liquid for at least 10 minutes. Do not try to remove anything sticking to the burn.

5. Be prepared
Always carry a first aid kit. You could save a life by learning emergency aid and first aid from a qualified organisation, such as the local ambulance services, the St John Ambulance Association and Brigade, St Andrew's Ambulance Association, the British Red Cross or any suitable qualified body (see Useful websites for contact details).

8. Safety code for new drivers
Once you have passed the driving test you will be able to drive on your own. This will provide you with lots of opportunities but you need to remain safe. Even though you have shown you have the skills you need to drive safely, many newly qualified drivers lack experience. You need to continue to develop your skills, especially anticipating other road users' behaviour to avoid having a collision. As many as one new driver

in five has some kind of collision in their first year of driving. This code provides advice to help you get through the first twelve months after passing the driving test, when you are most vulnerable, as safely as possible.

- Many of the worst collisions happen at night. Between midnight and 6am is a time of high risk for new drivers. Avoid driving then unless it's really necessary.
- If you are driving with passengers, you are responsible for their safety. Don't let them distract you or encourage you to take risks. Tell your passengers that you need to concentrate if you are to get to your destination safely.
- Never show off or try to compete with other drivers, particularly if they are driving badly.
- Don't drive if you have consumed any alcohol or taken drugs. Even over-the-counter medicines can affect your ability to drive safely – read the label to see if they may affect your driving.
- Make sure everyone in the car is wearing a seat belt throughout the journey.
- Keep your speed down – many serious collisions happen because the driver loses control, particularly on bends.
- Most new drivers have no experience of driving high-powered or sporty cars. Unless you have learnt to drive in such a vehicle you need to get plenty of experience driving on your own before driving a more powerful car.
- Driving while uninsured is an offence. See Annexe 3 for information on types of insurance cover.

REMEMBER that under the New Drivers Act you will have your licence revoked if you get six penalty points on your licence within two years of passing your first driving test. You will need to pass both the theory and practical tests again to get back your full licence.

You could consider taking further training such as Pass Plus, which could also save you money on your insurance, as well as helping you reduce your risk of being involved in a collision. There are three ways to find out more:

- internet – www.passplus.org.uk
- telephone – DSA head office on 0115 901 2633
- Email – passplus@dsa.gsi.gov.uk

Other information

Metric conversions

The conversions given throughout *The Highway Code* are rounded but a detailed conversion chart is shown below.

Miles	Kilometres	Miles	Kilometres
1.00	1.61	40.00	64.37
5.00	8.05	45.00	72.42
10.00	16.09	50.00	80.47
15.00	24.14	55.00	88.51
20.00	32.19	60.00	96.56
25.00	40.23	65.00	104.60
30.00	48.28	70.00	112.65
35.00	56.33		

Useful websites

www.sja.org.uk (St John Ambulance Association and Brigade)
www.firstaid.org.uk (St Andrew's Ambulance Association)
www.redcross.org.uk (The British Red Cross)
www.dft.gov.uk
www.direct.gov.uk
www.transportoffice.gov.uk
www.highways.gov.uk/traffic info
www.direct.gov.uk/highway code
www.larsoa.org.uk
www.collisionreporting.gov.uk
www.askthe.police.uk
www.secureyourmotor.gov.uk
www.parking-appeals.gov.uk (outside London)
www.parkingandtrafficappeals.gov.uk (inside London)

Further reading

Best practice

Further information about good driving and riding practice can be found in The Driving Standards Agency books *The Official DSA Guide to Driving – the essential skills* and *The Official DSA Guide to Riding – the essential skills*. Information specifically for drivers of large vehicles can be found in *The Official DSA Guide to Driving Goods Vehicles* and *The Official DSA Guide to Driving Buses and Coaches*.

The Blue Badge Scheme

Information on this scheme can be found on the Department for Transport Website: www.dft.gov.uk

Code of Practice for Horse-Drawn Vehicles

The Code of Practice is available from the Department for Transport, Transport Technology and Standards Division 6, 2nd Floor, Great Minster House, 76 Marsham Street, London SW1P 4DR.
Tel: 0207 944 2078

Roadworks

A leaflet giving further information on driving through roadworks can be obtained from Highways Agency Publications, tel: 0870 1226 236, quoting reference number HA113/04. For general Highways Agency information, tel: 08457 504030 or email ha_info@highways.gsi.gov.uk

Index

References are to rule numbers, except those
numbers in *bold italics*, which refer to the annexes

Part 5
Glossary

Glossary

Accelerate

To make the vehicle move faster by pressing the right-hand pedal.

Advanced stop lines

A marked area on the road at traffic lights, which permits cyclists or buses to wait in front of other traffic.

Adverse weather

Bad weather that makes driving difficult or dangerous.

Alert

Quick to notice possible hazards.

Anticipation

Looking out for hazards and taking action before a problem starts.

Anti-lock brakes

Brakes that stop the wheels locking so that you are less likely to skid on a slippery road.

Aquaplane

To slide out of control on a wet road surface.

Articulated vehicle

A long vehicle that is divided into two or more sections joined by cables.

Attitude

The way you think or feel, which affects the way you drive. Especially, whether you are patient and polite, or impatient and aggressive.

Automatic

A vehicle with gears that change by themselves as you speed up or slow down.

Awareness

Taking notice of the road and traffic conditions around you at all times.

Black ice

An invisible film of ice that forms over the road surface, creating very dangerous driving conditions.

Blind spot

The section of road behind you which you cannot see in your mirrors. You 'cover' your blind spot by looking over your shoulder before moving off or overtaking.

Brake fade

Loss of power to the brakes when you have been using them for a long time without taking your foot off the brake pedal. For example, when driving down a steep hill. The brakes will overheat and not work properly.

Braking distance

The distance you must allow to slow the vehicle in order to come to a stop.

Brow

The highest point of a hill.

Built-up area

A town, or place with lots of buildings.

Carriageway

One side of a road or motorway. A 'dual carriageway' has two lanes on each side of a central reservation.

Catalytic converter

A piece of equipment fitted in the exhaust system that changes harmful gases into less harmful ones.

Chicane

A sharp double bend that has been put into a road to make traffic slow down.

Child restraint

A child seat or special seat belt for children. It keeps them safe and stops them moving around in the car.

Clearway

A road where no stopping is allowed at any time. The sign for a clearway is a red cross in a red circle on a blue background.

Coasting

Driving a vehicle without using any of the gears. That is, with your foot on the clutch pedal and the car in neutral.

Commentary driving

Talking to yourself about what you see on the road ahead and what action you are going to take – an aid to concentration.

Comprehensive insurance

A motor insurance policy that pays for repairs even if you cause an accident.

Concentration

Keeping all your attention on your driving.

Conditions

How good or bad the road surface is, volume of traffic on the road, and what the weather is like.

Congestion

Heavy traffic that makes it difficult to get to where you want to go.

Consideration

Thinking about other road users and not just yourself. For example, letting another driver go first at a junction, or stopping at a zebra crossing to let pedestrians cross over.

Contraflow

When traffic on a motorway follows signs to move to the opposite carriageway for a short distance because of roadworks. (During a contraflow, there is traffic driving in both directions on the same side of the motorway.)

Coolant

Liquid in the radiator that removes heat from the engine.

Defensive driving

Driving safely without taking risks, looking out for hazards and thinking for others.

Disqualified

Stopped from doing something (eg driving) by law, because you have broken the law.

Distraction

Anything that stops you concentrating on your driving, such as chatting to passengers or on your mobile phone.

Document

An official paper or card, eg your driving licence.

Dual carriageway

One side of a road or motorway, with two lanes on each side of a central reservation.

Engine braking – see also gears

Using the low gears to keep your speed down. For example, when you are driving down a steep hill and you want to stop the vehicle running away. Using the gears instead of braking will help to prevent brake fade.

Environment

The world around us and the air we breathe.

Exceed

Go higher than an upper limit.

Exhaust emissions

Gases that come out of the exhaust pipe to form part of the outside air.

Field of vision

How far you can see in front and around you when you are driving.

Filler cap

Provides access to the vehicle's fuel tank, for filling up with petrol or diesel.

Fog lights

Extra bright rear (and sometimes front) lights which may be switched on in conditions of very poor visibility. You must remember to switch them off when visibility improves, as they can dazzle and distract other drivers.

Ford

A place in a stream or river which is shallow enough to drive across with care.

Four-wheel drive (4WD)

On a conventional vehicle, steering and engine speed affect just two 'drive' wheels. On 4WD, they affect all four wheels, ensuring optimum grip on loose ground.

Frustration

Feeling annoyed because you cannot drive as fast as you want to because of other drivers or heavy traffic.

Fuel consumption

The amount of fuel (petrol or diesel) that your vehicle uses. Different vehicles have different rates of consumption. Increased fuel consumption means using more fuel. Decreased fuel consumption means using less fuel.

Fuel gauge

A display or dial on the instrument panel that tells you how much fuel (petrol or diesel) you have left.

Glossary

Gantry

An overhead platform like a high narrow bridge that displays electric signs on a motorway.

Gears

Control the speed of the engine in relation to the vehicle's speed. May be hand operated (manual) or automatically controlled. In a low gear (such as first or second) the engine runs more slowly. In a high gear (such as fourth or fifth), it runs more quickly. Putting the car into a lower gear as you drive can create the effect of engine braking – forcing the engine to run more slowly.

Handling

How well your vehicle moves or responds when you steer or brake.

Harass

To drive in away that makes other road users afraid.

Hard shoulder

The single lane to the left of the inside lane on a motorway, which is for emergency use only. You should not drive on the hard shoulder except in an emergency, or when there are signs telling you to use the hard shoulder because of roadworks.

Harsh braking (or harsh acceleration)

Using the brake or accelerator too hard so as to cause wear on the engine.

Hazard warning lights

Flashing amber lights which you should use only when you have broken down. On a motorway you can use them to warn other drivers behind of a hazard ahead.

High-sided vehicle

A van or truck with tall sides, or a tall trailer such as a caravan or horse-box, that is at risk of being blown off-course in strong winds.

Impatient

Not wanting to wait for pedestrians and other road users.

Inflate

To blow up – to put air in your tyres until they are at the right pressures.

Instrument panel

The car's electrical controls and gauges, set behind the steering wheel. Also called the dashboard.

Intimidate

To make someone feel afraid.

Involved

Being part of something. For example, being one of the drivers in an accident.

Jump leads

A pair of thick electric cables with clips at either end. You use it to charge a flat battery by connecting it to the live battery in another vehicle.

Junction

A place where two or more roads join.

Liability

Being legally responsible.

Manoeuvre

Using the controls to make your car move in a particular direction. For example turning, reversing or parking.

Manual

By hand. In a car that is a 'manual' or has manual gears, you have to change the gears yourself.

Maximum

The largest possible; 'maximum speed' is the highest speed allowed.

Minimum

The smallest possible.

Mirrors

Modern cars have a minimum of three rear view mirrors: one in the centre of the windscreen, and one on each front door. Additional mirrors may be required on longer vehicles, or when towing a high trailer such as a caravan. Some mirrors may be curved (convex or concave) to increase the field of vision. The mirror on the windscreen can be turned to anti-dazzle position, if glare from headlights behind creates a distraction.

Mobility

The ability to move around easily.

Monotonous

Boring. For example, a long stretch of motorway with no variety and nothing interesting to see.

MOT

The test that proves your car is safe to drive. Your MOT certificate is one of the important documents for your vehicle.

Motorway

A fast road that has two or more lanes on each side and a hard shoulder. Drivers must join or leave it on the left, via a motorway junction. Many kinds of slower vehicles – such as bicycles – are not allowed on motorways.

Multiple-choice questions

Questions with several possible answers where you have to try to choose the right one.

Observation

The ability to notice important information, such as hazards developing ahead.

Obstruct

To get in the way of another road user.

Octagonal

Having eight sides.

Oil level

The amount of oil needed for the engine to run effectively.The oil level should be checked as part of your regular maintenance routine, and the oil replaced as necessary.

Pedestrian

A person walking.

Pegasus crossing

An unusual kind of crossing. It has a button high up for horse riders to push (Pegasus was a flying horse in Greek legend).

Pelican crossing

A crossing with traffic lights that pedestrians can use by pushing a button. Cars must give way to pedestrians on the crossing while the amber light is flashing. You must give pedestrians enough time to get to the other side of the road.

Perception

Seeing or noticing (as in Hazard Perception).

Peripheral vision

The area around the edges of your field of vision.

Positive attitude

Being sensible and obeying the law when you drive.

Priority

The vehicle or other road user that is allowed by law to go first is the one that has priority.

Provisional licence

A first driving licence. all learner drivers must get one before they start having lessons.

Puffin crossing

A type of pedestrian crossing that does not have a flashing amber light phase.

Reaction time

The amount of time it takes you to see a hazard and decide what to do about it.

Red route

You see these in London and some other cities. Double red lines at the edge of the road tell you that you must not stop or park there at any time. Single red lines have notices with times when you must not stop or park. Some red routes have marked bays for either parking or loading at certain times.

Red warning triangle

An item of safety equipment to carry in your car in case you break down. You can place the triangle 45m behind your car on the same side of the road. It warns traffic that your vehicle is causing an obstruction. (Do not use these on motorways.)

Residential areas

Areas of housing where people live. The speed limit is 30mph or sometimes 20mph.

Road hump

A low bump built across the road to slow vehicles down. Also called 'sleeping policemen'.

Rumble strips

Raised strips across the road near a roundabout or junction that change the sound the tyres make on the road surface, warning drivers to slow down. They are also used on motorways to separate the main carriageway from the hard shoulder.

Glossary

Safety margin

The amount of space you need to leave between your vehicle and the one in front so that you are not in danger of crashing into it if the driver slows down suddenly or stops. Safety margins have to be longer in wet or icy conditions.

Separation distance

The amount of space you need to leave between your vehicle and the one in front so that you are not in danger of crashing into it if the driver slows down suddenly or stops. The separation distance must be longer in wet or icy conditions.

Security coded radio

To deter thieves, a radio or CD unit which requires a security code (or pin number) to operate it.

Single carriageway

Generally, a road with one lane in each direction.

Skid

When the tyres fail to grip the surface of the road, the subsequent loss of control of the vehicle's movement is called a skid. Usually caused by harsh or fierce braking, steering or acceleration.

Snaking

Moving from side to side. This sometimes happens with caravans or trailers when you drive too fast, or they are not properly loaded.

Staggered junction

Where you drive cross another road. Instead of going straight across, you have to go a bit to the right or left.

Steering

Control of the direction of the vehicle. May be affected by road surface conditions: when the steering wheel turns very easily, steering is 'light', and when you have to pull hard on the wheel it is described as 'heavy'.

Sterile

Clean and free from bacteria.

Stopping distance

The time it takes for you to stop your vehicle – made up of 'thinking distance' and 'braking distance'.

Supervisor

Someone who sits in the passenger seat with a learner driver. They must be over 21 and have held a full driving licence for at least three years.

Tailgating

Driving too closely behind another vehicle – either to harass the driver in front or to help you in thick fog.

Tax disc

The disc you display on your windscreen to show that you have taxed your car (see Vehicle Excise Duty, below).

Thinking distance

The time it takes you to notice something and take the right action. You need to add thinking distance to your braking distance to make up your total stopping distance.

Third party insurance

An insurance policy that insures you against any claim by passengers or other persons for damage or injury to their person or property.

Toucan crossing

A type of pedestrian crossing that does not have a flashing amber light phase, and cyclists are allowed to ride across.

Tow

To pull something behind your vehicle. It could be a caravan or trailer.

Traffic calming measures

Speed humps, chicanes and other devices placed in roads to slow traffic down.

Tram

A public transport vehicle which moves along the streets on fixed rails, usually electrically powered by overhead lines.

Tread depth

The depth of the grooves in a car's tyres that help them grip the road surface. The grooves must all be at least 1.6mm deep.

Turbulence

Strong movement of air. For example, when a large vehicle passes a much smaller one.

Two-second rule

In normal driving, the ideal minimum distance between you and the vehicle in front can be timed using the 'two-second' rule. As the vehicle in front passes a fixed object (such as a signpost), say to yourself 'Only a fool breaks the two second rule'. It takes two seconds to say it. If you have passed the same object before you finish, you are too close – pull back.

Tyre pressures

The amount of air which must be pumped into a tyre in order for it to be correctly blown up.

Vehicle Excise Duty

The tax you pay for your vehicle so that you may drive it on public roads.

Vehicle Registration Document

A record of details about a vehicle and its owner.

Vehicle watch scheme

A system for identifying vehicles that may have been stolen.

Vulnerable

At risk of harm or injury.

Waiting restrictions

Times when you may not park or load your vehicle in a particular area.

Wheel balancing

To ensure smooth rotation at all speeds, wheels need to be 'balanced' correctly. This is a procedure done at a garage or tyre centre, when each wheel is removed for testing. Balancing may involve minor adjustment with the addition of small weights, to avoid wheel wobble.

Wheel spin

When the vehicle's wheels spin round out of control with no grip on the road surface.

Zebra crossing

A pedestrian crossing without traffic lights. It has an orange light, and is marked by black and white stripes on the road. Drivers must stop for pedestrians to cross.

Part 6
The Answers to
the Theory Test
Questions

Answers to Questions

ALERTNESS – SECTION 1

1 C	2 BDF	3 C	4 D	5 C	6 C	7 C	8 C	9 B
10 D	11 AC	12 ABCD	13 AD	14 AB	15 AB	16 ABCD	17 B	18 D
19 B	20 D	21 B	22 B	23 ABE	24 C	25 B	26 B	27 D
28 C	29 C	30 C	31 A	32 D	33 D	34 B	35 A	36 D
37 B								

ATTITUDE – SECTION 2

38 D	39 A	40 C	41 B	42 C	43 D	44 D	45 B	46 B
47 BCD	48 ABE	49 A	50 D	51 B	52 A	53 A	54 B	55 A
56 A	57 C	58 A	59 B	60 D	61 D	62 D	63 A	64 A
65 B	66 C	67 A	68 C	69 A	70 C	71 B	72 C	73 DE
74 B	75 D	76 B	77 C	78 AB	79 D	80 C	81 A	82 A
83 B	84 A	85 D	86 C	87 C				

SAFETY AND YOUR VEHICLE – SECTION 3

88 B	89 AB	90 ABF	91 BEF	92 C	93 ACF	94 C	95 B	96 D
97 C	98 D	99 D	100 D	101 A	102 AE	103 D	104 B	105 D
106 D	107 A	108 B	109 D	110 D	111 BC	112 BC	113 A	114 D
115 A	116 B	117 B	118 D	119 C	120 D	121 D	122 D	123 B
124 B	125 B	126 D	127 ABF	128 ABC	129 ABC	130 BDF	131 ADE	132 BD
133 B	134 CDE	135 B	136 B	137 C	138 B	139 DE	140 A	141 C
142 B	143 D	144 D	145 D	146 B	147 C	148 A	149 B	150 D
151 C	152 A	153 B	154 AB	155 A	156 D	157 B	158 BCD	159 C
160 CD	161 A	162 A	163 D	164 C	165 B	166 B	167 B	168 D
169 ABE	170 ADE	171 D	172 A	173 B	174 C	175 D	176 A	177 B
178 C	179 D	180 A	181 C	182 D	183 B	184 A	185 B	186 D
187 B	188 A	189 C	190 D	191 B	192 B	193 D	194 B	195 B
196 C	197 A	198 A	199 A					

SAFETY MARGINS – SECTION 4

200 D	201 D	202 BC	203 B	204 D	205 D	206 C	207 C	208 A
209 B	210 A	211 B	212 A	213 B	214 AE	215 C	216 C	217 BDEF
218 B	219 D	220 A	221 C	222 A	223 AD	224 C	225 B	226 B
227 B	228 C	229 C	230 B	231 B	232 BC	233 C	234 C	235 B
236 C	237 D	238 BC	239 B	240 ACE	241 D	242 D	243 D	244 A
245 D	246 BD	247 D	248 B	249 A	250 D	251 D	252 B	253 B
254 C	255 A	256 A	257 D	258 ACD				

Answers to Questions

259 D	260 CD	261 B	262 C	263 A	264 D	265 ACE	266 D	267 C
268 C	269 C	270 D	271 B	272 B	273 A	274 A	275 A	276 C
277 C	278 CD	279 A	280 B	281 A	282 C	283 BF	284 B	285 AE
286 A	287 D	288 D	289 C	290 B	291 B	292 C	293 A	294 B
295 B	296 CD	297 B	298 D	299 B	300 A	301 A	302 D	303 A
304 B	305 AE	306 C	307 B	308 BC	309 D	310 B	311 B	312 C
313 D	314 C	315 CD	316 AC	317 AB	318 A	319 A	320 B	321 B
322 ABC	323 C	324 C	325 C	326 ABE	327 C	328 D	329 D	330 C
331 C	332 D	333 ABD	334 ABC	335 D	336 C	337 AB	338 B	339 B
340 CD	341 D	342 ACE	343 ABE	344 A	345 A	346 D	347 D	348 A
349 D	350 A	351 A	352 B	353 B	354 ACE			

355 D	356 D	357 C	358 C	359 B	360 D	361 D	362 D	363 B
364 C	365 D	366 A	367 D	368 D	369 B	370 D	371 B	372 D
373 D	374 C	375 AC	376 C	377 C	378 A	379 D	380 C	381 D
382 ABC	383 C	384 B	385 AC	386 ABD	387 B	388 D	389 A	390 A
391 D	392 D	393 A	394 A	395 C	396 C	397 C	398 D	399 D
400 B	401 A	402 C	403 D	404 C	405 C	406 A	407 D	408 D
409 A	410 A	411 B	412 B	413 D	414 C	415 C	416 B	417 C
418 AE	419 D	420 C	421 C	422 B	423 B	424 D	425 A	426 C
427 D	428 D	429 B	430 D	431 B	432 B	433 C	434 D	435 A

436 A	437 A	438 B	439 B	440 D	441 B	442 A	443 BC	444 B
445 D	446 A	447 A	448 C	449 B	450 D	451 D	452 D	453 B
454 B	455 B	456 AC	457 BD	458 B	459 D	460 D	461 A	462 A

463 ACE	464 A	465 CD	466 D	467 A	468 BDF	469 C	470 D	471 C
472 DE	473 B	474 C	475 C	476 D	477 D	478 C	479 C	480 BD
481 BD	482 D	483 B	484 C	485 CE	486 C	487 D	488 A	489 A
490 C	491 B	492 ABDF	493 A	494 D	495 B	496 B	497 AB	498 BD
499 A	500 ACD	501 B	502 A	503 C	504 B	505 A	506 A	507 C
508 C	509 A	510 B	511 C	512 D	513 B	514 D	515 ABD	516 D
517 C	518 C	519 C	520 D	521 D	522 A	523 B	524 B	

MOTORWAY RULES – SECTION 9

25 ADEF	526 ADEF	527 D	528 D	529 D	530 D	531 A	532 B	533 C
34 D	535 C	536 A	537 C	538 A	539 D	540 A	541 C	542 C
43 C	544 C	545 C	546 C	547 B	548 C	549 B	550 B	551 A
52 B	553 B	554 D	555 CDF	556 C	557 D	558 C	559 D	560 A
61 B	562 B	563 D	564 C	565 A	566 B	567 D	568 A	569 D
70 D	571 A	572 C	573 B	574 B	575 C	576 A	577 A	578 B
79 D	580 D	581 B	582 D	583 D	584 B	585 C	586 D	587 D
88 C	589 A	590 D	591 B					

RULES OF THE ROAD – SECTION 10

92 C	593 C	594 D	595 B	596 A	597 C	598 D	599 ADF	600 AD
01 A	602 B	603 A	604 B	605 A	606 D	607 A	608 D	609 D
10 C	611 A	612 ACE	613 B	614 C	615 D	616 BD	617 B	618 A
19 D	620 C	621 A	622 B	623 CDE	624 B	625 AE	626 B	627 A
28 ABD	629 A	630 B	631 B	632 A	633 D	634 A	635 D	636 C
37 D	638 D	639 D	640 D	641 D	642 C	643 C	644 D	645 A
46 A	647 A	648 C	649 B	650 A	651 D	652 AB	653 A	654 D
55 D	656 A	657 D	658 B	659 ABC	660 D	661 A	662 D	663 A
64 A	665 B	666 C						

ROAD AND TRAFFIC SIGNS – SECTION 11

67 D	668 D	669 A	670 A	671 B	672 A	673 D	674 B	675 D
76 D	677 D	678 A	679 C	680 B	681 D	682 C	683 B	684 A
85 B	686 B	687 C	688 C	689 A	690 C	691 B	692 C	693 B
94 D	695 D	696 C	697 D	698 C	699 B	700 C	701 D	702 A
03 D	704 B	705 D	706 B	707 A	708 A	709 A	710 A	711 B
12 B	713 A	714 D	715 ACEF	716 C	717 A	718 A	719 C	720 D
21 B	722 C	723 B	724 B	725 B	726 B	727 D	728 A	729 C
30 A	731 C	732 D	733 A	734 C	735 B	736 D	737 A	738 B
39 B	740 C	741 C	742 A	743 A	744 C	745 C	746 B	747 D
48 C	749 B	750 A	751 C	752 D	753 C	754 B	755 A	756 A
57 C	758 BDF	759 A	760 C	761 C	762 B	763 B	764 A	765 C
66 A	767 B	768 A	769 B	770 D	771 B	772 A	773 D	774 C
75 D	776 C	777 B	778 C	779 C	780 A	781 B	782 D	783 B
84 B	785 A	786 D	787 A	788 B	789 B	790 D	791 C	792 B
93 A	794 B	795 A	796 C	797 A	798 B	799 A	800 A	801 C
02 C	803 A	804 B	805 C	806 B	807 A	808 C	809 A	810 A
11 C	812 C	813 B	814 B	815 B	816 A	817 B	818 B	819 A
20 D	821 B	822 D						

Answers to Questions

DOCUMENTS – SECTION 12

823 C	824 B	825 B	826 BE	827 C	828 C	829 B	830 D	831 AB
832 D	833 D	834 CDE	835 C	836 B	837 B	838 C	839 ABF	840 BCE
841 ABE	842 BD	843 D	844 A	845 C	846 ABD	847 D	848 B	849 C
850 A	851 C	852 C	853 D	854 B	855 C	856 D	857 B	858 A
859 B	860 D	861 A	862 AB	863 A	864 D	865 D	866 ABD	867 A
868 C	869 C							

ACCIDENTS – SECTION 13

870A	871 BD	872 B	873 ABE	874 A	875 ACF	876 A	877 ABD	878 ACE
879 DEF	880 ABE	881 ACF	882 AE	883 ACDE	884 C	885 BC	886 A	887 B
888 B	889 BDE	890 C	891 D	892 CD	893 D	894 C	895 B	896 D
897 B	898 BDE	899 A	900 B	901 AB	902 A	903 A	904 B	905 B
906 D	907 C	908 C	909 B	910 D	911 C	912 ABD	913 A	914 CD
915 CE	916 C	917 DEF	918 B	919 C	920 A	921 A	922 BE	923 ABCE
924 ADE	925 A	926 D	927 B	928 C	929 D	930 A	931 D	932 B
933 A	934 BE	935 D	936 A	937 BD	938 C	939 B	940 B	941 D
942 B	943 B	944 D	945 B	946 D	947 B	948 C		

VEHICLE LOADING – SECTION 14

949 AD	950 A	951 D	952 A	953 D	954 BD	955 D	956 B	957 A
958 D	959 BC	960 A	961 A	962 A	963 A			

Useful Contacts

AA driving school
0800 107 2045
www.AAdrivingschool.co.uk

Driving Standards Agency (DSA)
You can book your Theory or Practical Test

Online: www.direct.gov.uk

By phone: 0870 0101 372

By fax: 0870 0102 372

Welsh speakers: 0870 0100 372

Minicom: 0870 0107 372

To book your Theory Test you will need:

- The driver number on your licence

- Your debit/credit card details

To book your Practical Test you will need:

- The driver number on your licence

- Theory Test pass date and certificate number

- Driving school code (if known)

- Your preferred date

- Unacceptable days or periods

- If you can accept a test at short notice

- Details of any disability or any special circumstances

- Your credit/debit card details

Pass Plus scheme
For information on the Pass Plus scheme ask your Advanced Driving Instructor, see www.passplus.org.uk or call the DSA on 0115 901 2633

Driver and Vehicle Licensing Agency (DVLA)
www.dvla.gov.uk

For enquiries about your driving licence
Phone: 0870 240 0009

Or write to:
Drivers Customer Services (DCS)
Correspondence Team
DVLA
Swansea
SA6 7JL

The Highway Code
www.highwaycode.gov.uk

St John Ambulance
www.sja.org.uk
08700 10 49 50

St Andrew's First Aid
www.firstaid.org.uk
0141 332 4031

Saturday and weekday evening tests are available at some driving test centres. The fee is higher than for a driving test during normal working hours on weekdays. Evening tests are available during the summer months only.

Personal Information

My driver number

_____

Driving instructor's name and
phone number

_____

Driving instructor's number

_____

Theory Test date and time

_____

Theory Test pass date

_____

Theory Test certificate number

_____

Driving school code

_____

Practical Test date and time

_____

Acknowledgements

Illustrations: Chris Orr & Associates